The Only Dance in Iowa

A History of

Six-Player

Girls' Basketball

Max McElwain

University of Nebraska Press
Lincoln and London

∞

Library of Congress
Cataloging-in-Publication Data
McElwain, Max.
The only dance in Iowa: a history
of six-player girls' basketball /
Max McElwain.
p. cm.
Includes bibliographical references
and index.
ISBN 0-8032-3236-5 (cloth: alk.
paper)–ISBN 0-8032-8299-0 (pbk.:
alk. paper)–ISBN 0-8032-0439-6
(electronic)
1. Basketball for girls–Iowa–
History.   2. Sports for girls–Social
aspects–Iowa.   I. Title.
GV886.M34   2004
796.323'8–dc22
2004003693
Set in Janson Text and
Quadraat Sans by Bob Reitz.

To Barbara Boustead, Kathryn Kellow, Mary Ann Kenkel, and schoolteachers who came before and after them

Contents

Illustrations

Introduction

On a weekday afternoon in early March 1968, Henry Boone, the superintendent of schools in Woodbine, Iowa, faced 250 high school students in the gymnasium at a pep rally he required them to attend. There was good reason to stage a rally at this particular time—the Friday night before, the Woodbine Tigerettes had clinched the school's first berth in the Iowa girls' high school state basketball tournament, the Sweet Sixteen. The team's recent good fortune was not the primary reason for this occasion, however. Boone paraded in front of the student body the two head cheerleaders, members of prominent families in Woodbine, a farming community of thirteen hundred located in the Loess Hills of southwest Iowa. The girls did not display the happiness one would expect following their team's success. They were sad-eyed and dour, and as Boone motioned for them to step forward in front of the students, they both began to cry: they were forced to apologize to the school for skipping the Friday night game and attending a rock concert instead.

Woodbine's first girls' state basketball tournament berth was understandably meaningful to superintendent Boone.[1] In 1947 Boone had introduced competitive, interscholastic girls' basketball in the Woodbine schools; it was a relatively late start for the game in an Iowa small town. Previously, for almost a half century, Woodbine girls played intramural basketball.

Twenty-five years after the Tigerettes made it to the girls' state tournament, in that same gym in early November, the daughter of one of the stars of the '68 team stood at midcourt, hands on her hips, and yelled at her coach. "Listen! This isn't the way it says it on the practice sheets," she scolded the man, disagreeing with the way a practice drill was run. "No, I won't listen," the coach replied. *My, how things have changed.* The Woodbine Tigerettes are now the "Lady Tigers." And had a player told the Woodbine coach in 1968 to "listen," such an outburst would have merited a stern tongue lashing if not outright suspension.

That the Tigerettes had evolved into the Lady Tigers wasn't necessarily a sign of great progress. Tagging the feminine suffix *-ettes* on to the names of girls' teams had been found to devalue female athletes, and officials statewide have largely curbed the practice. But some scholars contend that *lady* equally demeans women athletes, evoking characteristics "decidedly unathletic" and "recalling the age of chivalry."[2]

The questioning of authority is a far different matter: in the golden era of Woodbine girls' basketball—the late 1960s and early 1970s, when questioning authority was considered a common experience for American teenagers—the players on the team were, for the most part, compliant as lambs. The restrictive nature of the game itself—adhering to rules that limited dribbling, stealing the ball, and who could and could not shoot—reinforced a disciplinary style of coaching. Eager submission to authority was then, and is now, thought by many teachers, parents, and players to be why the teams were so good—and irreverence why later teams were bad.

But the big change at Woodbine in early November 1993 was that these girls were playing organized full-court, five-player basketball, and they were the first girls in this town to do so. The unexpected decision made in February 1993 by the Iowa Girls High School Athletic Union (the IGHSAU) to discontinue six-player girls' basketball, played continuously in Iowa schools for almost a full century, was hardly a routine mandate that permitted the play of the conventional five-player game. Six-player girls' basketball was a seemingly inviolable institution in Iowa, the cultural significance of which was reflected in the lead story in the Sunday *Omaha World-*

Herald the week following the Union's decision: "The fall of the Berlin Wall was a shock. The breakup of the Soviet Union was a stunner. 'The Tonight Show' without Johnny Carson seemed unthinkable. And across Iowa, many people believed that six-player girls' basketball would survive the changes of time. They were wrong."[3]

More than one million Iowa girls had played basketball since the game was introduced in the state only eighteen months after James Naismith, assigned to devise a wintertime, indoor activity for college men, hung up peach baskets in Springfield, Massachusetts, in the winter of 1891–92. The Smith College physical educator Senda Berenson taught her female students the game shortly thereafter, and in 1893 girls in Dubuque, Iowa, played basketball at the city's YMCA. By 1900 girls were playing basketball in dozens of Iowa towns and cities, abiding by various sets of rules—or none at all—and often playing with boys. Although informal rules for "women's" basketball appeared in 1894, it wasn't until 1899 that Berenson, then head of the National Committee on Women's Basketball, and other physical educators attempted to standardize rules. "Rough and vicious play is almost worse in women's than in men's play," Berenson contended.[4]

This initial attempt at standardization provided for a court divided into three sections with five to ten players per team (depending on the gym size) who could dribble the basketball only one time and who risked disqualification with one foul. Eight-player ball was common: each team featured three shooting forwards, three guards, a center who battled for a jump ball following every field goal, and a "running" center whose responsibility was to pass the jump ball to her forwards. Players could not leave their third of the court—the forward or guard courts or the center circle. Other than the center jump ball following field goals, the positional structure and roles (and hence the game itself) was significantly different from the men's game. Its rules reflected the medical and moral concerns of educators, mostly women who feared that girls risked physical harm and exploitation were they to play basketball like boys. As late as 1900 conservative male and female doctors continued to warn an increasingly nervous public that "the physical activities of the 'new woman' were going too far and that women were irresponsibly using bodily energy that was required for healthy maternity and efficient housekeeping."[5]

The first official women's basketball rules that were developed in Springfield, Massachusetts, in 1899 brought only momentary order. The basketball court soon became the battleground for the fight over the propriety of women's competitive sport and other, larger, gender issues. Women physical educators, firm in their belief that "moderation" prevented the masculinization of female athletes and sexual exploitation, succeeded in curtailing interscholastic athletics. Two organizations whose goal was the prohibition of varsity sports led the charge in the 1920s, presenting a united attack against all kinds of competitive girls' sports. The Committee on Women's Athletics (CWA), formerly the National Women's Basketball Committee, tried to regulate high school and college athletics, while the women's division of the National Amateur Athletic Federation (NAAF) worked outside educational circles, fighting competition at the community level. NAAF, founded in 1922 to challenge the American Athletic Union (AAU), conflicted ideologically with such groups as the AAU as well as industrial working-class basketball leagues, which permitted fierce competition and, often, the five-player, full-court game for women. The battle over women's basketball was made explicit in its various sets of rules, which, throughout the twentieth century, were never static, always negotiable, and played out in constituencies that were often predicated on issues of class, race, and always gender.[6]

In Iowa the "moderation" educators met with mixed success. Girls' basketball spread quickly throughout the state, as it did throughout America. Iowa girls played basketball in the snow; they played in gyms with potbellied stoves in the middle of the court; and, as in 1920 when the Correctionville High School girls raised funds on their own to travel to the state tournament (they rewarded the community by winning the first state title), they proved eminently resourceful. But the Iowa High School Athletic Association (IHSAA), adamant that boys' basketball remain top priority, attempted in 1925 to discontinue sponsoring girls' state tournaments, thereby taking the position of national reformers who insisted on intramural instead of interscholastic competition for girls and that paid admission to watch girls' games was inappropriate.

Nevertheless, twenty-five men, mostly educators from small towns who understood the importance of the game to community life, vehemently disagreed with the move to shut down girls' basketball. "Gentlemen, if you attempt to do away with girls' basketball in Iowa, you'll be standing in the center of the track when the train runs over you!" one of the dissenters shouted at the IHSAA. Thus was born the Iowa Girls High School Athletic Union (IGHSAU)—the only girls' prep association in America—and the start of a half century's governance of Iowa high school girls' sports by men.[7]

IGHSAU-sponsored basketball was immediately successful: in its first year of existence, 1926, 159 Iowa high schools, nearly all from small towns, put girls' basketball teams on the court. The larger high schools as well as the universities and colleges aligned with the reformers against girls' interscholastic competition. By the 1940s 70 percent of the teams represented schools with fewer than one hundred students; one decade later, 70 percent of Iowa high school girls played basketball, the highest participation level for any schoolgirl sport in America. The six-player format was the only concession to "moderation" that Iowans made: the state tournament, first sponsored in the early 1920s by the *Des Moines Register* to boost circulation, developed into the sort of media spectacle that women reformers abhorred. By 1949 it drew forty thousand spectators. Players dressed in bloomers and abided by a noncompetitive ideology early in the century, but by 1950 bare midriffs had become the order of the day, and coaches were teaching players to "behave like ladies off the court, but play like boys on it"—anathema to the national reformers.[8]

But nowhere did the women physical educators fail more thoroughly in their attempt to wrestle control of girls' basketball from men than in Iowa. In fact, it was the work of organizations like the National Amateur Athletic Federation and Committee on Women's Athletics—both groups comprised entirely of women—that necessitated the Iowa Girls High School Athletic Union. The fifteen directors of the IGHSAU from 1926 to 1950 were men. Most of the girls' basketball coaches and officials in the 1920s were women, but two decades later, men so dominated the coaching ranks that a Union poll of more than two hundred female players found that 96 percent of them—most of whom had never had a female coach—preferred men over women as their coaches.[9]

The national debate over competitive women's basketball had kept the game out of the cities and big schools in Iowa. Meanwhile, the six-player game, already ensconced in the community life of small towns, continued to evolve. The three-court format, with its cumbersome center jump after each basket, was discarded in 1934 and replaced by a two-court game, favored by the AAU, that allowed for two dribbles and permitted guards to tie up the ball when forwards were in the act of shooting. Iowa girls, from all indications, *loved* competitive basketball, and their expertise at the game was proven after high school: more than 20 percent of the AAU's first-team All-Americans chosen between 1949 and 1960 were native Iowans. Legendary players left their mark on the game: there was Monona's six-foot-four-inch Norma Schoulte, who accurately made right- *and* left-handed hook shots from twenty-five feet; there was Havelock's Bernice Kaufman, whose trademark, an over-the-head toss shot with her back to the basket, accounted for 18 points in a 1943 state tournament game; and Union-Whitten's Denise Long, who scored 111 points one night; and Iowa's most prolific scorer, Ventura's Lynne Lorenzen, who became the all-time, national high school top scorer among girls *and* boys.[10]

But as late as 1951, when the state tournament became the first high school athletic event televised in Iowa and the tourney's sold-out status soon prompted a move across town from Des Moines' Drake Fieldhouse to the fifteen-thousand-seat Veterans Auditorium, Iowans felt compelled to defend the game. The Union's *Iowa Girls Basketball Yearbook* published that year included medical reports that insisted that competitive basketball presented no psychological or unusual physical risks for girls. "It is this type of Iowa girl— clean, healthy, vibrant, sportsmanlike, that has on three different occasions faced the champions of Texas," IGHSAU secretary R. H.

Chisholm wrote in 1950, a remark that characterized the ideological comportment of the game.[11]

It wasn't until shortly before the passage of the Educational Act of 1972 (Title IX)—the congressional legislation that required all schools receiving federal money to offer equal and fair opportunities for men and women or risk losing those funds—that the campaign against competitive women's basketball disappeared. Finally, national educators lauded Iowa for its unparalleled success at providing athletic opportunities for girls: the year before Title IX passed, 20 percent of the high school female athletes in America hailed from Iowa. "Ten years ago, those directing women's physical education would not vote for women's athletics but that has changed. We give thanks to the state of Iowa for changing that," noted Tug Wilson, president of the United States Olympic Committee before Title IX passed.[12]

As a result of the Title IX legislation, larger schools in Iowa joined the IGHSAU in the 1970s and started basketball and other sports programs for girls. And similarly, because of Title IX, three Iowa girls filed a lawsuit against the IGHSAU in 1984, claiming that six-player basketball violated the intent of the law. The girls' game, they said, was not "equal" to the boys', and the limits placed on players (only forwards could shoot, and only two dribbles were allowed) prevented them from earning scholarships to college, where the five-player game was played. The IGHSAU responded by permitting schools to choose between the six- and five-player formats.

Hardly surprisingly, the small districts clung to six-player basketball, and the larger school districts opted for five-player; as recently as 1991, four times as many high schools in Iowa played six-player ball as five-on-five. In two polls conducted by the *Des Moines Register* prior to the six- or five-player option mandated by the state in 1984, Iowans maintained a preference for the old game: 48 versus 27 percent favored the six-player game in 1977, and slightly more than 50 percent supported it in 1984. Another *Register* poll in 1993 helps show the cultural significance of the game. Only men (45 percent to 30 percent) and residents in cities over fifty thousand (40 percent to 25 percent) favored the five-player game, but their

numbers were large enough to eclipse those of the six-player proponents, who were, in most cases, residents in towns with less than
twenty-five hundred people, farmers, citizens fifty-five and older,
and women (who favored the old game 33 percent to 31 percent).
The change was inevitable: a unanimous vote by the Union on
February 3, 1993, dismantled Iowa six-player girls' basketball, the
longest-running sporting activity for high school girls in American
history.[13]

From the inception of American team sports in the nineteenth century through the cornucopia of amateur and professional athletics
that abound in the new millennium, sport has carried special freight
in America. Sport has been inextricably woven into the Protestant ethic and spirit of capitalism that directs much of American
behavior. At the moment when play ceased to be voluntary and
non-purposive—in other words, when play was transformed into
rationalized and commodified sport—it became an exemplar of the
values of the larger culture. From the introduction of "scientific"
football, designed to provide a training ground for future leaders, to
the corporate boardrooms of the twenty-first century that require
"team players," sporting metaphors pervade our society. Noting
that lexicographers have found seventeen hundred sports metaphors
that Americans use in everyday language, Michael Oriard has traced
the function of play from the Puritans through contemporary New
Agers and contends that conciliating the work-play dilemma figures
prominently in all American cultural matters. Spontaneous, creative
play becomes paradoxical when it is transformed into a national
sporting ethos.[14]

Iowans continued to play their game in part because of their
spectacular success with it. The game was so strong that it flourished
during the Depression, it was entrenched in the culture of the small
towns, and it inculcated cohesion for teams as well as communities.
Only Oklahoma played six-player ball after Iowa, and it discontinued the game in 1995. While sports may function similarly in
various regions, distinctive sports cultures do arise; Iowa six-player
girls' basketball, played continuously from 1893 to 1993, is one.

There were a number of characteristics about the sport that aided its longevity. First, Iowa had one of the highest participation rates for girls' basketball prior to the enactment of Title IX. And even a decade after Title IX, Iowa and five other upper midwestern states—Minnesota, Nebraska, North Dakota, South Dakota, and Wisconsin—led the nation in high school girls' sports participation.[15]

Girls' basketball in Iowa also received local monetary support. Iowa basketball is rich with tales of townsfolk collecting funds for uniforms or equipment, or approving bonds for new gyms. And the merchants of Des Moines always rolled out the red carpet in March, when fans came to the city for the tournament—and shopping.

Game attendance was a factor in the sport's long-term success as well. The state tournament attracted as many as ninety thousand spectators annually over its five days in Des Moines, eclipsing the boys' tourney attendance figures. As early as 1953, Iowa basketball led the nation in attendance in girls' *and* boys' high school sports.[16] The same held true for any game night during the cold Iowa winters—at least as many fans flocked to gyms to see the girls' game, which usually preceded the boys'. In fact, as Doug Bauer succinctly observed: "Many fans put on their coats after the girls' game had ended. They knew they had just seen the best basketball they would watch that evening, and they were going home."[17]

Similarly, press coverage was an important contributor to girls' basketball's lasting appeal throughout the state. The *Des Moines Register* was an early sponsor of the girls' state tournament, and small-town newspapers were often consumed with basketball coverage. In 1951 the first telecast in Iowa of a prep basketball state tournament—boys or girls—featured the girls in Des Moines; despite a shaky broadcast conducted during a blizzard, they attracted 260,000 viewers across the state. By 1966 television coverage had expanded into the upper Midwest, and, not surprisingly, the final six-player tournament in 1993 drew a national media response, including ESPN, *USA Today*, the *Chicago Tribune*, *Newsday*, at least fifteen television stations, and National Public Radio, which broadcast three different features.[18]

Another primary reason for the survival of Iowa girls' basketball,

which was largely the province of small towns and the rural countryside, was that it played an integral role in a culture of "schooling" that persisted in the Midwest. The lifeblood of rural communities was the school; and in many instances girls' basketball was
the most important issue in consolidation, or school reorganization,
which dominated the educational landscape beginning in the 1950s.
Iowans were used to controlling their education, and they were ex-
ceptionally good at it. The thousands of country schools in the state
produced the most literate citizenry in America in the twentieth
century. [19] But because the ways of the locally run rural schools
conflicted with the national ideology of Progressive Era leaders,
Iowa's country-school system was slowly dismantled throughout the
twentieth century. Iowans didn't want outsiders telling them how
to play basketball any more than they wanted to be told how to
operate their schools. The paradox was evident: just as outside forces
worked against Iowa country schools—some of the best schools in
America—so did they work against one of the most successful girls'
prep sporting activities nationwide. Playing a game that the rest
of the country found antiquated was one of many paradoxes that
characterized the sport, and for a time its uniqueness helped *preserve*
the game.

In order to examine such paradoxes in this cultural history of
Iowa six-player girls' basketball, I use such sources as archival records and newspaper accounts, private correspondence and public
discussions, scholarly writings and school publications. I also rely
on interviews with basketball players and their coaches and fans, di-
alogues that are presented in historical narratives, and ethnographic
forms like the "literary tale" or creative nonfiction, which incorpo-
rates the reportorial technique of the journalist with the narrative
style of the fiction writer.

This work begins with a description of the first week of practice
for an Iowa high school team changing from six-player to full-court
basketball. Such ethnographic enterprise figures prominently in this
book, notably the position in which I found myself as participant-
observer: I was returning to my hometown and was cast in an in-
sider-outsider role that raised a number of interesting questions. I

also discovered that after decades of non-Iowans questioning the validity of the six-player game, some of the "locals"—none other than friends, family, and teachers—now questioned the ability of the girls to play full-court basketball. This was evidence of the strength of the ideology in which girls' basketball had long been embedded.[20]

I focus on one small town—Maynard, Iowa—and how the culture of girls' basketball thrived there for most of a century. I also examine such concerns as school consolidations. But other institutions besides education helped to sustain the culture of girls' basketball. As mentioned, the media—the *Des Moines Register* in particular—sustained an ideology that strengthened high school basketball as its prominence waned elsewhere. I examine the motives and policies of this and other newspapers in addition to state tournament programs and other documents that illuminate the game and the broader rural culture.[21]

Iowa six-player basketball was introduced into a late-nineteenth-century culture characterized by distinctive gender arrangements, but the game outlasted the cultural norms in which it developed. I address the conceptual significance of issues of gender and tell the stories of the women who played the game and how they dealt with the gender "trappings," if, indeed, they perceived the game as constricting. The paradox of "playing like boys on the court but acting like ladies off it"—*apologetic behavior*—occurred when Iowans transformed the temperate six-player game into a competitive one. The Progressive Era educators and leaders who championed middle-class women's concerns fought against competitive basketball; but in the late twentieth century, this same impulse to promote the status and rights of female athletes was found in a broadly based women's movement that rallied *for* competitive basketball. In both cases, the six-player game was targeted. "The same people who didn't want basketball at first later fought to have six-player taken away," a veteran coach and former IGHSAU official noted.[22]

Even Title IX, whose 1972 passage ended the national campaign against competitive women's basketball and whose supporters cast it as a great equalizer, ushered in unintended hurts. Among them was the depletion of women in the coaching and athletic administration ranks, in part the result of male organizations extending their leadership over emerging girls' programs. Iowa was exceptional in this regard, though. While the number of female coaches for high school girls' basketball in other states (often more than 80 percent) fell dramatically when Title IX was passed, the number of women coaching Iowa girls' teams was already at an all-time low (1.5 percent); men *already* governed the sport. But by the early 1990s, women comprised 17 percent of Iowa's girls' coaches, the result of the climate surrounding Title IX for this state.[23]

Yet another paradox—as prominent as any—was that men governed the state's only girls' prep athletic association and continue to do so. The reason why Iowa is the only state to continuously play a girls' state basketball tournament since 1920 involves the formation of the Iowa Girls High School Athletic Union (IGHSAU) and its rules of governance. A handful of male administrators and almost one hundred coaches—men and women—turned against national opinion and supported girls' prep competition early in the twentieth century. But the power structure didn't shift until the Union permitted women officials to join in the 1960s and women coaches (who outnumbered male coaches before the advent of the IGHSAU in the 1920s) became more prevalent in the late 1970s. Until then, a male power structure dominated Iowa girls' basketball. In small towns across the state, school districts often provided only one coach—almost always male—who coached both the girls' and boys' teams and was, in many cases, the school superintendent.

But even in 1999 the Union was still explaining its overwhelmingly male leadership with the rationale that most superintendents and principals in Iowa were men. This rationalization was used because, according to the 1998–1999 constitution of the IGHSAU, four of the six elective members of the eight-member board of directors and the twelve members of the representative council were to be employed as superintendents, assistant superintendents, or principals in Iowa schools; the two board exceptions were one mandated coach and one required "woman coach or woman director of an activity sanctioned by the Athletic Union." The only high school girls' athletic union in America would thus have to create a constitutional provision in order to have women in its governing body. In 1999 only one more than the minimum number of women required—one—filled the eighteen governing seats of the Union. All twelve members of the representative council and six of the eight board members were men.[24]

Men governing a girls' association, female leaders promoting competitive basketball after fighting against it for nearly a century, the clash of acceptable on- and off-court behaviors for female players, the role of external criticism in the survival of the game—the paradoxes encapsulating Iowa six-player girls' basketball are pronounced. "The only dance in Iowa"—a description that former University of Iowa football coach Hayden Fry gave his team and that I find a more appropriate metaphor for girls' basketball—danced on for so long because of a complex arrangement of factors.[25]

ONE

The Curtain Is Raised on a New Game

"I think more girls will play." – Joe Monsen, *father of Lady Tiger Heather Monsen, when asked about the consequence of Iowa's change to full-court, five-player basketball for girls.*

"I think a lot of kids won't get to play." – Fred Monsen, *father of Joe Monsen and grandfather of Heather.*[1]

Once, believing that a main-street rock club would keep locals from spending their entertainment dollars in the big city and having found the ideal spot in a vacant grocery store with a vertical sign quite visible from Highway 30, my friends and I dreamed about opening the "No-Yewee-Tonight Club" (since main street was two blocks long, "tooling"—or driving around—consisted of a steady stream of u-turns, called "yewees"). And once, on a summer night, my friends and I were drinking beer while lounging in a red convertible in the park when Woodbine's only police officer, frightened over reports of a break-in at the town's only factory, ignored our public indiscretion and deputized several youths to help him solve the crime.

Such memories come and go, unlike the broad, imposing trophy case I was staring at outside the Woodbine gym. I was waiting for the first practice to begin in early November 1993, when the girls in this town would learn full-court, five-player basketball. Sure enough, front and center, the biggest trophies were still the state tournament consolation prizes from 1974 and 1969, when Woodbine beat the team led by the most storied high school player in Iowa history, Denise Long of Union-Whitten. During the first week of practice, I sat in the gym and watched the transition for two to three hours every afternoon. Sometimes I found myself staring at the floor, but even then I learned things: by remembering, comparing eras and people. Sometimes the girls running the floor seemed like their parents, many of whom I'd grown up with. Just as often, the players seemed their complete opposites. In fact, what I watched and how I recorded it may seem painfully mundane. But ordinariness is the traffic of small towns, and it is the cultural and social history of small towns that I pursue from the perspective of girls' basketball. [2]

When I walked up the steps to the coaches' office, I was met by girls' volleyball and basketball coach Bob Jasper, who, despite having his hands full of black-and-gold practice jerseys, managed to shake my hand. Earlier I had introduced myself to the principal, Fred Jackson, who was a bit frazzled; he had returned on Sunday from Washington DC, where he and several parents had chaperoned dozens of Woodbine High School students, including some of the basketball players, on a weeklong visit.

While waiting for practice to begin, I thought about the gym. When it was built in 1962, it was one of the largest and most attractive facilities in any community between Council Bluffs and Sioux City, an area that spanned over one hundred miles and included dozens of school districts. In 1962 the last of the country schools were closed down, sending "farm kids" into town to school. Accompanying them were dozens of country-school teachers, often as not steel-willed, Germanic women who brought their tough ways into town with them. It was no coincidence, I believe, that the students of these teachers, who have now retired or passed away, were readily acquiescent when a similarly severe high school basketball coach led them to success at the end of the decade.

Thirty years later, the gym looks no worse for the wear—and there's been a lot of it. The concrete blocks are painted solid yellow ten feet up the walls, then mixed with light and dark greens above that. A pastel block with a growling Tiger painted on it is the primary focus. Today there is a crow's nest on the south side of the gym—taping games is now an integral part of scouting opponents and providing potential college recruiters with film.

Hung on the north side, near the rafters, were the ten flags representing the schools in the Boyer Valley Conference, the athletic conference in which Woodbine competes. The names of the towns are pretty much the same as they were in 1970, with some variance: hyphens. The schools have consolidated, turning, for example, Irwin into I-K-M (Irwin-Kirkman-Manilla). In yet another variation, some schools remain separate academically yet share athletic programs; this occurs most frequently with football, which requires numbers no longer found in some school districts. In terms of proximity, consolidation is much easier in Iowa than in, say, western Kansas, where towns may sit an hour's drive apart. In southwest Iowa, it is rare to drive on any state or county highway much farther than ten miles before reaching a town. But Woodbine has succeeded at warding off consolidation of any sort and is the only school in the conference to do so. That's a "success" because consolidation, in the eyes of many, signifies failure. And Woodbine is clearly a town uncomfortable with failure.

The fact that the Woodbine school district remains independent says a lot about the community. The bearer of a long tradition of academic excellence—its normal school for training teachers at the turn of the century boasted of faculty members with degrees from "Eastern" colleges—consolidation would be something of an admission of failure, a rare experience indeed for this community. When in the late nineteenth century Cedar Falls was chosen over Woodbine and other towns as the site for the state teachers college, Iowa's cultural and educational landscape was etched irrevocably. There would be no state university in western Iowa.

The town produced a number of outstanding residents. A Woodbine student, John McKinney, was national scholastic spelling champion in the late 1940s. About that same time, Bus Brown, future mayor of the town, invented his trencher, a ditch-digging device, manufactured in town, that was so successful by the 1960s that a national trade publication named Bus Brown Manufacturing the largest small manufacturing company of its kind in the United States. Today, the company's chief product is the Tommy Gate, the hydraulic loading system that one can see on the tailgates of pickups, vans, and flatbeds in Des Moines, New York City, or London.

But easily the most storied native of Woodbine is Debbie Esser, the second of seven children born to humble dairy farmers who lived east of town. Arguably the greatest Iowa high school female track athlete ever, she led the Tigerettes to three straight outdoor track titles from 1973 to 1975, then excelled at Iowa State University, where for a period of time she held the international women's record in the 400-meter hurdles. Sadly, Esser's specialty did not become an Olympic event until she quit competing.[3] That a high school athlete is the most noted resident—male or female—of a town over 125 years old is quite revealing; few people in Woodbine, if any, know that a son of Elizabeth Cady Stanton, the prominent nineteenth-century women's rights activist, was an early mayor of their town (1880–81).

Harrison County, which is bordered on the west by the Missouri River, leads the state of Iowa in apple production; in the late 1980s Woodbine started hosting an annual apple festival, an event that draws more than six thousand visitors. Woodbine's two-block-long, brick main street in 1993 offered an authentic German bakery besides the usual coterie of small-town restaurants, a Hallmark shop, and the only men's clothing store in the county. Elevated on a plain, main street hovers above Highway 30, which runs north and south about two hundred yards away and lies between the railroad and the Boyer River. U.S. Highway 30, originally known as the "Lincoln Highway" when built in 1913, was the first transcontinental American motor route, stretching from New York City's Times Square to San Francisco. The mile-long passage through Woodbine is the oldest original section of the Lincoln Highway in Iowa.

With a stable population hovering at fifteen hundred, Woodbine was the only town in Harrison County not to lose population in the 1990 census. Logan, the county seat, is nine miles south on Highway 30 and consolidated schools with a smaller community many years ago. Dunlap, nine miles north, did the same more recently.

As practice began, I sat cross-legged on the stage, which faces the floor on the east side of the gym. During the 1960s, tournaments were held in Woodbine all the way up through the district finals because with bleachers set up on the stage, the gym could hold an overflow crowd of more than one thousand spectators. You knew there was a big tournament game approaching when the bleachers on the stage were up. People awaited one of those nights when a player like Dunlap's Mary Nelson, a six-foot-two forward custom-made for six-player basketball, would dump in 25 points in the first quarter over a helpless guard six inches shorter. The gym and accompanying buildings were important to me; three generations of my family were educated in this school, and my mother taught music there for more than twenty years. My grandmother, a graduate of the old normal school, was considerably smaller than her country-school teaching peers and many of her students; apparently, the implied power of a stack of bricks by her desk compensated for the lack of girth on her four-foot ten-inch frame.

I had become sports editor of the *Woodbine Twiner*, our local weekly newspaper, when I was fourteen, and throughout high school I published bylined stories that often ran sixty inches or more. I was paid by the inch, which, combined with the doubly good fortune of having an editor who never touched my copy and writing about the "golden era" of Woodbine sports, meant that I always had plenty of pocket change. In the banner year of 1969, when both Woodbine's girls' and boys' basketball teams qualified for the state tournament, my stories were usually the lead on page one, filling a quarter of the page and often nestled beneath sixty- or seventy-two-point headlines. Rising at 6 a.m. after a Tuesday night game and writing for two hours before school in order to make the 8:30 copy deadline left a lifelong impression on a fourteen-year-old. These memories came filtering back as I sat on that stage, watching the children of my friends, who were children themselves not long ago, running down that same hardwood floor.

First-Day Jitters

There were nineteen girls out on the first day, a good number compared with the turnout at other area schools. "For those of you who don't have a clue, watch this," said coach Bob Jasper (BJ) when he introduced the first shooting exercises, which were spelled out in five-minute increments on a practice sheet that lay on the stage. "For those of you who don't have a clue" spoke volumes; for all but a few of the girls who had participated in a summer "transition" camp at Creighton University in Omaha, this marked the first time they would be playing five-player basketball, dribbling the ball the full court. For the girls who had previously played guard only, they were shooting in practice for the first time. Three guards chose not to go out for basketball at all because of the changeover to the five-player game. "They were scared off," BJ said.

I was struck by the mendacity of this first session. For the first time since Woodbine girls began playing basketball, these girls were preparing for an entirely different game. After practicing shooting, the girls (whom BJ always called "ladies") began the first of several grueling, full-court exercises. The first one involved dribbling, both left and right-handed, the full length of the court, punctuated by dribbling behind the back when they switched hands. It was quite a change from six-player ball, which limited players to two dribbles— and to only half the court.

Before anyone had touched a ball, it was evident what hierarchy was in place: Candice, Heather, and Sara look like they were raised to play the five-player game, all muscular, athletic, and confident. Candice and Heather are the daughters of two well-known male athletes from my era, and their mothers were standout players on Woodbine's two state teams in the late 1960s. This trio hung together in shooting drills, and they were the acknowledged leaders, two juniors and a senior.

All of the twenty-three drills listed on the workout page took five to ten minutes each and were geared toward transferring skills from the one game to the other. Even the stationary passing exercises were taxing. Standing some twenty feet apart, the girls, paired up, drilled overhead passes to one another as hard as they could.

The ability to shoot a basketball both left- and right-handed is an invaluable skill, one so difficult that even professional players earning millions of dollars each season aren't able to shoot well with their "other" hand. But Coach would have his players shooting both left- and right-handed, and he had them practicing this on the first day. It was a frustrating drill, particularly when you consider that former guards had never developed their "shooting" hand, let alone the other one. It was obvious early on that BJ, who was approximately forty years old, was an active coach; he took the ball and demonstrated the drills himself. This was a big advantage for young, inexperienced players and an advantage for the coach himself. When one girl complained that she couldn't shoot left-handed, BJ showed her how and achieved better results.

One player, Meg, moaned, "I can't do that!" Early on, she appeared to be one of the more emotional, vocal girls, always talking and making comments after a successful or missed shot. It would be interesting to see how BJ reacted to this sort of player. . . . In the good old days, when I was in school and writing about the Tigerettes, they were coached by a middle-aged bachelor geometry teacher named LaVerne Kloster, whose authoritarian coaching ways were often credited by players, parents, and fans alike for his team's success. It was already obvious that BJ didn't operate that way.

And speaking of the good old days, it's hard to imagine that some of the legendary players of the 1960s—the six-foot string beans or husky post players who simply stood under the basket and popped in lay-ups over the heads of shorter guards—could manage the full-court rebounding drill that BJ demanded next. This was a three-player weave that had the players dribbling full-court, shooting, and rebounding, and then turning around and doing the same back again.

After an hour of hard running, the girls got a break by shooting free throws. Free-throw shooting was one of the hallmarks of Iowa girls' basketball. The state record sits somewhere around 120 consecutive free throws, and nearly every team has an 80 percent shooter. Some pundits have gone so far as to suggest that this is sex-based superiority. In stating his belief that high school girls are more accurate free-throw shooters than boys, an unidentified Iowa coach once told *Sports Illustrated* that girls have a unique sensitivity in the tips of their fingers. "They're born with it," he said. "They have something in their fingers boys don't have. Call it a gift, a feel . . . look at a girl's hands—soft, delicate. They're just better shooters. That's a fact that's clear as a sparrow's dew."[4] In fact, on the first day of practice, when the girls were required already to chart their free throws, most of the veterans were hitting at least 50 percent. That's quite an accomplishment considering NBA center Chris Dudley, who in 1993 signed an $11-million contract for three years, makes only 45 percent of his free throws, or that superstar Shaquille O'Neal holds an all-time NBA record for *missing* eleven straight free throws in December 2000.

Back to the dregs of full-court drills. To break the doldrums, one girl did a cartwheel back to the baseline. (I *knew* that watching this would get entertaining.) When they started practicing lay-ups—again, running the whole court—one player yelled "sorry" when she missed a shot. "Don't be sorry!" admonished BJ. At this point, I suddenly felt a chill, a rush from the realization that, from this early point forward, I was watching something young but with great potential.

Midway through that first practice, the apparent husband of the assistant coach arrived with the couple's baby. The baby, less than one year old, sat contentedly in her stroller in a corner of the gym for the next hour, perhaps with some prescient knowledge that basketball would baby-sit her for years to come. The baby finally began crying when she was in the arms of the student manager, a foreign exchange student from Switzerland; the baby's mother was busy on the floor.

In six-player basketball, following an opponent's basket the ball was put into play at center court. Thus the next drill, involving taking the ball out-of-bounds following a basket or a player yelling "outlet" on a missed shot, was, again, new terrain. So was dribbling full-court, posting up in front of the outreached arms of the assistant coach, and shooting a jump shot in the lane. "Well, I'm a guard! I'm new at this stuff!" sophomore Missy yelled after missing her first few attempts. "All right, I *am* a guard!" she screamed when she finally made one. Then she became the first player to talk to me. "Are you observing us?" she asked me. "Yes," I said from my cross-legged seat on the stage.

The shooting drill obviously caused the most excitement; after all, it had to be the source of anxiety for many of the players who previously weren't allowed to take shots. I noted that when BJ made an error on the court he'd say "I'm sorry," nothing a coach would have admitted thirty years before, during the Tigerettes' glory days. But excitement and all, the girls were running ragged. "Let's just run cross-country," groaned a blonde, athletic girl who joined her teammates in collapsing on the stage when they got to that end of the court. (She turned out to be Darcy, BJ's sophomore daughter.) And when after a water break the girls resumed a full-court drill, they laughed loudly when BJ showed them how to "sprint" to half-court—he barely reached the speed of a jog. Such laughter never erupted in the old days. When BJ swished a basket during a demonstration, the players roared "Whoosh!" Such a verbal outburst would never have occurred either.

Around 5:00 the drills became more complex, and the result was confusion and chatter. By then the assistant coach held her crying baby in her arms. When the chatter finally got to BJ, he ordered his first disciplinary action of the afternoon: sprints back and forth to all the lines up and down the court. Again, it was his daughter who verbalized her emotions. "I hate this game!" she moaned.

By 5:45 confusion and exhaustion reigned. Practice was over at 6:00.

STUDY HALL: DAY TWO

BJ had an open period at 8:30 in his room in the junior high building, the old normal school built at the turn of the century. It had been thoroughly updated, including the addition of a computer center with twenty-five terminals. As BJ and I talked, students regularly came over to his desk to ask about geometry problems. Many of the students in the room were on the basketball team.[5]

BJ acknowledged how tough the first day of practice had been. He talked some about the off-season practices; although Monday was the first state-sanctioned practice, several of his girls had played as many as seventeen informal, five-player games beginning last spring and through the summer. He knew he had some good players and predicted that Heather would become one of the best point guards in the state. In the middle of the period, the high school principal, Fred Jackson, rushed in to tell BJ that Logan High School and another team would have to cancel their junior varsity games on Woodbine's schedule: they didn't have "the numbers" to field a team.

Practice: Day Two

The Tuesday practice focused on defensive drills that BJ didn't get to on Monday. It seemed to be less taxing physically than the first day simply because there was some standing around while the coaches explained various defensive alignments. Early on, one of the toughest drills involved dribbling full-court, in particular the required dribbling between the legs when switching hands. A tough trick. "My legs aren't long enough!" yelled Missy when she had trouble. True, Missy was short-legged and husky. "That means you're dribbling too high," was assistant coach Lori Stockman's reply.

Beginning Tuesday and continuing thereafter, the team was divided into two groups (the apparent varsity and junior varsity squads) for weight-lifting sessions every other day. That in 1993 weight lifting had become a regular and accepted activity for high school girls—as it was for boys—symbolizes the wholesale changes resulting from Title IX. However, weight training was not entirely new for girls in Iowa. The female athletes at Manilla High School, a conference opponent of Woodbine, were lifting in the early 1970s, when Manilla won state titles in both basketball and track and field.[6]

Stockman was responsible for working with the lifters. Two years out of college, she played volleyball at Mankato State (Minnesota) and assisted at Woodbine with basketball and volleyball. She didn't teach; her husband worked for the Department of Transportation and was then working nights, which explained the presence of her child at practice. BJ's youngest daughter, who was about five, spent the first hour jumping rope before her mother arrived and whisked

her away. It's easy to see how coaches' kids get labeled "gym rats"—
they often have little choice.

BJ introduced a new wrinkle in full-court drills this day. He dragged several folding chairs out to midcourt and lined them up. They
looked ominous. The girls were paired off, offensively and defen-
sively, and after taking an inbounds pass, the offensive player had
to beat her defender to the basket down-court and score to avoid
twenty "step-ups" on a chair. It was brutal. As the drill got started,
one player who had apparently hurt herself earlier—or maybe she
was crying for some other reason—returned from the weight room
in tears. "You okay?" Stockman asked, and the player nodded and
walked away, joining the other girls in line for the drill.

About midway through practice, BJ called the players over to the
stage and introduced me for the first time. He mispronounced my
name, which is a rare occurrence in Woodbine. Several of the girls,
many of whom had taken piano lessons from my mother, chuckled.
I joked that I was glad somebody knew my name and told them I'd
appreciate speaking with some of them during the week.

Practice went much more smoothly on Tuesday, though certain
drills still met with the girls flopping their heads down on the stage
in frustration. One drill troubled them in particular: dribbling up
to the free-throw line, a player was supposed to bounce-pass the
ball to a teammate heading for the basket. Without fail, the passes
came late, preventing the other player from making a good shot.
Finally, BJ stopped the drill and demonstrated how the pass must be
thrown quicker. His second demonstration pass, thrown to no one,
went careening into the corner of the gym near the stroller holding
Lori's baby. It elicited a "whoops!" from the coach but not a peep
from the stoic child.

There was one fewer player this day; someone had quit or simply missed practice. The last hour was spent learning offensive and
defensive formations and exposed some new terrain in a half-court
scrimmage. The eight varsity players worked with BJ on one end,
and the other ten practiced with Lori, who roared directions with
baby in hand. The scrimmaging was getting physical by the end,
and BJ yelled "Nice practice, ladies!" at 6:00.

I spent the last half-hour talking with the boys' coach, Mark Massey, whose team couldn't officially begin practice until the following week but who held an "open gym" after the girls finished every night. He was anxious to get started after having traveled to Indiana to attend Bob Knight's coaches' camp the previous weekend with eight hundred other high school coaches from forty-five states. He should have been: he had four senior starters and a stable of young potential stars. Massey admitted he was a "my-way-or-the-highway" sort of coach, a philosophy undoubtedly shot with new zeal after meeting Bob Knight. He hadn't been too successful in Woodbine to that point; but he was loaded now, so the pressure was on.[7]

STUDY HALL: DAY THREE

I met with BJ at 10:00 this morning; again, he was busy tutoring geometry students. I asked two questions: could he help me line up some interviews with players, and would he talk about the differences between coaching girls and boys. The first was easily answered, and among the players I would be talking with on Thursday were two of the guards who didn't come out for basketball this season. Although those girls chose not to play, BJ said the changeover would clearly benefit his players. Franny Menken, the fourth forward in six-player, would have been a benchwarmer in the old game; she'd probably start now. Because of the strain of full-court play, at least eight girls, as opposed to six previously, would see significant playing time. That meant at least three other girls—Darcy, Carrie, and Meg—who had no varsity experience, would play a lot and maybe even start. "All eighteen or nineteen kids will play now, if not on varsity then on JV," BJ proclaimed.

He was a little more hesitant in answering the second question, though. BJ coached boys for ten years and was beginning his third with girls. "Boys seem to handle little jealousy things better. They duke it out on their own," he said. "With girls, you often have to settle problems. Both work hard—there is no difference there." I asked him about the maturity levels of boys and girls in high school.

"With certain girls on certain days, you want to leave them alone," was his reply.

BJ put in "a rough couple of first years" in Woodbine. Many of the girls' parents played in the "powerhouse years," and they wanted to win immediately. Between that golden era—1966–76—and 1991, when BJ took over, Woodbine couldn't win a game. Margaret Shorey, a former star under Kloster and the mother of Candice, was the assistant when Woodbine went to hire a new coach. Some folks wanted her as the head coach, and, coupled with the fact that BJ had no experience coaching girls, they questioned the school's decision to hire BJ. He explained: "Some people thought we should go from not winning any games to 1,000-1 again immediately. But it's okay now. The community told them to back off and shut up. The parents of some players, like the Shoreys, had questioned my hiring. So there was a question of whether I'd have a job."

BJ went 9-11 his first year, then improved to 11-9 last season, the best record in Woodbine since "Kloster-ball." It became complicated, though; BJ was getting mixed messages. BJ was told to win but then criticized for playing his best players instead of the older ones. "The policy had been to play juniors and seniors. I wanted to play the best ones. You've got to be kind of a jerk sometimes, and I don't do that well."

The matter had settled down now, and the only pressure to win was self-imposed. "I want to win every game," he affirmed. The changeover to five-player ball didn't lessen his desire for immediate success. BJ believed that the shocking decision to change the rules for the season, a decision made the previous winter and done without, according to him, any surveying of coaches, was made partially to alleviate the travel costs of schools playing six-player ball that would have to travel farther to find opponents. BJ felt the goal of the state was to consolidate schools, "to get all districts one thousand [students] or bigger." (Woodbine, which had about two hundred students in grades nine through twelve, was larger than only two schools in the conference, both consolidated.) Guards were not the only ones who packed it up with the change; at least one conference coach quit. And for some older coaches who were uncomfortable with the new game, 1993 proved to be a convenient time to retire.

We finished our talk about the first two practices. I mentioned that I thought they were physically exhausting. He didn't seem to agree. "I don't work the girls as hard as boys," he said. "I do feel uneasy about the first ones, though. I like to work on 'parts' first, then reach for the 'whole.' But I don't know what we've accomplished yet. I can be much more demanding." BJ and I finished up by talking more about players and the problems he encounters coaching his own daughter, a sophomore on the team. "She [Darcy] hints around that she wants to start. My policy is if a junior and senior are even, the senior starts. Same with sophomores and juniors. I get mad at her quicker than the others, and I don't treat her the same."

In My Mother's Parlor

Before practice Wednesday, I waited at the house to speak with Candice Shorey, the veteran senior who took her piano lesson from my mother. She is the only basketball player still taking lessons—several used to, but given the allure of girls' basketball in this town, when it comes to crunch time, music usually loses out. As a junior forward, Candice averaged over 30 points per game playing six-player ball.[8] Candice was sweet natured and shy; her reluctance to talk must have come from her father, with whom I grew up. Billy Shorey was the star athlete in our class. He played college football and returned to coach Woodbine's team and to farm. Candice's mother, Margaret, was a starting guard on the 1969 state team. Candice may have been better suited for the six-player game—she was big and muscular but not as athletic-looking as Heather, one of her teammates. But looks deceive: Candice battled Heather for the lead in most of the individual drills. Like her father, she was one of those rare athletes whose sweet disposition masked a ferocious competitiveness. Candice was at home on the court and often flashed a smile when she played, one that let you know she was enjoying herself. But she was not an easy one to talk to. I spoke with her for about ten minutes—she told me the names of several colleges she was considering—and then left our house to walk over to practice.

I was getting ready to leave, too, when Brenda Harper, a woman in her midthirties, walked out of the piano room. Brenda had heard about my project and was eager to talk. Brenda was curious about how I perceived BJ. She was as impressed with him as I was, but an earlier rift over his coaching had widened enough that some parents had started a petition drive to replace him the year before. I had forgotten about the letter in the *Woodbine Twiner* criticizing his decision to play some girls and not others. The parents of then-junior Franny Menken (one of the players BJ named as a likely starter in the five-player game who might not have started otherwise) wrote the letter, upset that in a parents' night game earlier that month, throughout which Woodbine held a double-digit lead, their daughter was the only member of the team who didn't play. The letter prompted a burst of support for the coach in the subsequent week's editorial page; two letters to the editor and the *Twiner*'s weekly editorial characterized BJ as "a victim of unrealistic expectations by a small but vocal group."[9]

Brenda went on to say how impressed she was with BJ—his coaching and his teaching. She was outraged that parents would petition to drive away such a good man, particularly since he'd been there only two years. Just up the road in Dunlap, parents had forced the school board to fire their basketball coach following the previous season, when he apparently didn't win enough games to satisfy them. Mike Melby, a Woodbine carpenter whose son dated one of the girls on the team, offered his thoughts on the topic: "If parents want to coach, they should go to college, get a degree, and do it themselves."

Practice: Day Three

As practice began Wednesday and the girls were shooting free throws, the boys' coach, Mark Massey, sat down on the stage before heading home. Wednesday night was church night, so there was no open gym; Woodbine—as well as many other Iowa communities—refrains from scheduling school events on one weekday night, which is reserved for church activities. Massey was on his way to a rules meeting in Denison, twenty-five miles away. Coaches are consumed with basketball even when they don't have practice.

Massey didn't think girls, by nature, shot free throws any better than boys. His explanation was that forwards in the girls' six-player game had more time to concentrate on free-throw shooting, not having to play defense. BJ later echoed these sentiments, adding that in a game situation forwards also usually got to rest a while when the ball was in the guard court. Massey predicted the girls' scores that year would hover in the 40s, like a boys' junior varsity game; BJ foresaw an offensive average around 50 points.

There were seventeen girls out on the third day of practice—missing was Karla, who wasn't in school on Wednesday. Practice might have taken its toll on her. All those step-ups on the folding chairs took their toll, too: one of the chairs collapsed during practice. It was a good practice, though. "It was a lot better, and we'll have one more on Thursday before we put in our defense," BJ said. Early on, Darcy, the coach's daughter, was "slacking"; as it turned out, she had bruised her tailbone sitting down on the stage. She wouldn't dress for Thursday's practice.

The full-court outlet-pass drill that consumed much of practice the first two days was really rolling now. It was remarkable how much improvement one could see over a couple of days. Besides being physically taxing, the drill involved a complex formation and still caused confusion on the third day; but BJ gave his team plenty of positive reinforcement. Even the guards' shooting had improved visibly in three days; Missy was nailing lay-ups and short jumpers as if she had shot them all her life. Rarely was there an allusion to the old game; it only occurred when a player executed a movement that was obsolete in the new game. "That's a great play in six-on-six, but not worth a darn in five-on-five," BJ told one of the post players when she made a pivot move under the basket.

When BJ saw that his girls were getting lackadaisical, he called for an "eye opener," a sprint back and forth between the lines on the court (baseline to free-throw line to baseline to half-court line to baseline to second free-throw line and back) that invariably left the players collapsing their heads on the stage. But it was a good practice, and they were still running hard at quitting time.

STUDY HALL: DAY FOUR

During my study hall debriefing I was scheduled to meet with two guards who chose not to go out for basketball that year. BJ was snowed with paper work: "I tried to get as much of it done before hoops began, but it's already piling up," he sighed. While waiting for the girls, I listened to BJ talk about the changeover.

> The six-player game was getting to be strictly an offensive show, mostly because of the three-point shot. Every team had two three-point shooters. They'd hit the post girl, who'd kick it back outside for the three-point shot. I hated six-on-six, it's not really basketball. The big post players who just dumped the ball in were a joke, unless they were good athletes. But the only thing forwards did was practice offense. Now, the only difference between boys and girls is that the girls will be slower and "lower"—below the rim. Everything else is practically comparable. I'd put Candice Shorey up against any shooter on the boys' team. But for a couple of years, free throws and shooting percentages will be half of what they were and will drop below the boys'. Girls will no longer get to rest up their legs after getting done at half court.

BJ believed the changeover came at an ideal time for him and his team. "We would have seniors sitting on the bench this year otherwise," he said. "In our particular case, the timing was perfect. Our guards graduated. Guards were always those girls who didn't want to work on their game in the off-season."

He along with most of his players were looking forward to playing Logan and Dunlap, Woodbine's fiercest competitors (and the two nearest towns). When Woodbine played Logan in volleyball, BJ coached against his wife, Jeri, who was that school's head volleyball coach. "If I could, I'd crush them," he said about playing against his wife's team. As for basketball: "As far as I know, Woodbine hasn't beaten Logan in thirty years. I hate to play that game. But we played 'em within one point in an off-season camp."

I wound up talking with six players that morning, including the two who chose not to go out for the team. The differences between these six girls were incredible—the difference between the sopho-mores and upperclassmen, between those who played and those who didn't, between personalities, between lives. Sandra and Alex were meek. They may also have been intimidated. They were only sopho-mores, and I can imagine the slights—real or imagined—they might have felt for having quit. Sandra suffered from asthma, which was a primary concern in her choice not to play. "I didn't think I could get up and down the court," she explained. "I was still making up my mind at the end of summer." Both Sandra and Alex played on a good junior high team in the same guard court with Darcy and Penny, who were still playing.

Sitting next to them in study hall that morning was a sophomore classmate who was on the team and a bit more talkative. Claire came from a family of athletes who starred on Dunlap teams. A former guard, she hadn't yet decided whether or not she liked the five-player game but was willing to give it a shot. "I thought we'd be running a lot more. We watched the boys practice last year, and all they seemed to do was run," said Claire. She had wanted Alex and Sandra to go out but respected their decision not to.

I next spoke with three veterans on the team—Kristin, Heather, and Sara—who, along with Candice, were the projected starters. Kristin, a senior, was one of those students for whom basketball was just one of many activities in which she excelled. After having visited Annapolis on the DC trip the week before, she was planning on applying to the Naval Academy. A former guard who had "shot some" in preparation for the change (she attended the Creighton University summer camp), Kristin said she felt more pressure play-ing in junior high under a "strict guy" like Phil Hummel, the ju-nior high coach who was from the "Kloster-ball" era and had led the track and cross-country teams to several state championships. "Jasper is a more relaxed, younger guy," she continued. Kristin's other school activities—student council and W Club, the letter win-ners' organization—didn't leave her feeling pressured. "I could probably take on a couple more activities," she said.

Heather, the high-spirited junior who BJ expected to become one of the state's best point guards, grew up playing basketball like boys.

In a way she had no choice—her father and uncles were star athletes and former coaches at Woodbine. "I won't say I felt pressure, but it was there," she confided. "I've always played some kind of ball. My parents are excited. They tell me if I work hard I can get a scholarship." Heather exuded self-confidence. She claimed practices thus far had been "monotonous" and admitted to having less patience with the younger players. Unlike many of her teammates, Heather had set lofty goals for the season. "I'd like to win the conference and at least advance a ways into districts," she said. "Next year, I'd like to get all-conference and maybe get a scholarship to a small college. But I'd rather see the team do well." Heather's use of "jockspeak"—evidenced by her diplomatic statement that she'd "rather see the team do well"—was part of the socialization that comes with the increasing rationalization characteristic of modern sport. It was similar to the social and cultural acceptance of high school girls' participation in weight training.

Unlike Heather, Sara, the daughter of the junior high principal, would be happy with a .500 season. And Sara, the team's tallest player at five-foot-eleven, admitted that she preferred the six-player game—not an unusual attitude for tall centers, who could dominate in the former game. Sara made an interesting comment. She didn't think the criticism of BJ had disappeared: "It's still there," she said. "But then every coach gets criticized."

PRACTICE: DAY FOUR

Day four introduced another new wrinkle in conditioning: the fearsome "crab walk," whose execution Heather immediately questioned. The drill involved bending over backward and "crabbing" upcourt on hands and feet. BJ's immediate response to the doubter and her teammates: sprints. That done, one crab walk down the court left Heather in tears, apparently hurt (either physically or emotionally). BJ guided her into a corner and had a brief, private moment with her. She bounded back to the court after the talk, good as new. BJ walked toward me smiling. "There's something else that's different between boys and girls," he confided. "After four or five days, girls can get a little owly. That's when you get on them. That's what I did. She wasn't any more hurt than . . . ," leaving the sentence incomplete.

There were only fourteen girls in practice this day, not counting Darcy, who was injured and in street clothes. Two more players— both sophomores—showed up at 5:00. They'd been bowling, apparently in connection with a school or church activity. The other four or so missing players caused some chatter among the players, who were talking about the absences during drills. The chatter provoked BJ's sternest lecture of the week thus far. In midst of a drill, he yelled "Stop!" then slowly walked in a circle around the players at midcourt, not saying a word. You knew something was coming. "Some of you seem to be worrying about those missing," he said. "Stop worrying about them. If you don't want to run, go sit on the stage. You must have your mind on the court."

Day four also brought a team vote on Saturday morning's practice time: 7:00 to 10:00 or 8:00 to 11:00. The girls opted for the latter. At quitting time, BJ made it clear one more time how questioning his authority would be handled. A player asked about defensive drills, and he told the team to do three instead of two—"because someone asked."

STUDY HALL: DAY FIVE

I was surrounded by sophomores again this day, only this time they were chatterboxes. It may have had something to do with it being late Friday afternoon, and the fact that I'd sprung the four of them from study hall, their last period of the school week. Missy, Penny, and Darcy all proved opinionated; Rhonda was more reserved. The forum broke conveniently into two sides: Missy and Penny, both guards, might have lettered this season as sophomores had the six-player game continued. It was clear they liked the old game better. Darcy and Rhonda, forwards, were enthusiastic about the new game. "I'm in shape, so I can run up and down the court," admitted Rhonda, a cross-country runner.

Penny and Missy were quite vocal for sophomores. Missy's father and his brothers were high school football players and wrestlers who didn't play basketball, and Missy said they didn't like the sport. The talkative foursome had some startling things to say about how other students and the faculty viewed the new game, too. "The crowds are going to laugh at us," Missy said. "But that's okay because we're doing it, not them." Darcy said that guys were already laughing at them. "My brother says our timing is off," she told me. "And some of the teachers laugh. It's not very supportive and kinda negative. Mr. Johnson [a teacher] was standing in the gym the other day, watching, and I heard him say about a player: 'obviously she's not a shooter.' It just makes you want to play harder." It sounded as if after years of unbridled criticism for sticking with the old game from outsiders, Iowa girls were now catching it from the insiders, too.

Practice: Day Five

Because it was Friday and an early-morning session was scheduled on Saturday, BJ let up on his charges this afternoon. Practice was low-key, and there was plenty of chatter. "Watch *The Wizard of Oz* last night?" one player asked another between drills. But at 4:45, for the first time this week, for the first time ever, the players scrimmaged full-court, uninterrupted.

> When I first came to Iowa, Dwight D. Eisenhower was president and six-girl basketball was the state's number-one sport. I couldn't believe Iowans took girls' basketball so seriously. And that was before I saw a game. . . . I'm not one to blow my own whistle, but before I came along no one had noticed that girls' basketball was dull. Duller than oatmeal, . . . I started to spread the word and slowly began to win converts.
>
> The final act was played out this week. . . . I'm proud.[10]

These were the remarks of the nationally syndicated columnist Donald Kaul, whose criticism of six-player ball helped build his career—and earned him the wrath of passionate fans. But his piece about the changeover on page one of the *Des Moines Register* (February 5, 1993) marked the end of an era.

The crowds are going to laugh at us. Missy was wrong about the crowds that winter of 1993–94. Of course, any naysayers in the Woodbine bleachers were quickly proven wrong themselves. Not only did the Lady Tigers win their first three games, they easily whipped those opponents by an average margin of almost 30 points en route to a 15-9 record. Woodbine was ranked as high as thirteenth in the state, and seven of the nine losses were to top-twenty teams, the result of the Lady Tigers competing in one of the toughest conferences in Iowa that season. Bob Jasper, who would coach just one more season in Woodbine, believed that the abundance of preseason work undertaken by many of the league's teams—especially summer camps—accounted for the success of most state-ranked teams. And, at least initially, the home crowd was won over. "We packed the gym that first year of five-player," BJ stated with pride. "We never had crowds like that before." Sara was a second-team all-conference selection, and Candice and Heather were named to the third team; all three received honorable mention for the all-Southwest Iowa and all-state basketball squads.

But more than five years after helping to usher in the new game in Woodbine, Bob Jasper was no longer convinced basketball was the most popular game with high school girls. After coaching one more season in Woodbine (1994–95), Jasper accepted the head girls' basketball and volleyball job at West Monona High School in Onawa, a community of three thousand about forty miles north of Woodbine. There, Jasper coached basketball for two more years before quitting and coaching volleyball only. "Volleyball is more popular than basketball with the girls," he said in 1999. "We'll get thirty to forty girls out because it is more fun than basketball. There's no full-court running. I don't know if girls were made for all that pounding."[11]

Each of Woodbine's trio of leaders during the 1993–94 season played basketball at the Iowa small college she attended—Buena Vista College, Northwestern College, and Central College. Heather and Sara both suffered career-ending knee injuries in college; only Candice played through her senior year. Darcy, the girls' teammate and BJ's daughter, transferred in her junior year to Lo-Ma High School, where she played volleyball under coach Jeri Jasper, her mother.

The same factors that made women's basketball the centerpiece in the century-long fight over control of women's sports were instrumental in the demise of Iowa six-player girls' basketball. Once more, the female athlete—in this case, high school girls—served as contested ideological terrain on the battleground of societal gender issues. While the construction of the "moderate" six-player game was the result of late-nineteenth-century gender arrangements, it took my watching the in-practice transition to full-court basketball and observing the cultural shift in the community that accompanied the change to understand fully what was being replaced. Iowa girls' basketball had been an elaborate, unique, longstanding, successful, and *powerful* culture that, for better or for worse, permitted young women a space where they played on their own terms and without the aggravation of having to compete with boys, which is an implicit and possibly unavoidable problem in the adoption of a gendered activity that involves physical prowess.

What I learned in the Woodbine gym, where curious but doubtful onlookers peered behind corners and questioned the wisdom of letting girls play full court, was that now a *whole* culture in rural communities had been stratified, marginalized, and, most ironic, gendered. Whereas the skill level of participants in six-player basketball was rarely questioned by insiders, the introduction of the "new" game resulted in the inevitable comparison of skills between boys and girls. Thus a basketball culture had been subverted and was now riddled with internal anxieties, ridicule, and disorder that were once the province of outsiders. The changeover from six-player "girls'" basketball to five-player "boys'" basketball meant that women were once again stepping onto men's turf, and the resulting cultural behavior was fearful, unaccommodating, and predictable.

TWO

Rural Education, Ideology, and Girls' Basketball

One could grow up in the town in the late 1950s and early '60s, as I did, watching girls' sports without the least notion that there was anything prophetic about a custom that in small Iowa farming towns is as deeply embedded in the psyche as the suspicion of skies and the certainty that a stranger is a Democrat. – Douglas Bauer, *Prairie City, Iowa: Three Seasons at Home*

They had won the state championship a few hours earlier, but when the high school girls' basketball team returned to Ida Grove in western Iowa in the wee hours of a late-winter Sunday in 1928, center Sarah Allen White remembers that the players were cold and tired. "There was no heat in the cars, only side curtains, and we huddled under blankets," she recalled. "As we were coming in at the foot of the hill into Ida Grove at one or two in the morning, there was a band and several hundred people. It was the biggest thing in Ida Grove." Similarly, in March 1956 nearly four thousand people rushed to the northeast Iowa town of Maynard to celebrate West Central's girls' state basketball title. Maynard had a population of 435. "The day of the championship final, Grandpa and Grandma Nicholson were the only people left in Maynard," remembered West Central player Carolyn Nicholson. Twelve years later, Union-Whitten High School's girls' state championship team was celebrated in neighboring Marshalltown, where the local newspaper described the gathering of over one thousand fans as "the biggest crowd since movie star Jean Seberg's homecoming."[1]

Throughout the century of its existence, six-player girls' basketball was played in other states—mostly in the Midwest and the South—but it was the dominion of rural Iowa. In 1950 girls' basketball was played in 700 of Iowa's 834 high schools; twenty years later that number had fallen to 332, primarily because of school consolidations. Because city schools didn't put teams on the court until the 1970s, the culture of basketball took hold in small towns like Farragut (15 state appearances through 1999), Guthrie Center (19), Mediapolis (21), and Wellsburg (18). Not until 1972—more than *fifty years* after the tourney's inception—did a city school, Cedar Rapids Kennedy, earn a state tournament berth. Rural Iowa culture was firmly implanted in its schools, the most prolific of institutional supports that sustained the phenomenon of competitive girls' basketball as it waned elsewhere. Other supporters included the Iowa Girls High School Athletic Union and the state media. Iowa six-player girls' basketball required such hearty endorsements in order to survive; national debates constantly loomed in its background, often involving issues larger than the rules of the game. Among the issues was centralization in modern society. Just as girls' basketball became the battleground for larger gender issues, Iowa served as a social laboratory for Progressive Era reformers' desire to engineer rural transformation through the reorganization, or consolidation, of country schools.[2]

A school serves to educate national citizens as well as to provide an important social institution in the local community. These functions are exposed as conflicting in instances of school reorganization, when national, centralized efficiency often threatens local identity and autonomy. Such was the case in Iowa, where Progressive Era reformers made school consolidation the centerpiece of their attempts to restructure the state's countryside. They were met with fierce resistence.[3]

The predominant force that shaped midwestern rural education was the fight for local control. It was a battle fought by farmers against reformers that began before the Civil War, when farmers initially opposed tax-funded public education. The struggle continued throughout the century as farmers insisted that their children's education remain firmly in their hands.[4]

Before 1850 midwestern schools, when they existed, were private subscription schools paid for by parents, or, increasingly as time passed, by school districts that resulted from the enactment of public education laws in the 1830s that accompanied the statehood of several Midwestern territories during the period. All of this changed because of the actions of two disparate groups: reformers and farmers. Practical but idealistic reformers were bolstered by both Puritan zeal and a belief that free schools would cure the nation's ills, among them, rising illiteracy rates and fear of a newly arrived immigrant population in the Midwest. Farmers were dubious of "book farming," things intellectual, and, most of all, a compulsory education tax. But the farmers were won over—they accepted free public education—when reformers had thoroughly persuaded them that they, the farmers, would remain in control. The farmers would build the schoolhouses and hire the teachers, and all property owners would pay for education, whether they wanted to or not. Beginning in the late 1840s several midwestern states began passing laws that required school districts to open their schools a minimum number of months each year and to collect taxes to support them.[5] By 1859 Iowa had three thousand independent school districts, and by 1900 the state led the nation in the number of schoolhouses—fourteen thousand.

An immediate result of the empowerment of small school districts was that by 1900 the Midwest led the nation in literacy rates. Like its neighbors Kansas and Nebraska, Iowa's illiteracy rate fell below 3 percent. These states, too, were national leaders in school attendance, well before compulsory attendance was instituted. The effects, which survive to this day, were twofold: On the one hand, an elaborate culture of schooling, infused with the belief that the quality and success of schools turned on local administration, was inculcated in rural midwestern culture. On the other hand, incessant fighting between rural citizens and state and national figures—over administration, funding, the preparation of teachers, compulsory attendance, centralization, and so on—conflated the yeoman myth with a rural and urban antagonism. Iowans fighting outsiders over girls' basketball rules was evidence that this oppositional force existed.

There was indeed something to the myth of the yeoman (the small, independent farmer) and Jeffersonian agrarianism: the idealized yeoman did exist in the Midwest, but he or she was a real, oppositional figure instead of the fictive player in the agrarian or pastoral myth. That figure was the parent and farmer who took full responsibility for his or her children's education, running the school and the district.[6]

"Bringing school to the kids" was the midwestern answer to providing rural education, and the formation of districts, with the schools centered in townships, gave farmers power and showed them how democracy worked. "The little independent school districts . . . gave parents almost complete control of that education in ways that would be virtually incomprehensible to later generations," the historian Wayne Fuller writes. He describes the school district as "the smallest self-governing political division in the nation," with the schoolhouse serving as a symbol of individualism and grass-roots direct democracy, and farmers gaining identity and transmitting values to their children. Farmers readily served on school boards— it was both a duty and a privilege—which integrated them into the social and political fabric of the community.[7]

But in the early twentieth century, an intruder appeared before rural education: consolidation. Enrollments had begun to decline, and rural education was blamed for migration to cities—an erroneous belief, Fuller contends. Professional educators seemed intent on disrupting a productive system. An example of the confusion and ineffectiveness of early bureaucracy in education was the 1908 report of the Country Life Commission, perhaps the most important rural reform movement of the Progressive Era. The Country Life movement hoped to transform midwestern rural life, a transformation that was to be accomplished in part through the consolidation of rural school districts, whose supervision by farmers and their families these national reformers no longer found acceptable.

Progressive Era reformers, hoping to increase educational opportunities for rural children, considered school consolidation the solution to many rural problems. "The rural school consolidation movement was decidedly a Midwestern phenomenon," argues David Reynolds, who describes the national reformers as a "cadre of urban elites" consisting of leading businessmen, social scientists, and religious leaders drawn together by a perceived agrarian demise in the wake of industrialism. [8] The commission blamed declining rural population on the country school after it asked farmers if their schools satisfactorily trained children for life on the farm. The majority of the fifty thousand farmers and wives surveyed answered "no"; they believed in fact that their schools prepared children for more advanced careers *off* the farm. The commission, however, interpreted the response as confirmation that the rural schools were ineffective and, in an effort to keep rural children on the farm, recommended incorporating "nature study" and agriculture into the curriculum. Equally ludicrous was the commission's suggestion that country schoolhouses function as "community centers"; that the buildings had been used for precisely that, in the heartiest of democratic fashion, for a half century reveals how little the commission understood the culture of schooling in the rural Midwest. Country schools already brought community residents together because they were almost always the only communal property a rural township held. [9]

Farmers, fearing loss of control and the intrusion of "city values," battled consolidation tooth and nail, and they were successful in Iowa through the 1920s. Standardized test scores differed little between rural and urban schools. In 1936 Iowa still had open over nine thousand one-room schools—one of the highest numbers in the nation—but they served just over one-quarter of the state's schoolchildren. Consolidation had consumed the country schools by the 1950s. In southwest Iowa, where I attended school, the last of the country schools surrounding town wasn't closed until 1962. [10]

As it turned out, rural residents didn't leave for the city because of inadequate schools; they were forced to do so when their schools were shut down. The strength of rural midwestern education was evident in the works of prominent writers and lesser-known memoirists as well as in the state's nation-leading literacy rates. The meaning of that strength and its pervasive worth is evident today in the culture of schooling that persists in the rural Midwest, which remains among the most literate regions of the country.[11]

On a January evening in 1952, woi, the first commercial television station in Iowa and the first to broadcast an Iowa high school sporting event—the 1950 girls' state tournament—hosted its popular show "The Whole Town's Talking" from Winterset, Iowa. The occasion: twelve citizens of this Madison County town of 3,579 had gathered to discuss consolidating the eleven school districts in and around Winterset. The consolidation would involve forming one school district and a single tax base. At the conclusion of the hour-long forum, witnessed by an estimated quarter million television viewers, the dozen participants, who favored consolidation by a 7–5 count, would vote again on reorganization.

"Country schools are outdated, and there's no competition when there's one or two students in a class," said Ollie Holland, a farmer and teacher who supported consolidation. "But I walk my daughter to school every day, and I'd like to keep it that way—there's no transportation, and I don't want her bussed," opined Ken Spiro, a reorganization foe. "You'd be junking one of the best elementary schools in Iowa, and the country folk are going to pay more." Another of the participants remarked that her school had no globe and no desktops and that the community's eleven schools were of unequal quality. To no one's surprise, the forum ended with the same 7–5 edge for consolidation.[12]

It was not surprising that a small-town-education forum in Iowa would draw some 250,000 television viewers in 1952, for this was the year that began the second of three decade-long waves of school reorganizations that swept Iowa in the twentieth century. Despite enactment of a state law for consolidation in the century's first decade, an early consolidated school movement failed, largely because of the 1920 agricultural recession that made it hard for farm families to finance schools and country roads. The second wave, called the community school movement, involved the elimination of the rural elementary districts—the country schools—as well as the continued shrinking of the number of high schools. This phase faced little opposition. A dramatically diminished rural population accounted for the success of the community school movement; sixty-five of Iowa's ninety-nine counties lost population between 1950 and 1960.[13]

By the end of the third wave (1985–95), the school-reorganization movement had run its course, and the number of school districts had been further reduced by approximately 20 percent, leaving 350 high school districts, which was little more than one-third the number in the early 1930s. It was abundantly clear that, as foreshadowed by the citizens of Winterset at midcentury, consolidation had become increasingly acceptable to Iowans. To close a country school was to remove an institution that held the rural small town together, but consolidation was better than the alternative: to dissolve (or voluntarily close by a vote) a school district completely. *Only twice in state history—in 1988 and 1997—have voters voluntarily dissolved an Iowa school district.*[14]

Guy Ghan, now retired from the Iowa Department of Education, was the state's authority on reorganization during the third wave of school reorganizations, having conducted 280 studies of different school districts between 1980 and 1995. According to Ghan, Iowans endorsed school reorganization because, similar to the nineteenth-century country schoolhouse movement, it was a matter of local control. Ghan maintains that the consolidation movement was driven by local decision-making, that the statewide impact was minimal, and that school reorganization was an inevitable occurrence that "always happened after the train came through":

> Schools are subject to many of the same economic pressures that have caused farms to become larger, for retail services to dramatically consolidate into larger communities, and for the populations to shift from the rural areas. In these towns,

in no case did I notice the school was first to go, but business was. . . . The school never led the charge. Main streets
changed, and there were no more mom-and-pop stores. What
the modern era has brought us [is that] no Iowa town is more
than one hour from a mall. When Wal-Mart comes into An-
keny, three hardware stores die. . . . Schools face the same
pressure, but they're a lot harder to change. You can't make
a living on a quarter section any more, and it's the same thing
with schools.[15]

An Iowa State University study that examined the impact of reorganization on perceptions of educational quality showed that closing
a high school was perceived to have a positive impact on academic
programs and participation in extracurricular activities: "While it is
often cited that closing a high school will reduce student participation in extracurricular activities, the results of this study did not in-
dicate that this was true for Iowa schools. They did confirm that . . .
all students who wanted to participate in extracurricular activities
were doing so. Further, students were satisfied with the variety of
activities offered in their schools."[16]

   Unlike Ghan, some scholars strongly disagree that consolidation
was a matter of local control. There is also evidence that consolidation may worsen such problems as the loss of stable communities
to support families and confusion over who should teach values and
beliefs. A study that compared community services between 1955
and 1980 in Iowa towns that had high schools with those that had
lost schools showed that the eleven towns that had lost high schools
had also lost services. The twelve with high schools reported having
the most services. Another analysis revealed that between 1970 and
1990 half the Iowa towns studied with high schools had population
gains of 5 percent or more, while three-fourths of towns without
high schools lost population. "When school doors shut in small
towns," says education researcher Craig Howley, "there's a loss of
community life. The loss of schools is parallel to the loss of institutions and society."[17]

   How the loss of a school is implicated in the demise of a town can be observed in Moneta, a northwestern Iowa community that was founded in 1901 and peaked in the 1920s with a population of about 130. At that time Moneta included among its several businesses a hotel, several gas stations, a bank, general store, two cafes, a town hall, hardware store, creamery, beer parlor, livery stable, and blacksmith shop as well as two grain elevators and the all-important railroad depot. In 1959 Moneta consolidated with Everly's school district, eliminating the high school; and in 1976 the elementary school was closed. Twenty years later, in 1996, the remaining twenty-six residents of Moneta voted to disincorporate their town. The mayor believed the school consolidation and the closing of the railroad that happened soon after led to the departure of the other town businesses. "When I was little, the street by the schoolhouse was lined with cars every weekend," he said. "Everybody came and played baseball. Everybody played—kids, parents, grandparents. It was a big deal."[18]

Understanding that rural schools are "special" and that some outside forces are harmful is vital in the discussion of Iowa girls' basketball. Six-player girls' basketball, considered obsolete by most of the nation long before it was eliminated in Iowa, was a cultural product of the rural schools and succeeded at a level on par with the country schools. In their stubbornness to fight against "outside forces," Iowans held on to the game with much the same tenacity that nineteenth- and twentieth-century farmers fought to control their children's education.

Throughout its arc of ascension to becoming the reigning high school girls' sport in America, Iowa six-player basketball was subjected to the same national forces that reconfigured sport throughout the twentieth century. The debate over the roles of men and women eventually surfaced on the basketball court, where the effect of having a game whose rules for women were always in flux unmasked the gender anxieties that marked the larger culture. The battle over gender-based rules manifested itself most clearly in the fight against vigorous competition for girls, which erupted in different areas of the country at different times. In 1907 the Illinois High

School Athletic Association banned girls' interscholastic basketball in that state, a precedent for administrators in other states. "The committee finds that roughness is not foreign to the game, and that the exercise in public is immodest and not altogether ladylike," the administrators ruled. In North Carolina, however, girls' basketball thrived until almost 1960, when the success of the anticompetition charge, the lack of institutional support, and an increasingly popular college men's game conspired against girls' participation in the sport. Their role transformed to fit with what has been identified as the primary athletic model in America: a ritual in which young men compete and young women cheer them on. In other words, North Carolina had returned to a conventional gender arrangement.[19]

Iowa girls' basketball's primary defense from such an attack was the Iowa Girls High School Athletic Union, the only such prep association in America and a powerful force from its inception in 1925. But the Union alone could not withstand outside educators' ideological attacks, among which were claims that vigorous play was harmful and that allowing the public to watch girls was playing to prurient interests. Supplementing the already powerful institutional support of the IGHSAU was an ideology that posited six-player basketball with rural education, small towns, and Iowa newspapers—notably, the *Des Moines Register*—resulting in a complex web of legend, myth, and narrative that infused the game with meaning when it was played and following its demise. Inspection of newspaper reports, school annuals, and IGHSAU bulletins help show how this ideology was constructed.

From its sponsorship of the first state tournament in 1920, when the championship game report was the lead story in the Sunday sports section, to the 1993 abandonment of six-player basketball, the *Des Moines Register* played an integral role in the development of the game and the ideology that sustained it. Apart from its sports coverage, the *Register* was nationally regarded for much of the twentieth century for its reputation as a regional newspaper. When Gardner Cowles bought the *Register* in 1903 he declared that its primary audience would be the entire state, a decree that permitted the newspaper to provide perhaps the most complete statewide coverage of any American newspaper. "We're one of the two things that unify Iowa," said a *Register* reporter, also noting the prominence of the state fair.[20]

But "the newspaper Iowa depends on" (the slogan set below the *Register* flag on the front page) gained even more respect for its editorial page. In 1933 a *Register* news bureau was opened in Washington DC to cover President Roosevelt's New Deal; his federal farm and public welfare programs, rural-electrification program, and bank-deposit insurance so closely affected the daily lives of Iowans that banks would often paste the front pages of the *Register* on their windows for townspeople. It didn't hurt, either, that Harry Hopkins, perhaps FDR's closest confidante and the Federal Emergency Relief administrator, was an Iowan who became a regular news source for Richard Wilson, the *Register*'s bureau chief in the capital. When he retired in 1970 Wilson—and the bureau he had built—held an unparalleled position in American journalism: the chief and his three reporters had each won Pulitzer Prizes. In 1975 the *Register* proudly presented the following text in a house advertisement: "In the history of journalism, only one newspaper has won more Pulitzer Prizes for national reporting than the *Des Moines Register*. Our congratulations to *The New York Times*." That wasn't all. Editorial cartoonist Jay Norwood "Ding" Darling was widely syndicated in American newspapers in the early twentieth century. And in 1925 Cowles hired George Gallup, a University of Iowa journalism instructor and doctoral candidate, to implement his new technique for measuring readership interest. The Gallup Poll was born.[21]

But the *Register*'s reputation suffered when the Gannett chain bought the newspaper in 1985. Soon after, Gannett released a mission statement revealing that the entire state was no longer the primary audience; the *Register* shifted its focus from the state of Iowa to the Des Moines metropolitan area. "The newspaper Iowa depends on" closed its satellite bureaus in Dubuque, Waterloo, and Sioux City; quit delivering the weekday paper in twenty-one western counties; and raised the price of editions outside Des Moines. "We're coming to grips with the fact that we're a different state

now," rationalized managing editor David Westphal, calling to mind
Iowa's population loss that accompanied the severe agricultural crisis
in the mid-1980s, when Gannett bought the paper.[22]

The sale of the *Register* to an outside chain like Gannett, spiraling
farm problems that transformed rural culture, impending school reorganizations that reconfigured neighborhoods and the countryside,
all were components in the unsettling narrative that had become
rural American life at the close of the century. As an icon wed to
rural Iowa culture, six-player basketball was inevitably affected when
its institutional girders were shaken, and the *Des Moines Register* had
been a girder for some time.

In 1920 the *Register* assigned two sportswriters, Jack North and
Bert McGrane, to organize the first girls' state basketball tournament, an action that was taken to boost the newspaper's circulation.
When the Iowa Girls High School Athletic Union was formed five
years later, the Union retained North and McGrane to manage the
tournament, a job the two sportswriters kept until the Union hired
a full-time executive secretary in 1947. For more than a quarter
century North selected the girls' all-state basketball teams for the
Register, officiated for several sports, and even served as the Iowa
softball commissioner, all the while managing the state basketball
tournament. The fact that North held multiple roles in the Iowa
sports world apparently went unquestioned, and his journalistic in-
tegrity was never impugned. Jack North was "Iowa's most recogniz-
able sports personality" at midcentury. When he retired from the
Register in 1960, after forty-five years of service, North was hired
immediately by E. Wayne Cooley to serve as the IGHSAU's publicity
director. And in 1969 the Union began bestowing upon a player
or coach its highest honor for service, the Jack North Commem-
orative Award, to "serve as a permanent reminder of he who con-
tributed most to the birth and nurture of the Athletic Union in
its foundling years." Thus, during the period when, in other states,
barring tournament play was a goal and eventual victory for physical
educators who resisted varsity competition for girls, Iowa moved on
a divergent path. Its state tournament was buttressed by the work
of journalists employed by the state's largest newspaper. The *Des*

Moines Register was clearly a significant institutional support for Iowa six-player girls' basketball as the sport dropped by the wayside in other states, and it is unlikely that other newspapers played such a significant role in promoting girls' athletics.[23]

Beginning with the first tournament in 1920, the *Register* provided at least as much news coverage of girls' basketball as of boys', or even of the Drake Relays, the world-renowned track-and-field meet held annually in Des Moines. With the most literate state of readers in the nation, the newspaper had a captive audience, particularly before television arrived at midcentury. Louita Goode Clothier remembered that she "was crazy about basketball" when she was growing up in the late 1940s in the southern Iowa town of Lamoni, which didn't have basketball then. "So the girls I read about in the *Des Moines Register* were my heroes. During the state tournament I devoured every word of the sports section." As interest in basketball continued to grow at midcentury—70 percent of Iowa high school girls played the game, and seven hundred high schools in the state offered the sport—the *Des Moines Register* both confirmed and constructed a complex ideology through its comprehensive coverage that strengthened the game in Iowa as it weakened elsewhere. Inherent in the ideology, from which few dissented until the Title IX era, was that Iowa six-player high school participants were "healthy, clean, and vibrant." This was according to an Iowa administrator at midcentury, that is, at the same time that physical educators in other states used medical issues to shut down competition.[24]

Nowhere was the "healthy, clean, and vibrant" ideology displayed more visibly than the cover of the official program for the state tournament each March. Late in the season, at the tail end of every cold Iowa winter, fans knew spring was around the corner when the IGHSAU selected its cover girl, a coveted honor invariably resulting in a photograph of the smiling, attractive recipient confidently bouncing a basketball on the front of the program. "Oh you're kidding—I don't believe it. I'm glad I'm sitting down!" gushed Jane Intlekofer, the 1970 selection from Monticello, whose response was typical of honorees. So was this biographical note: "Her personal church life is exemplified through membership in several religious groups, all of which present a personality of being totally home, church, and school minded." The cover girl never seemed to have a "steady boyfriend," though 1968's Janet Stone (Stratford, Iowa) enjoyed "corresponding with a boy friend serving in Vietnam." The cover girl, too, lived almost always in a small town if not on a farm: "She is a town girl, living in Jewell," the biography read on 1969's Becky Ioerger. Always healthy, clean, and vibrant and always from the farm or village, the cover girl was a cultural product idealized and ideologized in the tournament program in no uncertain terms.[25]

But there was something morally inconsistent about labeling the most sterling example of Iowa wholesomeness a "cover girl" besides the explicit sexism of a practice that would have infuriated the earlier reformers. So in 1992 a new element was added: the girl who graced the program cover was the initial recipient of the E. Wayne Cooley Scholarship Award, a $10,000 grant, dispensed over four years, to a recipient who "reflects discipline, perseverance, character, superior skill and achievement and citizenship traits which personify the life and expectations of the namesake." The 1992 scholarship winner, Leah Rae Willenborg of Dyersville, selected from 136 applicants, was class valedictorian as well as one of the state's best golfers and an all-conference pick in basketball and volleyball. The bespectacled Leah Rae was cast on the program cover as an academic, poring over books and papers in several photographs. Noteworthy is her remark in the accompanying biographical sketch: "Of over 200 trophies and awards, the one Leah is most proud is the trophy she received when she was eight years old and she 'beat all the boys.'" While it is unclear what she "beat the boys" at, one could attribute the nature of the remark to the post–Title IX anxiety that still hovered in 1992, twenty years after the passage of the landmark legislation, or to the timely question regarding girls' ability to play full-court basketball. In any case, the Iowa Girls High School Athletic Union was compelled to change its language, and the "cover girl"—at least in its earlier form—was no longer.[26]

The "healthy, clean, and vibrant" component was implicit in the media's ideological representation of six-player basketball. When the game was abandoned in February 1993, even Donald Kaul—

the game's preeminent critic—paid homage to the "wholesomeness" that had shrouded the sport:

> I suppose I could have done the easy thing. I could have liked girls' basketball. I could have pointed out its wholesomeness, its purity, the fact that it embodied the virtues of athletic competition like no other sport. I could have said that it was good, clean fun untainted by the mean-spiritedness and pseudo-professionalism that mars so much of high school and college sport. That would have been the easy thing to do, but I'm too much the feminist for that. I felt the game treated women cheaply and had to be destroyed. So I did it.[27]

Kaul, of course, had little to do with "destroying" the game. In fact Kaul played an important role in sustaining its popularity during the period his column, "Over the Coffee," appeared in the *Des Moines Register*. A self-described "knee-jerk liberal" from Detroit, Kaul was the ideal straw man for girls' basketball: the outsider on whom Iowans had always needed to project their fears.

For almost thirty-five years Kaul chided Iowans about their brand of girls' basketball, which, for him, was "like waiting for a bus, only with cheerleaders." Kaul harmlessly joked about "a guard who was hospitalized when her foot fell asleep and the trainer couldn't wake it," and first suggested sewing pockets into the girls' uniforms "so that the players would have something to do with their hands."[28] Kaul's criticism consisted of gentle jibes that might just as readily have been describing horseshoe pitching. But because he ridiculed a cultural symbol, he might as well have criticized tractors or corn. He was perceived to be passing judgment on Iowa's rural culture. It was no surprise that he received some hate mail, though more commonly locals simply dismissed him as a naysayer. That Donald Kaul criticized a cultural tradition in the very medium that helped construct the tradition itself shows how the ideology of Iowa six-player basketball was, at least partially, sustained. On a local level, opposition to that ideology was co-opted.

The ideological sphere of six-player basketball wasn't reserved for stars only, and the media supported this notion. For the several thousand Iowa high school girls who went out for basketball every winter, only a few earned star status, or even starting positions with their teams. But when *seven out of ten* high school girls in the state played basketball (the numbers offered by the Union in 1950), the level of devotion was apparently as high among "average" players as their more accomplished peers, even if their skill level wasn't. "High school senior learns valuable lessons on the sidelines," was the headline for a 1993 *Register* profile of an Adel-DeSoto player, Carrie Pedersen. Despite a disk injury and knee injury so severe that it required surgery and caused her to miss her junior season, as well as a request from her coach to be a team manager (a plea that would force less strong-willed teenagers to quit altogether), Pedersen refused to leave the game though she rarely played. It wasn't that she needed something to do: Carrie Pedersen participated in drama, choir, mock trial, and the National Honor Society and had been chosen homecoming queen in the fall. "I proved to myself that I could stick through something no matter how hard it was," she said. "I'm so glad I didn't throw in the towel. I'm so glad I went out this year just to prove to myself that even after any injury I could come back."[29]

Not all newspaper accounts were so optimistic or inspiring, however. Following the publication of a letter to the editor in the *Woodbine Twiner* in which parents complained about their daughter's lack of playing time (see chapter 1), nearly half of the local newspaper's editorial page was devoted to responses. A high school boy was "shocked" by the parents' letter, while another writer attributed "the lack of success of our girls' athletic programs" to the "bad luck" of not having tall players. Similarly, a lengthy editorial bemoaned the fact that Woodbine had had "short girls' teams for the last ten years" and "you can't coach height." This particular editorial concluded that some people had lost their perspective about basketball: "We need to remember it is just a game." But the attention paid to a seemingly trivial matter—a single girl's playing time—reiterated the importance of the sport in Iowa's small towns. Obviously, this player was as devoted to basketball as the girls who were chosen to play ahead of her. Nonetheless, the town's focus on winning games overshadowed her devotion to the sport. Winning had become a component in the ideology that linked basketball to the survival of small schools. Basketball was more than a game, the denial of which only served to confirm its complexity.

Another major component of the ideology, often discernable in news stories about the prominence of girls' basketball, was the sport's indispensability to the survival of small towns. In a four-part series the *Omaha World-Herald* ran that inspected the meaning of the game in the southwestern Iowa town of Farragut (population 500), the "Adettes'" 1971 girls' state championship is described as "probably the biggest moment in Farragut's history and unquestionably the most memorable." While casting the tourney experience as devoutly meaningful to those involved ("Other than bearing children, I can't think of anything in my life that's been more exciting," a former player confided), the articles assert that the well-being of the town itself has rested with the school and the fortunes of the basketball team. "With the fading of the Adettes as a girls' basketball powerhouse, there is little to distinguish Farragut from hundreds of other struggling Midlands towns," the newspaper concluded about the community, whose fifteen state tournament appearances rank it among the all-time leaders. "The school has survived consolidation talk so far." The "hub" of the community, say local citizens, is the school, but its status is uncertain as changes in state funding force Iowa's small school districts to consolidate further. Twenty-five years after the team's state championship, Farragut High School's enrollment had dropped 30 percent, the result of the county's number of farms falling from 2,600 to 1,400. An interdependent set of factors—agricultural problems, school reorganizations, girls' basketball—had transformed rural culture in this southwestern town.[30]

Even after the six-player game was dismissed, its ideology as a wholesome activity that helped keep small towns together was reified by the media. "Remember six-player?" asked the large headline in the *Des Moines Register*'s "Women's Basketball for 1997" section. The article focused on Lisa Brinkmeyer, a fifth-year senior at Drake University who was the last player in an NCAA Division I program who had played only six-player basketball in an Iowa high school. In the final six-player state championship game in 1993, Brinkmeyer scored 53 points as Hubbard-Radcliffe (enrollment 147) beat a much larger school, Atlantic, for the title. "It put Hubbard-Radcliffe on the map," Brinkmeyer recalled. "[Basketball] gave Iowa an identity, especially being one of the last states to play six-on-six—Iowa and Oklahoma." In 1998 ninety-three-year-old Esther Stensrude, on the occasion of Sac City's first state tournament berth since 1923, reminisced for the *Register* about the school's last trip to state. In the article, a Sac City banker, Jean Lange, observing how the town's main street would shut down for the Monday afternoon game in Des Moines, remarked that this was the only time a slow day on Main Street was good for the entire town. "It brings the community together," said Lange, a 1938 six-player all-state selection. Sac City's 1998 state berth was earned, of course, by a five-player girls' team; the legacy of six-player as being "good for the entire town" carried over to the new game. "It's kind of given us an identity," said a resident of South Sioux City, Nebraska, a blue-collar town across the Missouri River whose Cardinal girls' team won three straight state basketball titles in the late 1990s and gained national recognition.[31]

As the largest and most prominent Iowa newspaper, the *Des Moines Register* provided the most thorough coverage of the game. But other papers, dailies and weeklies, were comparable in that they gave girls' basketball equal billing as boys', and sometimes more depending on the success of the local team. As early as 1914 the girls' basketball teams from the neighboring southwest Iowa towns of Logan and Missouri Valley posed for team photographs, in which the players wore bows in their hair. By the time the first state tournament was held in 1920, few Iowans questioned the propriety of girls playing basketball, although this wasn't the case in other sports. "R. H. Eby and Dr. Dewell umpired the game without getting their hair pulled or faces scratched," the *Woodbine Twiner* reported on a two-inning, exhibition baseball game played by local women on Labor Day in 1920. Such remarks were rarely made about participants in girls' basketball. A sidebar commentary on the same baseball game read, "Say, fellers, you had orto [*sic*] to been at the big doins Monday and seen them there wimmen [*sic*] play ball. They were right there with the goods and done all most as good as the men did." Such commentaries had humorous intentions but nonetheless unmasked the gender anxieties of the era. Elsewhere in the same issue of this southwest Iowa newspaper was an admonition about "instructing women in their new responsibilities as voters," revealing another more serious fear surrounding women's changing role.[32]

Sixty years later, and less than a decade following Title IX legislation, all four of the photographs presented in the sports section of a 1980 weekend edition of the *Spencer Daily Reporter* featured high school female athletes. In those sixty years, the equal footing that Iowa girls' basketball was given to boys' was displayed in the state newspapers. It was a far cry from the paucity of coverage or condescension evident in other media, perhaps revealed nowhere more stridently than the *Wall Street Journal*'s 1969 front-page story, headlined "Is It a Peep Show or a Sport?" The *Journal* found it odd that in Iowa the star's name was Denise Long: "She is a girl."[33]

Other sources also show what basketball meant to local culture, and how the presentation of girls' athletic experiences reveals to what degree they are valued. The 1944 *Hawkeye*, the University of Iowa yearbook, reflects a collegiate sporting atmosphere in which women's athletics are clearly eclipsed by men's; it's striking because the campus departure of men for World War II service would ostensibly provide more visibility for women athletes. But the University of Iowa policies were clearly in line with those of the physical educators who were curtailing women's competitive sport throughout the nation at both the secondary and postsecondary level. Among those educators was the director of Iowa's physical education department, Elizabeth Halsey. "The department this year placed new emphasis on an extensive program designed in cooperation with national programs stressing more vigorous activities and physical fitness. Endurance, stamina and strength were added objectives in a training program including physical fitness classes, sport skills and techniques, body mechanics, dance, rhythms and varied recreational leadership activities," the *Hawkeye* wrote about Halsey's department. She permitted no competition beyond intramural activities. While the 1944 *Hawkeye* yearbook includes dozens of pages detailing UI men's athletics, categorized into "fall sports," "winter sports," and "spring sports," women's athletics are confined to four pages in the 375-page annual. They were described as activities sponsored by the "Women's Recreation Association Clubs" and "Women's Intramurals." The photograph introducing the predominantly male "spring sports" section, however, is a snapshot of a pretty UI coed walking briskly across campus with a tennis racket in one hand and a suitcase in the other.[34]

The secondary status accorded to women's athletics as displayed in the 1944 yearbook of Iowa's largest university is reflected in similar high school yearbooks only in districts that weren't yet playing competitive varsity basketball. At Woodbine High School in 1947, girls gathered twice a week under the auspices of the "Girls' Athletic Association" for basketball, softball, hiking, skating, and bicycling. Like their college-aged counterparts described in the UI yearbook, Woodbine girls held intramural games, and when they did participate in sectional tournaments, as the school's *Shipmates* yearbook describes, competition was underplayed. "During the blizzardous four nights we were able to obtain approximately $72 for our club treasury," read the yearbook account of a Girls' Athletic Association tournament, indication that vigorous competition was hardly a priority. And similar to the UI yearbook, Woodbine's devotes little room to its girls' sports—three paragraphs—but several pages to the boys'.[35]

Compared with other small Iowa high schools, Woodbine was late in coming to interscholastic competition. But elsewhere in the 1947 yearbook is a photograph of superintendent Henry Boone, who twenty years later would serve as president of the Iowa Girls High School Athletic Union. Boone introduced Woodbine to varsity competition with other schools in the late 1940s; one decade later, girls' basketball was allotted space equal to boys' in *Shipmates*, and in 1961 the yearbook's coverage of the "Tigerettes" was twice as long as the boys' report.[36]

Even as Iowa rural education experienced constant change and turmoil throughout the first nine decades of the twentieth century, it remained a firm supporter of girls' six-player basketball. After the last country schoolhouse was closed, the lingering strength of rural education carried over to six-player basketball, which endured intense scrutiny. But just as farmers had fought earlier to control their schools, Iowans battled outsiders to retain a game that evolved into the most successful girls' prep sport in America.

Besides the schools, there were other institutions that sustained six-player basketball. One of these—the Iowa Girls High School Athletic Union—is examined at length in later chapters. Another, the *Des Moines Register*, provided the most powerful media support, beginning with its sponsorship of the first state tournament and continuing through the decades with its thorough coverage of the game. Other sources, including small-town newspapers, were crucial in maintaining an ideology that supported six-player basketball for an entire century.

Many of the same factors that accounted for Iowa's excellent schools, including a stubbornness presented in the face of outside change, had shaped its uncommon and resilient favorite game. It only stood to reason, then, that the undoing of Iowa six-player girls' basketball would come in its own backyard.

THREE

Redheads, Blue Devils, and
Seventh-Day Adventists

In summers then, we didn't have air conditioning, and I'd be sitting on the front lawn in Montezuma, talking with neighbors. I'd hear a "bump, bump, bump," and I'd see Sandy under the street lamp. She'd say, "Coach, it's too hot to sleep." Today, you won't see kids shooting like that. – Montezuma coach Carroll Rugland *on player Sandy Van Cleave*

Myrna Kaune was dying, and she took her time doing it. Six years, to be exact, from when doctors discovered the colon cancer and removed the intestine until chemotherapy failed to stop the disease from spreading to her stomach and pancreas and killing her. Myrna lay in her bed on the farm in Fayette County for much of those six years, and the only Kaune child left in the household attended to her needs. Deb was in third grade when her mother was stricken, and the girl was just days from entering high school when her mother passed away. In between those years, Deb Kaune had her childhood as well as her mother taken away. When she wasn't attending to Myrna, she was cooking for her father, Delbert, and doing his laundry and cleaning the house. Delbert had his hands full: his wife was dying, and there wasn't any insurance to pay for the medical costs, so Delbert sold cattle and hogs to pay the bills. The Kaunes, who farmed just 120 acres, didn't even have a telephone until Myrna got sick—they had to drive nine miles to Maynard to use a switchboard.[1]

Myrna Kaune was sick for a long time, and often her illness was overwhelming for her young daughter and caretaker. "Once, Dad lifted her into the back seat of our Olds and we took her to Allen Hospital in Waterloo," remembers Deb. "After we left her there, I told him that I couldn't go back and see her that way. I had to be 'Mom' to myself, care for Dad, and still be a kid." The only place where Deb Kaune could still be a kid was the crushed-rock driveway outside her mother's window, just to the left of the corncrib. On that driveway, a wooden backboard and steel rim hung from a lone pole, and Deb Kaune repaired there to escape the burden of caring for her dying mother. Deb made this space her own world. She brought out a radio and a basketball and shot and shot and shot, patenting a turn-around jumper. "I'd pretend people were guarding me. I'd pretend I was at the free-throw line with a game on the line," she says. "I was dealing with stress in a different way."[2]

The stress—real in the house, imaginary on the driveway—took a different shape following Deb Kaune's freshman year at Starmont High School, a consolidated district comprised of students from the northeastern Iowa communities of Strawberry Point, Arlington, and Lamont. Within days of her mother's death in 1968, Deb was riding a school bus over twenty-five miles to Strawberry Point for her first year of high school when Maynard—the site of West Central High School—lay only eight miles from Delbert Kaune's farm. The problem was that the farm lay in the Starmont school district. And when Deb Kaune decided to transfer from Starmont to West Central High School, she took on a different type of stress—and enough that E. Wayne Cooley, the executive secretary of the Iowa Girls High School Athletic Union, would make the trek up from Des Moines to Maynard to get to the heart of the matter.

Folks in Maynard took their forward courts seriously, having grown accustomed to spectacular and championship-caliber basketball from their local girls—albeit sometimes amidst bizarre happenstance. In 1926 a sixteen-year-old Maynard girl named Irene Silka scored in the triple digits one night playing the old three-court game; the performance stood as the Iowa, one-game record for twenty-six years. Despite the added burden of a center jump following each basket and the requisite passage of the ball through the center, or "third," court on its way to either forwards or guards, Silka found time to score 110 points. A shortage of teachers during and immediately following World War II caused the discontinuance of girls' basketball in Maynard from 1943 through 1949. Within a decade following the game's revival, Maynard dominated the state tournament, riding the backs of Virginia Henniges—the only Iowa girl ever to play in four state championship games and the second leading scorer in school history—and the three Nicholson sisters, all forwards. The school won two state championships and twice finished second in the state from 1956 to 1959. During that time Maynard also had a forward named Donna Turner who, adjusting to having but two fingers on her shooting hand, shot underhanded lay-ups.

In the mid-1960s Maynard's forward court featured Mary Parsons, a youngster so painfully shy that her coach claimed she never said one hundred words to him in four years. Parsons returned to Maynard to play against her former coach as a member of the All-American Redheads, a barnstorming professional team that played full-court against men—and usually won. The forward court that Deb Kaune joined included a Seventh-Day Adventist who wasn't permitted to play on Friday nights—one of the two usual game days in Iowa—thereby making room those evenings for a freshman named Glenda Poock, who became the all-time leading scorer and, according to coaches, media, and fans alike, the greatest player in Maynard history.[3]

Deb Kaune's summer of 1968 shone brightly enough for a while. Her sister, seventeen years her senior, was married to an Omaha pilot, who flew Deb to basketball camp at JFK College in Wahoo, Nebraska. The women's coach there, Bob Spencer, was building a solid reputation for JFK as a girls' basketball mecca. Deb, while shooting those turn-around jump shots in front of imaginary crowds on the driveway, had sprouted up to five feet ten inches. "I can't ever remember being short. It was the era of miniskirts, and I had a hard time finding a fit," she recalls.

Deb fondly remembers the role basketball played for her while growing up:

> My folks knew basketball was important to me, and at the time of Mom's death, it was important to me to be successful at something. From taking care of my mother for so long, I have a lot of life experiences others don't have. She might have gone to one seventh-grade game, and I can remember watching the state tournament with her on our black-and-white TV. But Mom would stay home and Dad, who used to come out and shoot sometimes with me—he'd shoot underhanded—would take me and the Maynard cousins to watch basketball games to get away. He couldn't carry a tune but soon learned "The Star Spangled Banner." Little things like that are big moments.

In her only year at Starmont, Deb lettered in cross-country and track as well as in basketball, having been moved up to the varsity team at midseason. "There was a lot of animosity because I moved up," she says. "About the only girl who was nice to me was a player whose mother also had suffered from cancer."

The daily fifty-mile round-trip school bus ride to Strawberry Point started Deb thinking about attending school in Maynard the following year. Ironically, Delbert Kaune had once owned a farm in the Maynard school district, but he had sold it. The Kaune children and those raised on the neighboring farm one-half mile west had grown up in the Starmont district; but the kids from the next farm west, the Kellys—not even one mile from the Kaunes—attended Maynard. But the shorter bus trip to Maynard was only one factor being considered when Deb Kaune found herself in a quandary in the summer of 1969. And it was not the deciding one.

> I grew up seeing Maynard winning—all their trips to state and the community support—and I'm a kid without a community. There was lots of turmoil when the Starmont reorganization occurred. Dad always sold corn to Maynard; we grocery-shopped in both. And when Mom got sick and we needed a phone, we got a Fayette telephone. I had aunts, uncles, and

cousins in Maynard. So I had lots of discussions with Dad about what a risk transferring would mean, like losing friends. I went to the Maynard school board president for support, checked with my relatives about eating meals with them, and chatted with the superintendent about paying tuition.

There was one other person to consult, and he didn't figure to be a hard sell, though the ensuing conversation was hardly the equivalent of what was spewed from the rumor mill just starting up. "I would be remiss if I didn't say that I spoke with [West Central coach] Gene Klinge," says Deb. "I wanted him to know my ideas and whether I would fit into his program. So I went to his home, and we sat down and talked. 'Recruitment' is a heavy term today, and that isn't what happened then. *I* went to *him*. But he is a coach, and as with any coach, he thought about spots [on the team] he had to fill."[4]

"Some people believed I'd recruited her, and that created a ton of hard feelings," says Klinge. "Cooley came up here, but when push came to shove, there wasn't anyone who would stand up for the accusation."[5]

The tuition charged for out-of-district students—$700 per term, or $1,400 for the school year—was hardly an incidental for a family that had only recently obtained telephone service and had no medical insurance. So Delbert Kaune did what he had done before in times of need—he sold cows and pigs. And in the fall of 1969, he drove Deb each morning the one mile over to the Kellys, where she sat on the porch with classmate Cindy Kelly and waited for the school bus. To Maynard.

In accordance with state regulations, which required that a student transferring to a school without parental residence in the new district sit out of interscholastic athletics eighteen weeks from the start of the school year, Deb Kaune refrained from playing basketball during her first semester at West Central and became eligible for the Blue Devils in the winter term. Her sitting out the early season was great for getting the rumor mill up and running. Some said Gene Klinge was going to pay her tuition if she played basketball for him; others said she was going to transfer back to Starmont. She heard it all on Sunday mornings after the services at the Arlington Lutheran Church, which sat in the Starmont district. "After being a kid without a community, here I am, now in the middle of communities," she said. "After my sophomore year at Maynard, when the rumor was flying I was going back to Starmont, my old bus driver from there stopped by and asked, 'Can I pick you up this fall?' There was also the story going around that Wayne Cooley had come up to Maynard to investigate the recruitment allegations. Well, I never met Wayne Cooley until he gave me a medal at the state tournament." The rumor mill was still churning the first time Starmont played West Central after Kaune's transfer. "I didn't sleep well, and there was a lot of anxiety before that game, but afterward it was okay."[6]

Deb Kaune became eligible to play the second semester of her sophomore year, and she gradually worked her way into the starting lineup. It wasn't as if Maynard basketball was going to dry up and blow away if she hadn't transferred; Gene Klinge had such a successful program in place that, as Kaune says, "he would watch the fifth- and sixth-graders and know who he was going to develop and how."

In 1970 in fact, there was such a jam-up in the forward court that Deb Kaune's arrival sent Gail Meyer packing to the guard court. Meyer had started playing basketball in fourth grade, and she was taught from the outset to dribble left- and right-handed as well as to shoot. With Kaune's arrival, Klinge made Meyer a guard, and Gail acquiesced, putting her shot away (until college anyway) only somewhat begrudgingly. Gail Meyer, "a tough nut who was willing to tell Gene off" according to Kaune, instead became a fiercely aggressive guard who, like Kaune, merited first-team all-state status as a senior. "I probably averaged five fouls per game as a senior," Meyer says. "We played aggressive defense—playing for interceptions, forcing the back door."[7]

Deb Kaune and Gail Meyer were classmates as well as teammates, but the two never became close friends, largely because of Gail's move to the guard court. For a ferocious competitor who had grown up *shooting* the basketball, being relegated to the guard court had to temper the dream of playing the game after high school, even if Gail, ostensibly, succeeded in the one court as easily as she would have in the other. "Deb and I were never close," admits Gail, "and it might have been because she came in and I had to become a guard." And Gene Klinge sensed the tension between Kaune and Meyer. "When we were seniors, he never put Gail on me [in practice], or even in a scrimmage when I was on the floor," remembers Deb. "I can remember her saying, 'Why doesn't he put me in more?' "

Gail Meyer would take her shot off the shelf after high school, when she played for the Northern Iowa Area Community College (NIACC) basketball team in Mason City and then on an industrial-league team for Minnesota's Mayo Clinic. "NIACC was just starting up the five-player game, and I got to play forward again," she says. "I was always a big fan of six-player because it gave the chance to an extra player, but in college six-player held you back."

Firmly ensconced in the forward court, Deb Kaune spent her last two high school summers—1970 and 1971—at basketball camps perfecting her game. "Klinge told me, 'I don't need you as a softball player but for basketball.' " Kaune was one of thirty-two girls chosen for the initial Iowa High School Girls Basketball Academy held late in the summer of 1971 in Ida Grove, where local industrialist Byron Godbersen—the father of two high school-aged, basketball-playing daughters—worked with the IGHSAU to bring the state's first academy to the western Iowa town. Godbersen flew Deb, who was in Illinois attending a camp, to the academy. She joined the other players and several coaches from across the state in Ida Grove, where basketball courts had been set up in Godbersen's boating factory, and such celebrities as astronaut James Lovell and basketball Hall of Famer Bill Russell were brought in as speakers. "It was one of the neatest experiences," recalls Deb. She was also one of the six girls awarded a five-hundred-dollar scholarship. Members of the Godbersen Scholarship Team were selected on the basis of athletic ability, scholarly achievements, and personal qualities.

Led by Kaune and Meyer, the Blue Devils breezed through the 1970–71 season undefeated before losing to Allison-Bristow in the first round of the state tournament. In that game the team blew a 10-

point lead with six minutes to play, squandering an 18-rebound performance by Meyer. Typical of Gene Klinge, he scheduled Allison-Bristow for a regular-season rematch the following winter. Before 1,400 fans in Allison in 1972, West Central responded by easily winning, 72–51. "Gene wanted to see if we would meet the challenge, so he went out and scheduled them, and we whomped them," recalls Deb. "It was also a challenge for him to coach against Dale Fogle."

Klinge was a senior at Upper Iowa University in Fayette in 1962 and had already signed a contract to work as an assistant football coach when the West Central girls' basketball coach quit as the school year ended. Klinge was offered the job and took it. "I got to Maynard by mistake," he says. Three years later, Klinge had the Blue Devils in the state tournament, and they returned again in 1969 and in both 1971 and 1972. "Mel Kupferschmid [the previous coach at Maynard] had set the tone for the kids in town, and the tradition was there," Klinge says. "And it became perpetual."[8]

If back in the early 1970s Gene Klinge was wise enough not to let his two star players beat up on one another in practice and to schedule a team that had ended his undefeated season the year before, he also knew how much control he might wield *off* the court. And Klinge, by several accounts, wielded total control. Says Meyer: "[We] had to be home by 10:15 weeknights, 9:00 and in bed by 9:30 game nights, and 12:15 and in bed by 12:30 weekends. If you broke rules, you had to have 100 percent of your teammates vote to keep you on the team, and there were at least two who didn't get it. But that's how kids were brought up. . . . We couldn't date during the tournament. You couldn't tell a kid that now. People are a lot more liberal now."

Glenda Poock, the leading scorer in West Central's history, says:

Once I missed curfew—I was a half hour late with my church group—and I told him [coach Klinge]. He wasn't pleased. I never had any problem with him, but some people didn't like him. He laid a guilt trip on me when I didn't go out for track—I didn't like to run. "But young kids look up to you." So as a senior I went out for track. He even gave me static about my boyfriend—now my husband—because he saw me sitting too close to him in a car. So I moved. Today that wouldn't work. But he knew what strings to pull.[9]

Says Deb Kaune:

He called parents to check curfew, but I never got a call. Your hair couldn't be in the way when you played, and boys were taboo, though I met my husband, whom I was dating before my senior year. Klinge was successful because he knew what he wanted, knew how to coach, knew who would develop. He had a program. He said to me: "We'll get you the ball; I expect you to score until you get double-teamed, or tripled." He adjusts, gets the most out of kids, but he's also very much into his records. He could be sarcastic: if the guards threw the ball away, he would sing "Three Blind Mice." And he'd say to me, "You're captain, and you can't drink or smoke." And he put wrath in it. It was total commitment then. He had great faculty support, and the other teachers would be at the games screaming their guts out.

Gene Klinge could get teenagers in bed by 9:30 and teachers screaming their guts out at games, but there was one element that not even he could control. Gene Klinge's wrath held no sway with the Seventh-Day Adventists.

In the winter of 1972, led by seniors Kaune and Meyer, the Blue Devils cruised into the state tournament with a 26-1 record, bolstered by having exacted revenge on Allison-Bristow with a victory over the team late in the season. The victory, their eighteenth, came after their only loss and was followed by two performances from Deb Kaune that were even grander than her dreams on the crushed-rock driveway. Playing against her old school and teammates, Kaune poured in 78 points in a win over Starmont. Then, in her final home game in Maynard, she scored 88, a career high—and the top single-game total in Iowa that season—that raised her average to over 48 points.

In Des Moines the controversy over players transferring schools was raised again when West Central faced Montezuma in the state tourney's opening round; but Deb Kaune was not the focus of attention this time. Montezuma coach Carroll Rugland had become the legal guardian of a Minnesota player he had met at a summer camp and invited her to live with his family and play for him her senior year. The player, Sue Meredith, like Kaune, led her team in scoring. "It was all done within the rules, but I'll guarantee it'll never happen again," Wayne Cooley remarked at the time. "It's identical to what happened to the Kaune [Deb] girl at West Central, but the Montezuma case is more severe," said Cooley. The state regulation that required players to sit out eighteen weeks when transferring school districts didn't apply to out-of-state players. Cooley quickly changed that rule. The pairing of the two transfer players wasn't the only curious matchup during that Wednesday night game in Des Moines: Gene Klinge and Carroll Rugland had grown up together and played basketball at Monona High School in the late 1950s. "I'm sure glad we played Gene, and if we had to lose, lose to him, because I knew he wouldn't say anything about transfers," joked Rugland.[10]

Montezuma, whose eighty-eight-game winning streak and two-year reign as state champs had ended in 1971 (presumably creating the need for a good transfer player), did indeed lose to West Central. So did Manilla on Thursday night. On Friday evening, when West Central would have been better served focusing on beating Roland-Story and earning its first tournament final in thirteen years, distraction again reared its head. This time, however, it was internal—at least initially. The World Wide Church of God, or Seventh-Day Adventists, forbade its members to participate in outside activities from sunset Friday to sundown on Saturday. Among the Maynard church's members was Chris Jennings, the Blue Devils' junior forward who was responsible for getting the ball into the hands of Deb Kaune. Jennings, who had already missed five games on Friday nights during the season, herself averaged over 15 points a game. According to Ralph Cole, a Maynard fan who seldom missed a basketball game at home or on the road, Kenneth Jennings was usually milking cows in the barn when his daughter did play and would listen on the radio. Jennings was perhaps the best all-around athlete at Maynard, but the sundown-to-sundown ruling had taken its toll. As a sophomore, she recorded the second-fastest time in Iowa for the 100-meter hurdles, but because preliminaries for the state championship race were held Friday night, she was unable to compete for the title. A third baseman for the Blue Devils softball team, Jennings once left the field when the sun set on the diamond on a Friday night during a weekend tournament, then reappeared at Saturday's sunset. Jennings' religious practices were apparently the only way to keep her out of athletic competitions. "She got hit with a line drive once, getting her teeth knocked out," says Gene Klinge, "and it didn't bother her. She was a tough kid."

And Gene Klinge remains convinced that had the news media not concentrated on the Jennings dilemma, the Blue Devils would have had Chris on the basketball floor for their Friday night semifinals game against Roland-Story. "The media played up the religious angle all week: 'Is she gonna play?'" he said. "I think her folks would have allowed her to play if not such a big deal had been made about it."

In fact, Chris Jennings's parents were driving to Des Moines on Thursday when they heard on WHO Radio that Glenda Poock would start in place of Chris on Friday if the Blue Devils won that evening. This was news to all the principals involved, for the decision not to play wasn't reached until Klinge, Chris, and her father huddled in a hallway at Vets Auditorium following the West Central win over Manilla. "Gene was under the impression her parents would let her play, but he called us into the room and told us otherwise," recalls Gail Meyer. "I really thought if we would get this far, she would be able to play," Klinge told reporters after Thursday's game. "It's a sore subject, and as far as I am concerned it's a dead horse now."[11]

As she had on Friday nights thus far, freshman Glenda Poock took Jennings's spot in the starting lineup. Despite a stellar 70-point performance from Deb Kaune, the Blue Devils lost a six-point lead late in the game and lost the semifinal to Roland-Story 91–90. West Central did beat Everly in Saturday night's consolation game, but the one-point loss proved heartbreaking.

"We lost, but it wasn't because Chris wasn't there," says Meyer. "We had a letdown in the guard court. But Chris never said anything bad about her parents."

"We found Chris in the hotel room in tears after the game," recalls Kaune. "The other students were so disappointed in the loss that they didn't show up at events for a while. But Chris never talked to us about it. I had a lot of compassion for her. She and I were buddies because of the controversies we both were involved in. She felt, as many people did, that the newspapers had overplayed the whole religion thing."

Indeed, the state media had focused on Chris Jennings's sunset-to-sunset dilemma: one newspaper columnist declared "Jennings, Koufax in Same Boat," comparing the high school player's situation with that of baseball great Sandy Koufax, who declined to pitch in a World Series game when it fell on a Jewish holiday.[12] Friday sunsets opened a window of opportunity for Glenda Poock, however, who soon became, according to her Klinge, one of the premier players of her era and "by far" the best player he had coached.

There she was, four years old and already photographed in the Iowa Girls High School Athletic Union's annual yearbook. Glenda Poock was leading cheers for the Maynard Blue Devils before she even started kindergarten—the yearbook photo showed an exhilarated Glenda at courtside in 1961. A beneficiary of the Maynard girls' basketball tradition begun by coach Mel Kupferschmid in the 1950s and maintained by Gene Klinge, Poock grew up immersed in basketball culture and graduated in 1975 as the leading scorer in school history.

Like Kaune, Glenda Poock was a five-foot-ten farm girl with enough daily chores that playing basketball might have been a significantly intrusive activity. And, as with Deb Kaune, Glenda Poock's older sister had graduated before Glenda even started school, so she played ball alone after helping with chores on the farm, which lie about one mile west of Westgate, a village just five miles west of Maynard. Werner Poock usually kept about five thousand chickens and raised hogs, too. "He was an old German farmer," says Glenda. "You didn't argue with Dad. The only thing he ever said about my playing basketball was, 'once you start you don't quit.' He never criticized me or the coach."

There wasn't a lot to criticize when it came to Glenda's basketball talents. When asked to account for her abilities, Poock shrugs and offers, "God?" She attended parochial school until, as she put it, "Coach Klinge got me in eighth grade." One year later, she was starting in West Central's forward court in place of Chris Jennings on Friday nights. Already, Poock was mastering a jump shot that fan Ralph Cole called "deadly from ten to twelve feet"; it enabled her to score 3,993 points during her West Central career, including 71 in a state-final loss to Manilla in 1975.

Glenda Poock was happy to play six-player basketball: "It was unique," she says, "but I got to play both." Indeed, she played four years at William Penn College in Oskaloosa, Iowa, earning All-American honors in 1975. "Coach Bob Spencer was an Iowa boy, so he knew what we were up against," she says. "Those of us coming from six-player started on fundamentals a couple of weeks before the others."

Deb Kaune is more ambivalent about the six-player game. "Our teams and later ones could get up and down the court," she says. "Where did six-player get you? There were no scholarships then, not like now. We played with the same size ball as boys." Kaune, plagued by knee problems, was also ambivalent about playing any more basketball after she graduated from high school in 1972. *Look* magazine's company team in Des Moines and William Penn College showed interest in her, but Kaune enrolled at the University of Northern Iowa. "All I had was the five-hundred-dollar [Godbersen] academy scholarship, and we got work-study wages," she says. She played one season at UNI, then one year at Upper Iowa. Following her junior season, Kaune gave up basketball and was married—to the man for whom she broke training rules at Maynard. "I put my time in. I'm glad I didn't pursue basketball afterward because of my knees," she says. "But I had done my time, which included such things as watching other players. I watched Mary Parsons play a lot on tape—watched her movements across the lane—on a 16 mm projector in Klinge's biology room. Basketball was my way out, my way to success. Glenda had it naturally, but I had to practice at it."

So Deb Kaune became a physical education instructor, and she worked as an assistant basketball coach for almost ten years. "I enjoy working with kids and teaching. But from the standpoint of when I coached, kids today don't realize the commitment it takes to succeed. It doesn't end with the season. And they're bombarded with so many things today. I also don't like pressure from parents. I don't think a parent ever talked back to Gene Klinge."

The Mary Parsons whose graceful movements Deb Kaune studied was, according to Gene Klinge, so awkward before he got hold of her that he "would have liked to cry" the first time he saw her play. But three years after Klinge had yanked her from the guard court and shaped what became the first of the Maynard prototype forward—a five-foot-ten jump shooter—Mary Parsons was traveling the country with the All-American Redheads. She was a redhead now herself, bashing men at their own game as a member of a barnstorming women's professional team that was a sort of female equivalent of the Harlem Globetrotters.

When Gene Klinge came to Maynard in 1962 and found the gangly freshman Parsons out for his team, he wouldn't have bet a pair of the red socks Juanita Parsons would knit him every season that Mary would one day play professional ball. "She had no coordination at first. It was awful," says Klinge. "And she was a bashful kid, never dated, never married. I don't think she ever said five words to me. I made her a forward; we played one-on-one. Basketball became her whole life, and she became a good post player."

Mary was the daughter of Walter "Buster" and Juanita Parsons, who had moved to town in 1953 and operated a general store on the highway that is Maynard's main street. In 1997 the Parsons still lived in the store, two blocks from the school. The Parsons remember hiring a woman to mind the store in 1956 when Maynard made its first of four straight state tournament appearances and the family made the two-hour drive to Des Moines. It's unlikely, though, that the popular soda fountain had many patrons that week.

Nine years later, Buster and Juanita were again leaving the store during tournament week, this time to watch Mary play for West Central. "Mary had been playing guard, but when Klinge came here, he told her, 'I'm going to make a forward out of you.' She had 51 points the first game she started, and Klinge was so surprised," says Buster. "She lived and ate basketball. We had to tell her to leave it on the court." In her junior season the Blue Devils made it all the way to the title game, and, in an unusual circumstance, ex-guard Parsons fouled out in the loss to South Hamilton. "Mary was a post forward now, shooting from either side, and the guard on her kept 'flopping,' and Mary got called. I was so mad," recalls Buster.[13]

The Blue Devils slipped to third place in Parson's senior season, but any disappointment might have been eased by the presence in Des Moines of scouts for the All-American Redheads, a touring professional women's team that played five-player basketball against men in more than one hundred games each year. The Redheads, headquartered in Caraway, Arkansas, comprised mostly southern women and traveled as far as Alaska to compete and entertain. "We met with their representatives in Des Moines, and then with the coach that summer in Spirit Lake, where Mary was playing in an all-star game," recall the Parsons. "They wanted our okay." Mary Parsons left Spirit Lake with the Redheads, a team of seven women who toured the country in a limousine that had "World Champion Girls Professional Basketball Team" painted on its sides. She played with the Redheads for four years, and the Parsons sometimes traveled to their games. "We drove quite a few miles. She loved it, playing five-player," says Buster. "We thought at first she'd get homesick and come home. They did trick stuff, but they seldom lost a game against men. And Mary learned to shoot from anywhere."

Playing pro ball also brought Mary Parsons out of her shell. "The Redheads brought her out of it," says Buster. When Mary Parsons left to go barnstorming, Gene Klinge was concerned about his timid forward. The next time he saw her was when the All-American Redheads played in Maynard against the male faculty, including Klinge. "It was a shock. She'd dyed her hair and was outgoing," he says. "In high school she rarely talked to me." Hers was a quiet admiration for her coach says Juanita Parsons about her daughter's respect for Gene Klinge: "If he'd said the moon was made of cheese, Mary would say yes, it is."

Mary Parsons left the Redheads in 1970. She then played briefly for an AAU team in Shreveport, Louisiana, before embarking on a corporate career there with AT&T. "She worked at some of Klinge's camps, but she never played again. She coulda been a coach," says Buster. "She never played again, but when she built a new house down there, she put up a basket." And she idolized Larry Bird, as did other players from her era, and bought stock in the Boston Celtics, giving shares to a nephew and niece.

The Parsons' general store on the highway is closed now, but Buster and Juanita still lived there in 1997, right across the street from where Ruth Nicholson used to sit huddled in her car in the dead of winter forty years ago, waiting for her daughters to finish a basketball practice that might run two and one-half hours long.

From 1951 through 1957, Maynard girls' basketball fans continuously watched a Nicholson—always one, sometimes as many as three—play in the Blue Devils' forward court. Ruth and Glenn Nicholson raised four daughters who graduated from Maynard and played forward for the team: Lu Ann (a 1951 graduate) and Betty (1953) played in an era when the school was rejuvenating a program that had been shut down from 1943 to 1949—the result of a teacher shortage caused by World War II. Carolyn (1956) and Glenda (1957), members of the Iowa Girls' Basketball Hall of Fame, led the Blue Devils to their first state tournament berth since 1924 and to the state title in 1956, and they finished as the third and sixth highest scorers, respectively, in school history. Betty, Glenda, and Carolyn joined mother Ruth, 89, for the following session at Ruth Nicholson's home in Maynard in June 1997.[14]

RUTH: We had so many Nicholson girls, they [the coaches] didn't
          know which one to call on. And they were all forwards.

CAROLYN: My first game in seventh grade, I played guard, then
          changed. We always used our assets . . . take that as you'd
          like.

GLENDA: We were muscular. I grew five inches between the ninth
            and tenth grades.

CAROLYN: We shot all our team's free throws. I shot a modified hook
            shot. Glenda set blind screens for me. In my final game in
            '56, we beat Sylvia Groning and Garrison 62–51 for the
            title. Maynard beat Garrison four times that year. Glenda
            graduated in '57 and played on two state teams.

BETTY: Carolyn, Glenda, and I were all in the same game once, in
            '53. The teams wore skirts then.

Question (MCELWAIN): How did they [the Nicholson girls] get good?

RUTH: It just happened.

BETTY: Parents' abuse (*joking*), 'cause they went through so much.
            Grandpa Nicholson gave me some nerve.

RUTH: In '59, there was that awful blizzard, and we were snowed
            in at Vets Auditorium.[15] I left to go, and we had a preg-
            nant woman with us. We saw a light at a farmhouse near
            Hansell, out in the country, and stayed all night. We made
            it to Oelwein the next day.

CAROLYN: Basketball got us out of a lot. Coach [Bill] Mehle laid
            down the law, and he once had the three of us against
            the gym wall. He told us to decide between farming and
            basketball. "Do you want to milk cows or play ball?" We
            chose basketball.

RUTH: They were afraid their hair would smell like milkmaids'.
            But it didn't keep boys from coming around.

CAROLYN: Bill Mehle came to Maynard for three years, [19]52–55,
            and scouted me in eighth grade. He'd won state at Hansell
            [1947]. Mel [Kupferschmid] came for the [19]55–56 sea-
            son.

BETTY: We have the greatest admiration for these men. Mehle
            taught us basics, because we didn't know how to dribble.

CAROLYN: When Mehle left, I was crushed. I saw him at the Hall
            of Fame induction and told him that. Then Mel [Kupfer-
            schmid] came from Fayette. He was not quite as stern or
            tough, and never mad. He'd play one-on-one with me.

GLENDA: Mr. K. could get his point across in a joking way. I'd hit

him in the chops. We called both coaches "Mr.," though
Mel was also "Koop." He was in his twenties. Both Carolyn and I contact Mel at Christmas. Our key to success
on those four teams in the late '50s was that there were
only a total of twenty-two girls on them. And we have to
mention our chaperones at state. Irene Harrington, the
third-grade teacher, took care of us, cut up lemons, served
as a watchdog at the Kirkwood Hotel, where we stayed in
Des Moines. No boys, no calls—we abided by her rules.
We respected her so much and didn't doubt her.

CAROLYN: When we went to state, it was the first time I was away
from Mom and Dad. Even after graduation, when I had
lined up a job and apartment in Waterloo, I couldn't go
and went to Oelwein to work instead.

GLENDA: We had a loving family. Growing up, we had no television,
so we listened to the state tournaments on a radio in the
kitchen. We'd put popcorn in a dishpan and have some
Kool-Aid.

RUTH: I fed them cold potato sandwiches, then would hide and
see what they'd do.

GLENDA: She would put cold coffee in a pop bottle, put the cap on
it, watch us drink it, and laugh.

RUTH: I had five kids in seven years.

BETTY: Daddy [Glenn] would love to be here. He died in '87. He
wore a shirt and tie to all the games.

RUTH: He ate basketball for breakfast, asking 'em about it.

BETTY: He didn't give a lot of advice, but you knew it when he did.

GLENDA: He'd say, "Shorty, you'll have to make a decision." The
only time he kicked me was when I was taking oats to
the barn, and my brother Jim was on a ladder [that was]
leaning against it. I threw an apple at fifty feet and hit him,
which shook the ladder.

BETTY: The only time he kicked me was when I let a team of
horses get out.

RUTH: Do you know how we [Glenn] met? He was practicing
baseball in a cow pasture on our parents' farm near Hazel-

ton. He was on the town team. And he walked through our
yard.

CAROLYN: When I was an eighth grader, Mr. Mehle came to the door
in junior high and watched me practice. My heart was
pounding. He told me to practice with the varsity. So I
practiced hard, but he never told me to come back. So,
again, he knocked on the junior high door. He wondered
where I was. "You come to practice until I tell you not to."
I scored 15 [points] in my first game and moved up. That
first game when Mehle pointed at me, then to the scorer's
table, I didn't know what to do.

GLENDA: We had hoops in our barn, where we also did square danc-
ing—it [square dancing] was big too. We rotated it around,
different kids taking turns having square dances. All the
high school kids came, and moms made sandwiches and
Kool-Aid.

CAROLYN: After we won the title in 1956, there was a motorcade
of probably four hundred cars, some from Des Moines,
that drove the twenty-five-mile stretch from Westgate to
Oelwein to Maynard. They did it three times. There were
4,000 people in Maynard, population of 435! The day of
the final, Grandpa and Grandma Nicholson were the only
people left in Maynard. The semifinal the night before, I
can remember late in the game legendary Garrison coach
Ben Corbett yelling so clearly at us, "Don't foul, don't
foul!" It's all I heard. He wanted to play us the next night,
since we'd beaten them three times already that year. Of
course, then it was four times.

GLENDA: There were only thirty-one in my graduating class. Each
year, Iowa Wesleyan College chose one "guest player" in
high school to come visit, and I was the one in 1957. . . .

CAROLYN: I didn't get the same honor the year before. I felt jilted. . . .
I was too small at five foot four.

GLENDA: So I went to school there [Iowa Wesleyan], where I had
[Garnavillo Hall of Famer] Sandy Fiete as a teammate. I
made All-American the first two years at Iowa Wesleyan

then got married and slowed down. I did play in the 1959 Pan American Games in Chicago and won a gold medal. Carolyn was inducted into the Iowa Hall of Fame in '71, and I was in '72.

CAROLYN: At the time, we were the only two sisters to score 1,000 points in a season. I scored 54 once as a sophomore, and Glenda had 61 in a state tournament game.

BETTY: Talk about roommates . . . I played for Brammer Manufacturing, an industrial-league team, and Norma Schoulte was my roomie for two years, [19]54–55. We slept four in a room. Norma was six foot four, and I had to sleep with her! She was a shy girl. I gave it up after we played Hanes Hosiery from Winston-Salem, North Carolina. They were wicked.

CAROLYN: There were some weird fans . . . Ralph Bonjour of Fayette was a bachelor who wore a plaid shirt and overalls and took pictures at the games. He gave me a blue wooden box full of slides of the '56 champion team. There were sixty double slides, mostly warm-up shots and good photos. But he couldn't take pictures on Friday nights because he was a Seventh-Day Adventist.

GLENDA: I had a weird one, too. There was a guy from Fredericksburg who telephoned and wanted me to meet him at the Maynard cemetery and run off to California with him and his ma. He sent me a box of chocolate cherries. I never saw him.

Deb Kaune's situation showed how seriously neighboring school districts considered the game. Kaune's transfer from one district to another heated up a rivalry that was quelled only with the intervention of the state athletic union. The daughter of a poor farmer, Kaune exemplified the stubbornness and toughness that characterized so many of these players, many of whom were raised on farms— often a challenging environment.

Deb Kaune's ordeal involved more than simply changing basketball uniforms; she relied heavily on the consultation of family members, weighing their support, in her decision to leave Starmont. But she also considered the basketball culture that thrived at West Central of Maynard. Such passion for the game was hardly confined to her experience. In the last half of the twentieth century, Iowa rapidly reorganized school districts—from 1980 to 1995, the number of Iowa high schools with girls' basketball teams dropped from almost five hundred to four hundred, a 20 percent decrease. And the level of interest in and success of girls' basketball in a particular community was sometimes considered in consolidation plans. Such was the case when the school districts in Hubbard and Radcliffe reorganized.

When Les Hueser's Hubbard-Radcliffe team won the final six-player state tournament championship in 1993, the title was his first in a thirty-nine-year career and came in the nine hundredth game he coached. Of similar interest was the fact that the state crown was won by a school district that had only recently consolidated two schools. Hubbard and Radcliffe—two towns in north central Iowa seven miles apart—had "shared" sports as well as some animosity for several years before reorganizing. "Hubbard was German and Radcliffe was Norwegian, and they hated each other with a passion," Hueser said. "In the fifty-eight games Hubbard played Radcliffe in six-on-six, Radcliffe won only two games. Some kids walked out when we consolidated, and both towns wanted the high school. We [Hubbard] got it."[16]

Similarly, when several tiny high schools in western Harrison County consolidated in 1962, the reorganization brought together longstanding rivals. Both Pisgah and Mondamin high schools had had recent success in girls' basketball, but they graduated only fourteen and eighteen seniors, respectively, in 1961, forcing a consolidation with nearby schools Modale and Little Sioux (even smaller, with just eleven graduates). West Harrison High School was the result of a mandate by the Iowa State Department of Public Instruction that forced small districts to reorganize or risk losing state aid and closed down the remaining country schools. According to local newspaper reports, school boards and study groups from the various towns worked on the reorganization for three years—beginning in 1959—

and more than 86 percent of voters approved of the merger when it was voted on in 1961. The result was that in the fall of 1962, West Harrison opened with the largest elementary school in the county and the second largest high school (258 students). While newspapers rarely reported how the reorganization affected athletics, the merger was on the minds of players. "We hated Mondamin, and now we had to play basketball with them," remembered Sharon Elkins, a former Pisgah player whose passion toward the subject needed little rekindling almost forty years after she had graduated. [17]

Two other Harrison County high schools consolidated in 1962, but their circumstances differed slightly from their West Harrison neighbors. In 1960 Magnolia's high school enrollment of sixty students made it the twenty-fifth smallest of 562 high schools in Iowa and, without reorganization, it would have likely lost state approval. Logan, the county seat, whose high school had almost two hundred students, chose to consolidate with its smaller neighbor nine miles away; 92 percent of the two districts' voters who cast ballots approved, and Lo-Ma High School was born. But confusion reigned in the countryside: area country schools were closing their doors in 1962, and there were still sixteen school districts within twenty miles of the new Lo-Ma school, and the Pisgah and Mondamin districts had reorganized into West Harrison. According to a local newspaper, fifty-six persons, mostly parents who were concerned about district boundary lines, filed objections to the proposed Lo-Ma district. Among the concerns was whether, as the proposal detailed, Magnolia would keep its elementary school while Logan got the high school. [18] That's what happened, and the arrangement has worked for nearly forty years.

Reorganization had different effects on the Lo-Ma girls' and boys' basketball teams, both coached by Eugene Evans. "Magnolia hadn't been successful in girls' basketball, and my eleventh and twelfth players had been three-year letter winners there," Evans recalled. "I had no Magnolia girls starting. But it was different for the boys. There were three from Magnolia who started." [19]

While some communities overcame animosities to make consolidation work, others used such tensions to keep reorganization at bay. Betty Emrich, a retired physical educator, recalled that during a boys' game in 1941 between her school, Mechanicsville, and its primary rival, Bennett, a prankster set off a fire alarm at the Bennett High School gym. Later that night, a fire—its origin unknown and apparently unrelated to the prank—*did* burn the school down. "They [Bennett] have been holding a grudge ever since, to the point of using the fire as an excuse not to consolidate," said Emrich.[20]

Winning a state championship brought Hubbard and Radcliffe together. Simply qualifying for the boys' tournament was a community effort in 1998 at BCLUW High School, located in Conrad in northeast Iowa. An "alphabet soup" school that included students from Beaman, Conrad, Liscomb, Union, and Whitten, BCLUW had at least one player from each of these small towns, a situation that strengthened the ties among the communities. The success of this team reaffirmed a study the Research Institute for Studies in Education completed on the impact of reorganization; it showed that school mergers can have positive effects on extracurricular activities. The night before the BCLUW boys' team left for the tournament, a half dozen middle-aged women cheered them on at a pep rally. Their fans were players on the 1968 girls' state-championship team from Union-Whitten, including the all-time-great Denise Long. "There's something special inside you. Reach down. Call on it," Long told the boys, thirty years younger than she. The rally was remarkable in two ways: high school boys received a pep talk from *women* who had been stars, reinforcing the unusual prominence of Iowa girls' basketball, and a cross-generational tie revealed itself in this small school district.[21]

A 1950 graduate of Churdan High School in west central Iowa recalled that until reorganization decreased the number of high schools in Greene County from eight to three, sports rivalries between the towns were "absolutely fierce"—"first cousins played on opposite teams." Similarly, another Churdan graduate remarked how basketball opponents often knew one another well. "We not only played against each other all the time in sports, we all knew each other from 4-H competition at the county fair."[22]

Whether school reorganization strengthened social ties between communities or exacerbated longstanding tensions, consolidation—in all of its multiple presentations—laid bare the cultural roots of rural school districts. Six-player girls' basketball had provided a prism through which to understand rural education and the larger culture. Aspects of Deb Kaune's experiences illustrate this. The fathers of both Kaune and the Nicholson sisters allowed their daughters to play basketball only if they promised "not to quit," reflecting rural Iowans' deeply held value of persistence. Furthermore, Deb Kaune took on the role of caretaker for her dying mother, for which she "gained a lot of experience others didn't have." This was an educational experience that was common earlier in Iowa as well as other sections of rural America, when farm kids were often expected to take on adult responsibilities beyond their household chores.[23]

While many of Deb Kaune's experiences exhibited the enduring social and cultural traditions in rural Iowa, others were indicative of change. Earlier in the century teenage farm children often left school temporarily or quit altogether when required to help out at home. Usually, the adolescent who left school to work on the farm was male, but in family situations like the Kaunes', when the daughter was the only child at home, girls dropped out too. The fact that Deb Kaune stayed in school, as well as played basketball, is evidence of the modern notion that quitting school is unacceptable. Also, the game's significance in Kaune's life shows how Iowa basketball had evolved into a *modern sport;* this was further evidenced by the growing number of summer basketball camps organized for girls, several of which Kaune participated in.[24]

The Iowa Girls Basketball Academy, held in Ida Grove from 1970 through 1974, was a complex and thoughtful affair. The brainstorm of boat manufacturer Byron Godbersen, the academy comprised thirty-two girls—one forward and one guard from each of the sixteen tournament districts. The girls, chosen by the Iowa Girls High School Athletic Union, enjoyed the amenities of the lakeside resort and castle located on the grounds. Six high school coaches—all men—worked with different groups of players during each session of the four-day camp, permitting girls to learn various techniques; and a girls' weight-lifting team from Manilla, Iowa, demonstrated proper lifting techniques. (Although weight training was generally unheard of in girls' prep sports in 1971, it may have been a key to Manilla's success. The school would win state championships in basketball and track within a few years.) The academy was "dedicated to refining skills, building character, promoting sportsmanship, and developing leadership," and to help accomplish such goals, Godbersen and the Union brought in such speakers as astronaut James Lovell, the chairman of the President's Council on Physical Fitness, and former NBA great Bill Russell. After the camp's final scrimmage, Godbersen presented each girl with a framed achievement award and an academy patch for her basketball uniform; and the academy awarded six players a five-hundred-dollar college scholarship. The Iowa Girls Basketball Academy gave girls the opportunity to meet other players beyond the limited circle of their small towns. And the academy, the first such clinic held for high school girls in Iowa, provided strong evidence that the game had become increasingly specialized and rationalized.

Deb Kaune's relationship with her teammate Gail Meyer could best be described as "competitive." Kaune's transfer to West Central resulted in the talented Meyer's shift to the guard court, meaning that Meyer lost her chance to shoot the basketball. One of the most common charges made against six-player basketball—and the one that eventually caused the demise of the game—was that guards were prevented from developing ball-shooting skills that could earn them college scholarships. Gail Meyer's unhappy retreat to the guard court shows a pertinent and common aspect of the game.

Chris Jennings was a prominent West Central player whose religious beliefs kept her from playing in the semifinal state tournament game that her team lost by one point. As a Seventh-Day Adventist, Jennings wasn't allowed to participate in activities from Friday evening through Saturday evening, and her absence caused a stir in the state media. Her situation elucidates what can happen when religion intersects with sport; in conservative rural Iowa, Wednesday evenings are uniformly referred to as "church night," an evening set aside exclusively for religious activities. Neither practice nor games can be scheduled for this night. Like the school, churches helped define rural communities and were an instrumental ideological component of the Country Life movement's attempt to preserve the agrarian myth by transforming it. This would be accomplished when rural churches took the lead in promoting school reform, including the transformation of curriculum. The movement largely failed, although such components as school reorganization eventually succeeded, as did—for the most part—the movement's goal of making the country town a "nonethnic," Protestant place. Catholics and Lutherans of German descent often viewed rural school consolidation as a way of forcing their children to attend public schools, resulting in the closing of parochial schools and the decline of ethnic communities. The Wednesday "church night" itself is a Protestant practice that dates back to the early twentieth century and remains a respected ritual throughout rural Iowa towns today.

Glenda Poock was West Central's leader in career scoring and exemplifies the player who was raised in basketball culture. An All-American college player, Poock, was a quintessential "tough" farm girl—she lived by the advice of her father, a chicken farmer, who told her, "once you start, you don't quit." Mary Parsons "never said five words" to Maynard coach Gene Klinge, but when she returned to town as a member of the All-American Redheads, she had lost her shyness and gained red hair. Parsons's transformation can be viewed in the larger context of social construction, identity, and agency.

Finally, the shared experiences of the Nicholson family—mother and three basketball-playing daughters—encapsulate girls' basketball culture as well as the larger rural culture. Their characterizations of coaches, fans, and other players suggest how deeply a basketball tradition was inculcated in Maynard for a half century, and their remembrance of family affairs shows how basketball worked to strengthen family ties, which, in turn, strengthened their affection for the game.

The seemingly idyllic world of the Nicholson sisters—eating popcorn in the kitchen while listening to the state tournament, hosting

square dances, and playing basketball in the barn—evokes pastoral-
ism and the garden myth often ascribed to the Midwest. But pas-
toralism and the Midwest have had an adverse connection. A primary legacy of the Progressive Era Country Life movement was its
attempt to redesign the midwestern landscape through the concept
of the "country town," a new kind of place that combined the best
of rural and urban communities. Thus rather than invoke pastoral-
ism or the garden myth, a more accurate assessment of how rural
Iowa culture supported girls' basketball can be gained through a
different geographic metaphor—six-player basketball as a "middle
landscape" in the constant battle over rules between those physical educators who championed competition and those who did not.
Iowa six-player basketball was, in the truest sense, a compromise: its
leaders sustained Victorian Age beliefs—among them, that strenuous physical activities were harmful to women—but added a competitive dash. This compromise was the only path of survival for
a phenomenon that was simultaneously conservative and progressive.[25]

The middle landscape is a compromise, which is precisely what
Iowa educators accomplished when they preserved six-player basketball: they stayed with "girls' rules," the game that national reformers invented to combat the more competitive five-player game.
But Iowa leaders parted ways with national reformers when they rejected the reformers' emphasis on intramural competition and aver-
sion to tournaments, which Iowa used to help construct the most
elaborate girls' sporting activity in America and ward off the national
decline of basketball in the 1950s and 1960s. Mary Channing Coleman, the founder of the North Carolina Girls High School Athletic
Association, adamantly opposed varsity competition for girls and
took such drastic measures as shutting down tournaments. Whereas
the anticompetition movement had a national impact, in Iowa and
Oklahoma statewide support for women's basketball persisted.
These states comprised an American "middle landscape" where six-
player basketball not only survived but thrived close to the end of
the century.[26]

But the Nicholsons played basketball in the 1950s, when Iowa schools were closed at a record pace, and the sisters' rustic world was rapidly vanishing. By 1992 the number of farms in the United States would fall below two million for the first time since 1850, and Iowans were describing their state in less than glowing terms: "I live in the Third World, in Iowa . . ." a local writer contended in 1995. "Typically a Third World country has natural resources and human labor that it's willing to sell for a pittance, resources and labor that developed countries want, especially at bargain prices. . . . Does that fit Iowa? You bet." Similarly, Wes Jackson, an ecologist and geneticist who founded the Land Institute in Kansas and wants to preserve small-town America, argues, "We're a poor people in a rich land. Our institutions don't work. . . . Why can't a fat country like ours have an idea of small-town life? Towns have been the seedstock of our culture." In 1970 twenty million Americans—about one in ten—still lived in towns with populations under ten thousand; by 1990 that number had been reduced to less than sixteen million, or one in sixteen.[27]

The Nicholson girls were fed cold potato sandwiches—their lives were hard and their parents economically strapped like so many of the other Maynard families. But the Nicholsons remember their youth in largely glowing terms, and the experiences of Maynard players as well as those of many other Iowa women who played high school basketball throughout the twentieth century show a connection to their ancestors through physical and mental strength, persistence, and, importantly, humor. Above all, the girls respected authority. "He didn't give a lot of advice, but you knew it when he did," Betty Nicholson said about her father. "You come to practice until I tell you not to," Carolyn Nicholson recalls the Maynard coach telling her. The aforementioned personality traits were consistently present in Iowa players, a steady barometer that showed what this culture was like—and revealed it on the basketball floor.[28]

In rural Iowa family ties mean everything and were (and often still are) the arch consideration in nearly all matters. Farms were kept in the same family from one generation to another, and well into the twentieth century the work sometimes compelled parents to withdraw children, both boys and girls, from school when necessary.

Earlier, before there was a state education bureaucracy, the luxury
of having a farmer-controlled school system allowed parents to de-
termine when school terms started and ended. Rural school systems
were so malleable in the late nineteenth century that semesters were
scheduled to accommodate fall harvest and spring planting. By the
mid–twentieth century, however, basketball had become so funda-
mental an experience in many Iowa girls' lives that it competed with
farm chores for their time. As the experiences of several Maynard
players showed, parents and teachers usually accommodated both
activities.[29]

But sometimes choices had to be made, as Carolyn Nicholson's
comment revealed: "Basketball got us out of a lot. Coach [Bill]
Mehle laid down the law, and he once had the three of us against
the gym wall. He told us to decide between farming or basketball.
'Do you want to milk cows or play ball?' We chose basketball."
Nicholson's memory also shows the implied force that coaches used
and with which players unquestioningly complied.

Sometimes girls were told that they couldn't milk cows even if
they wanted to. "No, Dad won't let us—he's afraid we'll be hurt and
can't play in athletics," said Mt. Union's Jan Krieger, who, when
named the cover girl for the 1978 state tournament program, was
asked if her father let her do farm work. Krieger, an all-stater who
averaged 40 points as a senior forward, was the fourth of nine girls
raised on a northern Iowa farm; and her three older sisters were all-
state selections, too. Like Jan Krieger, Elaine Paulsen was chosen as
a state tournament program cover girl (1974) and had three sisters
(and a mother) who excelled at basketball. Elaine, in fact, was the
only female in her family not to play at state. Unlike Jan Krieger,
Elaine Paulsen drove the tractor and threw straw bales on her father's farm near Elk Horn in southwest Iowa. Questioning program
cover girls about their work habits on the farm was hardly idle conversation, and the selection of girls from strong basketball families
was hardly incidental: the Union officials who picked cover girls understood the close ties between rural culture and girls' basketball.[30]

The game was important enough that Maynard coach Bill Mehle
picked Carolyn Nicholson for his high school team when she was

still an eighth-grader, a common practice that wasn't halted until well after midcentury. And in rural Iowa, where formal dress was rarely seen outside church doors, game night was special enough that parents like Glenn Nicholson wore a shirt and tie. It took a state tournament appearance to draw the teenage Carolyn away from Mom and Dad for the first time, and upon high school graduation, the prospects of leaving the farm for Waterloo so overwhelmed her that she took a job in Oelwein, smaller and closer, instead. Waterloo was less than an hour from the Nicholson farm, which makes Carolyn's action an excellent example of how tight-knit and provincial farm families were.

The lives of residents in rural school districts were governed by low numbers and scarcity. Glenda Nicholson recalled that the West Central teams that played for the state championship four consecutive years used a total of twenty-two girls. There were but thirty-one seniors in Glenda Nicholson's graduating class, an average size for a rural Iowa school in the 1950s. Maynard had, after all, only 435 residents. So when more than four thousand fans flooded the town following its 1956 state title, the numbers seemed overwhelming. Nothing before or since, not even the huge auctions that occurred routinely during Iowa's farm crisis in the mid-1980s, has drawn such hefty crowds to small towns across the countryside. As other states shut down the game, Iowa girls' basketball reached its zenith because of the unfaltering support of small towns and their schools.

FOUR

Harlots and Ladies and the Prettiest Girl in Town

Small towns in Iowa had girls' basketball, but Ames was too sophisticated for such pastimes. Girls who liked sports could swim or play tennis. But otherwise we watched the boys, cheering and caring so intensely whether they won or lost that we regularly wept or shouted ourselves hoarse. – Susan Allen Toth, *Blooming: A Small-Town Girlhood* (1998)

Although Iowa six-player basketball survived world wars and the Great Depression, stubbornly ignored naysayers and educators, and might have outlived its own usefulness, sometimes it didn't take much to make the game go away. Other times players and coaches and entire towns fought uselessly to keep it alive. It was like the random work of a tornado: a coffee can could rest unmoved on a fence post left shrouded in the earth when a barn exploded ten yards away.

While girls danced the decades away on the court in Maynard, a town four times as large and fewer than fifteen miles up the road lost basketball for forty years. Ruth Lang and her Sumner teammates shucked their cotton stockings and garter belts one cold Iowa night in 1934 at an out-of-town game, and their insubordination got back to superintendent Thomas "T.J." Durant. "He had a thing about high school girls showing their bare legs, telling us that it wasn't 'ladylike,'" says Lang, who was a five-foot-eight jumping center in the three-court game. It wasn't as if Ruth was some kind of prima donna or discipline problem: at the height of the Depression, when access to automobiles was sometimes scarce in rural Iowa, Lang would walk the five and one-half miles back to her farm from Sumner after basketball practice in the winter—a one and one-half hour trek.[1]

T.J. Durant had bought the elastic garter belts and heavy stockings for the players out of his own pocket. "He bought 'em," said Ruth, "after we told him we were too poor to, which was true, but we didn't wanna wear 'em." The belts and stockings were not only cumbersome to wear while playing basketball, but, as Ruth said, "when you slid on the floor, it really hurt. And how were you gonna hold 'em up?" Lang and her teammates wore the required uniform but occasionally played without the belts and stockings when the team traveled far enough away that Durant wouldn't be at the game. They went for two seasons before getting caught without them. "If we didn't play a nearby town like Hawkeye, we'd get away with it," Ruth recalled. After one game day when Ruth and her teammates were naughty and decided to leave their belts and stocking at home, Durant marched the mutineers into his office. "Professor Durant wasn't at the game, but some lady told him. He threatened to throw us out of school. He called the only players who wore the things— the Diercks twins, Leona and Leota—'ladies,' then said, 'the others of you are harlots!'."

Durant, who died the next year—his thirty-sixth as the Sumner superintendent—didn't expel Lang and her bare-legged teammates, but he did eliminate girls' basketball following that 1934 season. The sport wasn't resumed until 1974. "Not wearing the stockings was a good excuse to keep basketball out," said Ruth. "My daughters would have loved to play. My oldest daughter was six feet tall, and so was her daughter, who did play."

If showing some leg wasn't convincing enough to shut down basketball in Sumner, hearsay that a player had died playing basketball during her menstrual period certainly was. During the town's forty-year hiatus from the game, the rumor spread that a local high school girl had passed away during practice when the school still offered the sport for girls. According to a Sumner coach, a girl who played basketball did in fact die, but it was two years after she had graduated; she was the victim of a heart condition. "It was a good story and another reason to keep basketball out. Some people believed it," remembered Lang.[2]

The anxiety created by myths about the dangers of physical activity during menses was reinforced by the educators responsible for curtailing competitive women's basketball. (Ruth Lang remembers it was even said that you shouldn't wash your hair during your period.) But these educators hadn't been successful in the smaller towns of Iowa; few communities the size of Sumner (population two thousand) and larger had basketball until the 1970s. The fact that basketball could be shut down in the 1930s when players refused Victorian attire or beliefs, particularly outdated attitudes concerning health matters, reaffirmed the existence of a national fight against the girls' game. But as late as 1969—just three years before the passage of Title IX—the value of girls' basketball was still challenged and ridiculed.

The anxiety shown over girls playing basketball during menstruation was a Victorian response to "ovarian determinism," which has been defined as the use of biology to rationalize female inequality. The higher standard of living for American girls in the late nineteenth century meant that they were better nourished, healthier, and educated, marrying later and having fewer children, and menstruating earlier and having more regular periods than women in the past. This "ovulatory revolution" prompted physicians, educators, and parents to question—as ridiculous as it appears today— whether young women could simultaneously use their brains and their ovaries. Because women crossed into a "male" realm when they entered sport, both advocates and critics quickly presented their views about the female body and the appropriateness of its appearance in the athletic arena.[3]

Detractors like the superintendent who didn't think bare legs were proper might have pointed to *Life* magazine's 1940 five-page photo essay for evidence of the kind of sexual commentary that infuriated some women educators and sport leaders. "With her soft brown hair, her sparkling eyes and lovely figure, she is just about the prettiest girl in town," read the lead paragraph, which focused on sixteen-year-old Virginia Harris, a co-captain of the 1940 state champion Hansell High School basketball team. "When Hansell High School, where she is a senior, holds its parties, she is dated up far ahead. When she walks home from school, she never has to walk alone." Among the several photographs of Harris was one of her partially nude, capturing her undressed from the waist up but seen only from the back, as she sat up in bed and was inspected by a male doctor for the state tournament's "health contest." "In spite of her pretty looks, Virginia did not win a prize, but one of the other Hansell girls took second place," read one of the photo captions.[4] The contest was soon discontinued, largely because of the *Life* publicity.

The garter belts and stockings that Ruth Lang was forced to wear and the "health contest" in which Virginia Harris was encouraged to compete provide historical evidence of how gender distinctions were imposed on girls. These distinctions varied in explicitness, from the overt nature of the six-player rules to the more subtle practice of having high school girls' teams be accompanied by a woman chaperone. Usually a chaperone, an older woman and often the coach's wife, appears in many of the team photographs in the state tournament programs until the Title IX era. By 1992 chaperones had all but disappeared from the photos, though they were often replaced by women assistant coaches who may have performed some of the same tasks as the chaperone but under the guise of a less gendered term. A "chaperone," after all, was a woman who performed matronly duties, such as ensuring appropriate behavior from teenaged girls, ostensibly sustaining the Victorian notion of protecting the virtue of her charges.

Chaperones were held in high esteem even though they provided a measure of control. Glenda Nicholson recalls the woman—her third-grade teacher—who accompanied the Maynard team to state: "[She] took care of us, cut up lemons, served as a watchdog at the Kirkwood Hotel, where we stayed in Des Moines. No boys, no calls—we abided by her rules. We respected her so much and didn't doubt her." Similarly, Union-Whitten player Cyndy Long thought to include the team's chaperone, the coach's wife, in her poem about her state tournament experience: "Mrs. Eckerman banging frantically on her floor; And the lobby boy trying to peak through our door" (see chapter 5). High school boys' teams had no equivalent to the chaperone, only male coaches, an interesting fact considering the adolescent male behavior, ranging from harmless pranks to criminal acts, that sometimes occurred at boys' state tournaments. The point is that the chaperone was in place not so much for discipline but to sustain an ideology where girls were perhaps most vulnerable—away from the court and in the privacy of their living quarters.

Wives of girls' coaches often played important roles beyond serving as chaperones. Hubbard-Radcliffe coach Les Hueser, describing his wife Bev as "the best press agent around," recalled that in his early coaching days he knew his team was playing badly when he looked into the stands and saw Bev "holding a finger on her nose." "She knows everything," said Hueser when, during an interview, his wife rattled off the exact total of his basketball wins as she worked in another room—notably and ironically, the kitchen. Pat Klinge, the wife of Maynard coach Gene Klinge, "kept books" (the common name for recording statistics), which was another activity that often fell in the hands of coaches' wives.[5]

In matters on the basketball floor and off, behavior was governed by gender—the social organization of sexual difference. If girls failed to recognize that the activities in which they participated were gendered in a particular way, violation of these rules made it apparent, as Ruth Lang discovered when she left her garter belt at home. Consideration of how gender informed and influenced the conduct of girls' basketball raises many questions: What was the significance of uniforms? What role did coaches play in maintaining gender distinctions? Did female and male coaches differ in their teaching methodologies and perceptions of the importance of the game? How were the relationships of female players with male classmates affected by the girls' participation in sport?

A convergence of social, political, and cultural conditions ensured the survival of Iowa six-player girls' basketball for one century. Among those conditions was the constant imposition of gender distinctions on girls. An examination of newspapers, high school yearbooks, and Iowa Girls High School Athletic Union publications and documents as well as remarks by coaches and players, show the distinctive ways in which roles were defined.

The Gendered World

Flipping through a book of photographs taken in the early twentieth century in southwest Iowa's Harrison County, one observes the gendered nature of this world. In a picture of a corn-judging contest in the Logan Opera House, all of the dozens of judges are men. Similarly, women fill every pew in a 1900 photograph of the Logan Presbyterian Church sanctuary, taken presumably to document some religious function. The Mondamin Cornet Band of 1902 was composed solely of men, in contrast to the Lincoln Highway Kensington Club, which provided a place where women could gather to work on sewing and catch up on the latest news. That basketball would be similarly bifurcated, staying in step with the times, was hardly surprising.[6]

To study the world through the prism of gender involves the discovery of unchallenged assumptions resulting from prescribed behavior. The 1968 Iowa High School Girls Athletic Union basketball tournament manual offered the following instruction for the championship team postgame celebration dinner: "Immediately following the Championship game, after the Championship squad has showered and dressed, team personnel will go directly to the Kirkwood Hotel where the honor dinner will be administered. . . . Wearing apparel for the Squad Members will be Bobby Sox, skirts, sweaters or 'what have you.'" Similarly, there were not any doubts about who was to dine at the traditional postgame dinner; the Union invited the winning team's coach, superintendent, principal, and education board members, *and wives*. The assumption that the person holding each of these administrative positions was male was correct; in 1968 there hadn't been a woman-coached state championship team in more than thirty years, and there were two female superintendents in the entire state at that time.

Just as the number of women coaches had dwindled throughout the century, so had the number of Iowa women working as superintendents, though that figure had never been high. Nonetheless, following a wartime "surge" of fourteen women superintendents among the 866 school districts in 1945 (a number ostensibly heightened because of male administrators being gone for military service), the figure dropped to six in 1950 and did not reach double digits again until recently. Country school teachers were almost always female, and women were employed in significant numbers as county superintendents, at least until the country schools under their governance began to close. Statistics gathered for five-year periods beginning in 1935 reveal the corresponding decline: thirty-eight of the ninety-nine county superintendent positions were filled by women in 1935; the number fell to thirty-two in 1940 and 1945, to sixteen in 1950, and by 1955, to only nine.[7]

Similarly, the percentage of female teachers, elementary and high school, working in each Iowa county over a twenty-five-year period beginning in 1930 slipped slowly but steadily. Whereas 83 percent of all Iowa teachers in 1935 were women, just twenty years later the number had fallen to 73 percent, the result—in part—of men moving into the high school teaching ranks. During the 1953–54 school year, 60 percent (5,151 of 8,548) of Iowa high school teachers were men, who were always hired to coach boys' sports and almost always to coach girls' athletics. The gendered pattern of public school teaching placed men in the high schools and women in the kindergarten and elementary classrooms.[8]

Inspection of the official programs of the Iowa Girls' State Basketball Championships reveals how gender arrangements shifted over time. The cover of the 1948 state tournament program is a caricature of a curvaceous but muscular girl dressed in contemporary uniform shorts, a ribbon adorning her head, posed with one foot on a basketball and holding a mirror as she applies lipstick. A puzzled referee, whistle in mouth, scratches his head as he watches. The scene is superimposed on an outline of the state of Iowa. The drawing encapsulates the reigning comportment of female athletes at midcentury: prescribed apologetic behavior for the Iowa girl, who was tough as nails on the court but never forgot her feminine side, much to the befuddlement—and pleasure—of male onlookers.[9]

The drawing also demonstrates that the state was not immune to national anxiety over the effect of sports on gender arrangements. As attacks on competitive women's sport grew harsher in the first half of the twentieth century, athletic women—college-aged and industrial-league basketball players in particular—were stereotyped as unfeminine, even called "mannish lesbians," regardless of their true sexual orientation. High school girls were much less often the target of such stereotypes, though the unspoken implication was that "this is what will happen if girls compete like boys." Thus female athletes made up for their on-court lack of femininity in their behavior, appearance, and language off the court; doing so was expected and made their lives easier.[10]

Iowa high school girls were, for the most part, sheltered from the national attack on their increasingly peculiar brand of basketball. The Iowa Girls High School Athletic Union responded to the national attacks with an ideology of its own, exemplified by the appearance on tournament covers of the best that Iowa had to offer: the wholesome, versatile, small-town girl. In 1969 the Union minced few words in describing the intent of its cover girl: "The Athletic Union . . . salutes Miss Becky Ioerger for the splendid image she has given to Girls' Athletics over the last four years."[11] Not until 1992 was the tournament program's traditional "cover girl" replaced with a Union-sponsored scholarship winner, who was photographed participating in activities other than athletics. The shift implied that, in the post–Title IX era, there was no place for the sexist title of "cover girl." The attitude, energy, and competence of the girls featured remained unchanged, but the language had evolved. Once again the tournament program had served to expose contemporary gender beliefs.

The "splendid image" that Becky Ioerger displayed included, among many other activities, her membership in Future Homemakers Association, one of the highly successful curricular activities implemented during the Progressive Era and the girls' counterpart to Future Farmers of America. FHA, as it was commonly called, was a key component of the vocational education movement that historians have described as a turning point in public education for young women: when sex segregation and the treatment of women based on their special characteristics and needs became a formal agenda of public schools. Homemaking was cast as a vocation and a cornerstone of the modern social order and seen as a remedy for the deterioration of family life. [12]

The strength and staying power of vocational education can be seen in the following passage from a rural newspaper, the *Woodbine Twiner*, in 1960. Most telling is the bifurcation of the sexes, attained through the creation of such organizations as FHA and FFA, whose Woodbine High School chapter opened in 1930 with fifty-two boys—more than half the males in school: "Members of the Woodbine FFA Chapter, working in teams, will try to visit every farm family in the community. They will review with the man in the family rules for safe operation of corn harvesting equipment, reminding him that his responsibility includes his family and his community. A farmer who agrees to follow these rules will have a 'Safe Operator' sticker placed on his tractor. The farm housewife will receive a 'Remember' card to place on the dining table to remind all who gather there that safety is a family affair." [13]

Like the FFA, Woodbine's FHA was a successful organization. By 1961 the school's chapter had grown to eighty members, which, according to the yearbook, made it "next to the largest club in the state." While the FFA chapter disappeared in the 1960s, the Woodbine FHA remained active until 1993, when it became the Family and Consumer Science Club. A yearbook photograph that year reveals a handful of boys in the new group. In contrast, however, the FHA chapter in neighboring Missouri Valley—a town twice the size of Woodbine—had half as many members in 1969 as Woodbine had in 1961, perhaps signaling a decline in interest in homemaking. Missouri Valley yearbooks from the late 1960s nonetheless reveal traditionally gendered activities: its all-girls pep club numbered over one hundred, Future Farmers of America was going strong, and the

Key Club (the Junior Kiwanis Club) was male only, while the Future Nurses club included one brave boy.[14]

A glimpse of the 1976 yearbook at Manilla High School shows how gendered organizations like FHA intersected with girls' basketball and other activities in Iowa schools. The entire starting lineup of the 1976 state runner-up Manilla Hawkettes, who finished the season 30-1, were members of the school's large and active FHA group. The forty-girl group raised money for various community and school causes through such activities as bake sales, powderpuff football games, suppers, and dances. The yearbook also reveals that the president, vice president, and secretary of Manilla's senior class that year were female, as were many of the class leaders—often athletes—photographed for annuals in the 1970s. That basketball players were socialized as both future homemakers and class leaders reflects the flexible gender roles that held steady in Iowa. For example, electing female class presidents was hardly unusual in Iowa. And the coaching great Gail Hartigan, a Manilla graduate, didn't find her school's weight-lifting program for girls in the early 1970s unusual: "It didn't seem extraordinary at the time." Crossing gender lines wouldn't and didn't appear "extraordinary" when done routinely. Thus instead of readily casting gender roles as intractable, it is possible to view them as malleable arrangements, as the stories later in this chapter will show.[15]

"Treat Us Like You Would Boys"

Early in his first practice in 1992 as coach of the Council Bluffs Lewis Central High School girls' team, Steve Padilla suddenly stopped talking after barking orders to his team. Padilla, who was coaching girls for the first time after a career as a boys' coach, grew quiet as soon as he had yelled. It occurred to him, he said later, that perhaps he shouldn't be yelling at girls like that. So he asked what they thought, and they yelled back at him to treat them like he would boys.[16]

Throughout six-player basketball's century of existence, nearly one million Iowa girls were coached almost exclusively by men. While Mrs. Daisy Tague had the distinction of winning Iowa's first girls' state basketball championship in 1920 in her first year of coaching at Correctionville, the status of women coaches declined sharply with the advent of the male-dominated Union just five years later. In 2001 women comprised fewer than 10 percent of the head coaches for Iowa's high school girls' basketball teams. Thus in an activity whose well-being depended heavily upon the maintenance of gender distinctions, the role of coaches—particularly male ones—is important and complex. Maynard's Gene Klinge wielded so much control over his players that he decided how close to their boyfriends players would be permitted to sit. While all coaches generally aspire to gain as much control as possible—over players as well as game situations and final outcomes—males coaching younger females carried the additional responsibility of protecting their charges' virtue as well.

"We couldn't date during the tournament," Maynard player Gail Meyer said about Klinge's rules. "You couldn't tell a kid that now." Similarly, teammate Glenda Poock moved when Coach Klinge saw her sitting too close to her boyfriend in a car. "Today that wouldn't work." Any inspection of how girls' relationships with boys were affected by the females' participation in athletics must consider not only contemporary gender arrangements but also how the authority of coaches (usually male) affected teenage behavior.

The journalist Douglas Bauer has written about the power that girls' basketball held over its athletes during the season, recalling the following incident when he dated a player during his high school days in Prairie City:

> On the eve of a game, we would drive from school to her home . . . and park in front and look out into the early falling dark:
>
> "Can I come in?"
>
> "Not tonight," Sue would say, smiling. "Coach says we should rest. If we win tomorrow night, we'll be tied with Pleasantville."
>
> "Just to talk?"
>
> "We're talking right here." Not only her feet were quick.
>
> "What do you want to do this weekend?"

"Depends. If we lose, Coach says we might have Saturday practice."[17]

In many American towns the words of Doug Bauer's girlfriend likely would have marked her as a prude or a girl simply brushing off a boy. But not in Iowa—the remarks of Bauer's girlfriend were not only socially acceptable but expected behavior in schools where basketball was deeply engrained in the local culture. Scholars have shown that elsewhere in America, girls' popularity was based on such ascribed characteristics as possessions or appearance, while boys' status resulted from achievements, especially in sports. Other scholars discovered that being an athlete was well down the list of characteristics that resulted in high status for girls. Such was simply not the case in Iowa, where female athletes—especially in small towns— were revered for their skills and, consequently, gained popularity.[18]

The fact is, in rural schools the small number of students encourages involvement in many extracurricular activities. When Iowa high schools led the nation in girls' participation in athletics at 70 percent, that figure had to have climbed to over 90 percent in the small districts in order to offset the absence of sporting activities offered in the city schools. One reason why small high schools may have preferred interscholastic athletics over the intramural programs favored by reformers was that many districts didn't have enough girls to organize multiple teams within their own school.

A few rural states like Iowa stood up to the national physical educators who spent the first half of the twentieth century striving for moderation instead of competition. The women leaders who formed the Committee on Women's Athletics (cwa) and the women's division of the National Amateur Athletic Federation (naaf) in the 1920s and 1930s did so with the express purpose of attacking male-run athletic organizations on both the national and local levels, groups such as the American Athletic Union (aau), and municipal sports activities. The cwa worked within the physical education profession in high schools and colleges, and the women's division of naaf focused on the community level. These reformers strove to prohibit varsity sports and to institutionalize their beliefs in moderation. They didn't necessarily advocate *less* exercise but a different kind, an expanded realm of female activity.[19]

In many states that expanded realm included cheerleading, an activity whose popularity blossomed in postwar America. As the appeal of girls' basketball diminished at midcentury in such states as North Carolina, young women took up cheerleading, a similarly public activity that required young women to develop coordination and poise and perform before large crowds. Basketball and cheerleading developed into class-governed activities: rural and working-class girls preferred the physical challenges of basketball, while suburban and urban, middle-class teenagers chose the more feminine cheerleading.[20]

Because of the institutional support that protected Iowa from the national decline of competitive girls' basketball at midcentury—the Iowa Girls High School Athletic Union, schools, and the media—cheerleading never triumphed over varsity sports in Iowa as it did in North Carolina. The "natural order" in Iowa was never comprised of high school girls cheering on boys. That happened, of course, but usually after the first game of the basketball doubleheader, and the boys just as readily cheered on the girls those nights.

Across the nation, particularly in the South, cheerleading increasingly gained institutional support. At the 1977 annual meeting of the National Federation of State High School Associations, the director of the Texas-based World Cheerleader Council presented an elaborate program, remarking, "If these students [cheerleaders] are to be successful in fulfilling the role of their position, there exists a need to provide leadership training sessions where the appropriate skills will be acquired." While other states were setting up cheerleading clinics, Iowa physical education leaders like Ruth Johnson were battling for athletic opportunities for girls. In 1974 Johnson complained to Davenport administrators when the eleven supplemental coaching contracts for girls' sports at the school included two contracts for cheerleading sponsors. "[Cheerleading] is basically supportive of the boys' program and not athletic opportunities for girls," she wrote.[21]

Although cheerleading was an important part of the pageantry surrounding Iowa six-player basketball, it rarely competed with the game as a status symbol for girls, as yearbooks and tournament programs reveal. Cheerleading as well as related activities like pep club often did not merit as much coverage in high school annuals as the girls' sports teams. In fact, it wasn't uncommon for girls who quit or were "washed out" out of basketball to wind up as cheerleaders, as accurate an indicator as any that Iowa and such states as North Carolina had taken divergent paths.

Two events in Iowa that occurred at midcentury elucidate the different courses girls' basketball took in these two states. After *Life* magazine printed the photo of a partially nude Iowa high school player (Virginia Harris) undergoing a male doctor's inspection in a "health contest" at the 1940 state tournament, such thinly disguised beauty pageants were discarded. Not so in North Carolina, where competing in beauty contests joined cheerleading as a substitute for competitive basketball in that state's developing sporting culture. Then in 1954, as national physical education leaders effectively discouraged nearly all states from continuing state basketball tournaments, the Iowa Girls High School Athletic Union selected E. Wayne Cooley as its executive secretary. Other states, including North Carolina, shut down their tournaments, but Cooley transformed Iowa's—already the nation's most notable—into an entertainment extravaganza that was grandiose even by Iowa's standard.

The cumulative result of these different reactions to national pressures was that a different "natural order" surfaced in Iowa. Because the state did not accept outside educators' notions about competition and its pernicious effect on girls, few Iowans shared the nation's anxiety over the athletes' potential loss of femininity or susceptibility to "mannish" behaviors and appearances. Iowa's female high school players avoided such labels as "jock" in part because they often participated in every extracurricular activity their small towns offered, and a bifurcation of femininity and athleticism never developed. Elsewhere, women athletes had to endure a second-class athletic status and gender controversies as well as overcome the male characteristics attributed to sport. But Iowa high school girls were never second-class athletes and, at least until the Title IX era, were rarely embroiled in gender controversies. In Iowa's "natural order,"

its players could bare midriffs in 1950, a time when elsewhere reformers, quaking over the sexual danger they claimed followed competitive basketball, covered up girls.

The late Leon Plummer is an example of just how influential a
successful small-town girls' basketball coach could be in the lives
of his athletes. Before dying suddenly of a heart attack in 1976 at
age forty-one, Plummer took ten teams to the state tournament in
the nineteen years he coached at Farragut, a town of five hundred in
far southwest Iowa. Twenty-five years after winning the state championship in 1971, players from that team maintained that Plummer
remained an enduring influence in their lives. "He really molded
young women," said a former player. "The patience, the discipline,
the teamwork, the hard work, the fun, the respect. I'm who I am
partially because of him." Plummer made his players work on spe-
cific goals each summer, like practicing free throws or working on
dribbling. "He probably instilled in all of us the idea of having a
goal and working toward it," said another player. Just as Maynard's
Nicholson sisters noted that their coaches were always addressed
as "Mr.," the Farragut coach similarly was called "Mr." or "Coach
Plummer," a signal of respect from his players. The Farragut players
didn't question his directive, including the time he instructed them
to go to church the Sunday morning after the team won the state
title, even though the girls had stayed up all night celebrating.[22]

Successful coaches like Gene Klinge and Leon Plummer appeared to earn the devotion of players as well as gain control over the
girls' lives. "If he'd said the moon was made of cheese, Mary would
say yes, it is," the mother of Maynard player Mary Parsons had
said about her daughter's coach, Gene Klinge. Male coaches who
succeeded at coaching high school girls' teams possessed qualities
that presumably lead to success: leadership, good communication
skills, and the ability to teach—all nongendered traits. But most
men who have coached both girls and boys readily admit differences
between the two, and regardless of Steve Padilla's team's plea to
"treat us like boys," most male coaches say that they coach girls and
boys differently. These differences are presented by the coaches in

gendered language, which one must examine to learn how and when coaches maintained gender distinctions.

Men who coached Iowa girls' basketball as often as not started out hoping to do something else. "To be honest, I thought it [coaching girls] would be easier to win," said Carroll Rugland, who had coached girls for forty years by 1997. "Many girls' coaches were hired as football coaches, and they cared more about that." Gene Klinge, upon college graduation in 1962, had already signed a contract to work as an assistant football coach when the Maynard school board offered him the head girls' basketball job. Thirty-six years and 735 victories later, Klinge led all active Iowa girls' coaches in wins. Importantly, Rugland and Klinge—who both were honored as national coaches of the year by the National High School Athletic Coaches Association and were high school classmates who played basketball together—were members of a quite informal "old boys' network" that comprised the Iowa coaching fraternity.[23]

Over the course of a career, male coaches often coached both girls and boys, sometimes at the same time. Such was the case for Tom Ramsey, whose girls' teams at Farragut High School in the 1980s were better than the boys'. Ramsey had a running start with the girls: Farragut had gone to the state tournament ten times under the legendary Leon Plummer, and a strong tradition was in place. Ramsey also inherited an awareness from Plummer that girls were more emotional than boys. "There are different things you have to deal with," Ramsey said. "With boys, it's ego. With girls, it's emotions." Plummer, who started out as an assistant football coach at Farragut, shared that belief. "I think he always preferred girls," his widow said. "He thought they worked harder for him. The male ego gets in the way with boys."[24]

Eugene Evans served nearly a half century as an Iowa educator, including positions as school principal and superintendent; during that time he also coached both girls' and boys' basketball and served as president of the IGHSAU in the 1970s. Evans learned early that coaching methodologies varied. "In one game my first year coaching girls," said Evans, "we were terrible, and I chewed on the girls at halftime. In the second half, they were even worse, if that were possible. So the second time we played this team, I told my players, 'Let's see if we can have some fun.' And we played much better." Evans said he did not discipline girls in the same manner that other coaches with reputations as disciplinarians did. "I had to figure out [girls] individually, what they're not like, what they're like," Evans said. "I couldn't drive them like a Bob Knight would."[25]

But Eugene Evans knew of numerous successful coaches, including female coaches, who were strict disciplinarians. "Look at Gail Hartigan," he says. "With her, it was 'my way or the highway.'"

Late in a district semifinal game at Treynor High School in southwest Iowa in mid-February 2000, an errant shot from the visiting Malvern team resulted in the basketball being lodged between the rim and the backboard. It was that kind of night for Malvern: Treynor easily won the game en route to a seventh straight state tournament berth in Des Moines a couple weeks later. Instead of waiting for a confident player to swat the ball down (and there were several girls on the floor athletic enough to accomplish that), Gail Hartigan, the forty-seven-year-old coach of the Treynor Cardinals and the most successful female coach in Iowa girls' basketball history, jumped up off the bench and, ignoring the heels and dress she wore, sprinted crosscourt to a closet outside the gym. In seconds she returned with a broom that she used to jar loose the ball, handed the broom to a custodian, then jogged back to the bench, where she took her seat. People who knew Hartigan and witnessed the act probably thought: there goes Gail, micromanaging again.

In 1994, in the first post-six-player, four-class state tournament, Hartigan became the first woman to coach a championship team since 1937. Crossing barriers became common for her: in August 1994 she became the first woman to win high school coach-of-the-year awards from the *Des Moines Register* and the *Omaha World-Herald*. Perhaps Hartigan's most notable—and ironic—accomplishment is that after fighting to save the six-player game, she coached her five-player team into the state tournament seven straight seasons. Hartigan's remarkable record of 333 wins and 95 losses—the all-time best mark among Iowa female coaches—prompted an important question. What, indeed, were the conditions that permitted the disenfranchisement of female coaches in, of all activities, women's sports?

Perhaps the most credible respondent to such a question is Gail Hartigan herself. Hartigan describes herself as "lucky" that her father bought 160 acres of farmland near Manilla, a southwest Iowa town of fewer than one thousand residents. Whereas Denison, from where Hartigan's family moved, didn't offer girls' athletics, Manilla became a hotbed in girls' sports in the early 1970s. Hartigan was one of the earliest disciples of weight lifting, which Manilla coach Larry Bullock demanded of basketball players as well as of his track-and-field athletes (though both squads were comprised primarily of the same girls). "We did not know it was extraordinary to be lifting weights until we went to a clinic like the Ida Grove one," Hartigan said. Bereft of women models as a young assistant coach, Hartigan learned her profession from such successful male coaches as LaVerne Kloster (Woodbine), Larry Bullock (Manilla), and Leon Plummer (Farragut) at the summer basketball camps held regularly throughout Iowa. Besides learning successful teaching methodologies, Hartigan took from these men a traditional, hard-nosed, no-nonsense approach to coaching that cast her as a disciplinarian. Hartigan's successes at Treynor, where she has been the head coach for twenty-four years—the longest such tenure for a woman in the state—have been attributed to her reputation as such.

That's not the case, she argues. Or at least not anymore. "Around 1992 some players came in to see me after the season," Hartigan said. "They said I was yelling so much that they hated the game. So I changed. I now look at myself as a facilitator, though I haven't changed everything. I don't get stressed out when players wear weird socks. And having my own family changed me, too." Hartigan claims she was forced to change because high school students have changed. "You could yell at girls easier twenty years ago," she said.

Vadonna Hall, a former six-player girls' coach and boys' golf coach, echoed Hartigan's sentiments almost exactly. "The common response of girls is, 'I can't stand being yelled at,'" she said. "They whine and complain and hold grudges. Girls take criticism personally, and their tears tick me off. When boys get mad, they fight, come back, and the problem is over." But whereas Eugene Evans dealt with girls' problems "individually," Hall's method was to talk to the whole team so they wouldn't take the criticism personally.[26]

Gail Hartigan claims that she became "less harsh" as a coach because of behavioral changes in today's adolescents. "Girls are emotional and boys still act like boys, but this is changing," she said. "In the past, men weren't allowed to express their feelings. And you could yell at girls easier twenty years ago." The belief that high school- and college-aged females are more emotional than boys is a popular opinion shared by male coaches as well. "Women tend to be a little more emotional at times. But they're also a little less selfish," Paul Sanderford, a former University of Nebraska women's basketball coach, has said. And Woodbine's Bob Jasper, who coached boys for ten years before taking over the girls' team, said, "With certain girls on certain days, you want to leave them alone." Such statements can be construed in a couple of ways.

These coaches believe that experience has shown them that girls *are* more emotional than boys; this is, to the coaches, an established psychological difference between the sexes, and the coaches adjust their styles accordingly. But gender is defined as the "*social* organization of sexual difference," so these coaches are actually maintaining *gender* distinctions, for "adjusting a coaching style" is surely an activity that can be called "social organization." Also, such preoccupation with psychological or biological difference is a perpetuation of the Victorian belief that girls are better off not playing strenuous sports, such as basketball, because their emotional nature is not suited for competition.[27]

Still, there are *cultural* differences between girls and boys on a basketball floor that are difficult to overlook. "Never before in a locker room did I see so many basketball players put on so much lotion," said a girls' coach who had previously taught boys. "I'd say, 'You're about to pick up a basketball. Why are you putting on lotion?'" This coach also quickly learned that a "hair scrunchie" is a ponytail holder, and that it can interrupt practice when it falls out. But to acknowledge biological or psychological differences is to acknowledge gender distinctions, something female coaches are as likely as their male counterparts to do.[28]

Gail Hartigan has noticed changes in her players over the years, but she has not seen opportunities for women as coaches change significantly. She believes that coaching high school girls is a "zero-sum game" for a woman and that the future will promise no noticeably larger numbers of female coaches:

> A big advantage I've had is that I talked my superintendent into letting me teach half time. Before that it was like I had two jobs because I had three kids. So I stayed home in the morning, and the first year of that [1988] I went to state. It's an unusual arrangement and there's less stress, but I don't know many others with it. Lots of women need money, so they don't do it. There are still few women coaches because they get married, and then it's harder. Most husbands don't want their wives in the limelight. I've been lucky there, too, because I have an understanding husband. So there are reasons why high school women coaches don't stick around, and it's not going to change.[29]

Gail Hartigan, like so many other female coaches and physical education teachers, dismisses "women's libbers" and the feminist implications the description implies. But yet her actions belie her words, and she of all people understands the stifling effect that unchanging gender roles has had on women in coaching. But as physical educator Ruth Johnson points out, adopting a feminist tract within the confines of Iowa's conservative rural culture and a male-run girls' athletic union was hardly a successful strategy. Downgrading women's libbers can be understood as yet another instance of apologetic behavior; until the post–Title IX era, it hardly seemed plausible for women athletes to be feminine and feminists concurrently.[30]

Economic considerations steered Vadonna Hall's coaching career, too. But unlike the convenient half-day teaching assignment that Hartigan was able to obtain, Hall—like most female high school coaches—found no such sweet deal. "Nobody wanted to pay me for

my master's degree in physical education," said Hall, who became
a counselor after coaching. "Because of gender roles, women had a
hard time staying in coaching."

FASHION AND THE GAME

Few artifacts reveal as much about gender arrangements in a particular era as clothing, and societal attitudes toward women could be
understood in part by the way the players dressed. For Ruth Lang
and her teammates, the requirement that they wear garter belts
and heavy stockings was a way to enforce gender roles. While the
violation of these rules in Ruth's particular town had a consequence
that was perhaps unusually severe, the wearing of such garments was
commonplace throughout America. In the first quarter of the twentieth century, it was common for female players to wear bloomers
and hats as well. Some communities fretted over the sexual implications of the bloomers (and later, shorts), while others worried less
about the showing of flesh than how basketball uniforms could blur
the distinctions between girls and boys. Collars and sleeves were
added to women's uniforms when they were judged to resemble too
closely the men's shiny satin outfits.[31]

But just twenty years after Ruth Lang dispensed with her garter,
many Iowa high school girls were wearing two-piece uniforms that
revealed their midriffs. Another twenty years later—in the 1970s,
the Title IX era—the earlier fascination with uniforms was all but
lost, a sure sign that girls' basketball had truly arrived. What happened on the court was more important than how players dressed.
Such passages as the one that follows, taken from a 1958 yearbook,
would be ridiculed by most players many years later: "At the beginning of the year, we wore the black suits that were purchased
last year. However, we worked so hard that they were torn. At the
middle of the year we received new black suits, which had gold trim.
We won seven games and lost eleven."[32] The fact that these players
cared more about their uniforms than their record was characteristic
of earlier times.

Basketball uniforms, however, represented more than social attitudes. Beginning with the first state tournament championship

game in 1920, when Correctionville players raised money among townspeople for uniforms, the provision of uniforms has served as a primary component of the sport's ideology: girls learned responsibility by having to find sources to pay for their uniforms. In 1938 girls at Dunlap High School played basketball, volleyball, kitten ball (similar to softball), and ping-pong under the auspices of the Girls Athletic Association (GAA), an intramural group. The GAA called its coaches "supervisors," the implication being that the "supervisor" was responsible for a less strenuous activity than the coach. Nonetheless, like their peers participating in more competitive IGHSAU-sponsored programs, the Dunlap girls raised funds for uniforms. "Early in the fall, members of the GAA campaigned for basketball suits," read an account in the 1938 *Archive*, the Dunlap High School yearbook. "They sold enough magazine subscriptions to partially pay for gray satin suits and twelve sweaters. Eight girls bore the burden of battle in fine shape, winning 11 and losing only 3."[33]

The awkward garb that Ruth Lang and teammates were ordered to wear was the customary look of the day. High school girls often wore stylish sailor collars and bloomers in gym class as late as 1925, a sign that the physical exercise was likely moderate. In the first two decades of the twentieth century, players were typically covered from neck to toe, usually wearing ankle-length bloomers, black stockings, and long-sleeved blouses. Headgear—ostensibly to keep hair out of eyes—included hats (some with ruffles or pompoms), beanies, ribbons, and bows. By the late 1920s, uniform fashion rules had relaxed to allow above-the-knee bloomers as girls "showed skin" for the first time. One decade later, the more contemporary basketball "shorts" made their appearance along with a skirt made of satin—the most available fabric during war time—described as a sort of "evening dress" on the court.[34]

The most dashing design for uniforms came at midcentury, at the hands, appropriately, of a coach's wife. O. E. Lester was a well-traveled coach whose wife, Ruth, had designed uniforms for the several schools at which he taught. At Hartley, in northwest Iowa, Mrs. Lester designed an outfit that exposed several inches of a player's midsection. The comfortable midriff hardly raised a stir and quickly became popular throughout the state. In less than a quarter century, Iowa girls had gone from covering themselves head to toe in various useless garments to baring their midriffs, a telltale sign that the work of the anti-competition reformers elsewhere in America never took hold in rural Iowa. The balances that developed throughout the United States between local and national cultures weighed in heavily on the side of local institutions when it came to women's basketball in Iowa.[35]

But the decorative and restrictive basketball uniforms were an extension of gender arrangements off the court. A 1945 photograph of Helen Ehlert, a country-school teacher near tiny Magnolia in southwest Iowa, shows the young woman in pants, waving to her husband as she rides a horse away to work. Only dire circumstances permitted her to wear slacks: because Americans often found it difficult to buy gasoline, tires, or even a car during World War II, Mrs. Ehlert was forced to ride a horse, which was hard to do in a dress. It wasn't until the 1970s that many rural Iowa school districts permitted high school girls to wear pants to school.[36]

Finally, the gendered nature of basketball was visible without ever inspecting a uniform or counting dribbles. The Iowa game, like its counterparts throughout the nation, was gendered by its mascots and team names. Although the awkward name "Adettes" didn't prevent Farragut High School from attaining success on the floor, such titles, according to one study, violated rules of gender neutrality. Over half of the postsecondary institutions that scholars Eitzen and Zinn examined used sexist names that de-athleticized women by "implying their fragility, elegance, and propriety." Only 6 percent of the college teams that were studied used a feminine suffix like -ettes. But In Iowa high schools, the usage of such suffixes as well as adding the prefix "lady" was much higher.[37]

Uniform styles, the use of chaperones, team names, coaching strategies—all were elements of Iowa six-player girls' basketball that maintained gender distinctions in the social organization of the sport. But the Iowa game enjoyed unparalleled success because it

was a compromise, or middle landscape, in the battle over basketball rules. Because the compromise required the regular crossing of
boundary lines, gender distinctions were always in flux. Two stories
from disparate eras—the 1930s and 1960s—will shed light on the
gender arrangements operating in each period.

FIVE

The Longs, the Langerman Twins, and Others Before and After

"Hi, Gang, I'm going to show you how to play basketball. This is the basketball, you may bounce it once . . . twice . . . but never . . . no *never* thrice!" – Cyndy Long, *pep rally at the Union-Whitten High School, January 12, 1968*

See the zany Celtics fan decked out in green, sidling up to Larry Bird as "The Star Spangled Banner" introduces yet another NBA final at the Forum in Los Angeles. Disapproving viewers would like to believe that the legion of face-painted crazies who make spectacles of themselves at televised sporting events are guilty of misplaced idolatry, and, worse, are owners of small lives with inconsequential histories. Yes, this green-clad fan does own a history that includes, two hours earlier, arriving at the Forum simply to watch Larry Bird do his customary running of the stairs before game time. "That's why I love Larry Bird—his work ethic. He was the ultimate player because he couldn't run or jump but he went inside and he went outside. Denise stayed inside, and I was outside. My favorite spot was one foot outside the free-throw line. If I'd had the three-point line, I'd have lived there," says Cyndy Long. Long idolizes Larry Bird enough that she once grabbed her sleeping bag and basketball and drove alone in her Volkswagen Beetle to French Lick, Indiana, where she camped outside and queried the local bartenders about their famous native son. Cyndy Long always sent Larry Bird birthday cards and even bought shares in the Celtics. Now Long watches Bird at the Forum. She has sat by Oscar Robertson and talked with Danny Ainge; and when Jack Nicholson, "drunker than shit," inspects her green attire, all he can mumble is "ugh." Cyndy Long has visited the hotels where the Celtics stay, but she has never talked with Larry Bird. Standing next to him for "The Star Spangled Banner" is going to have to do for now.[1]

I am going to start dedicating each poem to one of you,
It will make them more fun and more interesting, too.
I will start out this poem by describing a friend,
That I dedicate this poem to and probably never again.
For the benefit of 'Mary Hammill':
Who has so many bumps we call her the camel.
——December 12, 1967, vs. Hubbard; uw won 80–69

Cyndy Long may have preceded the era of the three-point basket, but she stayed outside anyway; that's where she scored most of her 41 points in the most storied state tournament final in Iowa history— Union-Whitten's 113–107 overtime win against Everly in 1968 that featured 64 points from Denise Long and 76 from the losing team's Jeannette Olson.

Cyndy Long was used to staying outside. When Union-Whitten coach Paul Eckerman told her and her cousin Denise to "sleep there," referring to the outdoor basketball court in Whitten, Cyndy took his advice literally and dragged a mattress the one block from her home to the court. On hot summer nights, the Longs shot baskets until they tired of it, slept a spell, then shot some more. I called Coach and told him, "We got our mattress," and he thought we were kidding. The Longs still play full-court ball with any boys who dare, a life-long preoccupation that finds Cyndy squaring off against some rough-and-tumble teenagers at the Eldora Training School, a state reform facility, and, recently, at the Marshalltown Games. "I was the only girl," said Cyndy, who turned forty-five in 1997, the time of our interview. "A lot of women are like, 'I don't wanna hurt my knees'—not me."

The only boys the Longs couldn't keep up with were the big ones in the NBA. They found that out in 1969, when in the thirteenth round of the draft, the San Francisco Warriors selected Denise Long, the all-time, national leader in scoring for high school girls' basketball. The first woman ever drafted by the NBA, Denise took her selection seriously enough to attend training camp, accompanied— to no one's surprise—by Cyndy; the Long girls shared an apartment in Redwood City. Cyndy Long was always taking care of her famous cousin; she even wore her coat and signed autographs when Denise grew weary of the activity. Fans easily mistook five-foot-ten Cyndy for five-foot-eleven Denise, both of whom had shiny black hair that hung below their shoulders off the court. "I *liked* dressing up as her," said Cyndy, "but I was never jealous of her." And it was Cyndy who answered the telephone when *The Tonight Show* called and wanted Denise as Johnny Carson's guest.[2]

Cyndy Long, only a high school sophomore in 1968, had grown accustomed to responding to the emotional needs of Denise and the Union-Whitten Cobras. Every game day of that fabled season she scribbled a poem, and were the language of codependency fashionable in 1968, Cyndy Long would have merited the role of primary enabler. "Cindy reads poems to the team before a game to help the players get over any nervousness," was how a local newspaper described Cyndy's poetic charge, a preoccupation that Paul Eckerman might have found disturbing initially but accepted when he discovered that it worked. "Coach Eckerman would call me a hippie—I was a free spirit and wore armbands—and pull my long hair. He'd say, 'you're trying to make me mad.' He was tough on me and everyone, except for Denise. He had a great work ethic that made us tough, but he liked my poems. I locked myself in the bathroom and wrote 'em. They helped relax us. I was the funny one. I was the rebel—I was the one who ran away from home—and Denise was straight. I wrote the poems to calm everyone and to keep Denise from getting nervous." Cyndy's basketball scrapbooks include the poems along with the game reports published in various newspapers that invariably misspelled her name "Cindy." She dutifully corrected them all in pen, even the 1968 *Look* magazine commendation "for

Much to the chagrin of some national educators, girls' basketball in Iowa became a strenuous sport. "Play like boys on the court but act like ladies off it" became the reigning paradigm. Photo courtesy of Bloom Publishing Company.

(*Above left*) The cover girl on the state tournament program (here, 1969's Becky Ioerger of Jewell) represented the "healthy, clean, and vibrant" ideology that was a foundation of the game. Photo courtesy of IGHSAU.

(*Above*) Jan Kreiger, the 1978 program cover girl, was forbidden to do farm work because her father was afraid she would get hurt and not be able to play basketball. Photo courtesy of IGHSAU.

(*Left*) The covers of the state tournament programs were often a reflection of gender arrangements operating within the larger culture. Photo courtesy of IGHSAU.

(*Above*) The girls' basketball team from Logan posed for this photograph in 1914. From *A Pictorial History of Harrison County, Iowa*. Photo courtesy of Bloom Publishing Company.

(*Right*) Helen Boustead of Woodbine was set for gym class in her uniform with a sailor collar and bloomers in this 1925 photo. Photo courtesy of Bloom Publishing Company.

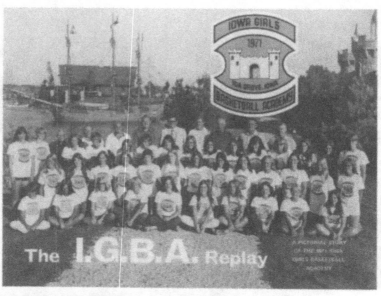

(*Above*) The fortunate players selected for the first Iowa Girls Basketball Academy in Ida Grove in 1971 attended camp at a lakeside chalet. Photo courtesy of IGHSAU.

(*Left*) The fight over girls' basketball rules became more intense with the passage of Title IX in 1972. Photo courtesy of Bloom Publishing Company.

E. Wayne Cooley directed the Iowa Girls High School Athletic Union for nearly a half century. Because of his leadership, Iowa became a "utopia for girls' athletics," according to *Sports Illustrated* in 1973. Photo courtesy of IGHSAU.

Cyndy Long of Union-Whitten, 1968. Photo courtesy of Cyndy Long.

outstanding achievement in Iowa girls' basketball." But Cyndy Long was the *other* Long.[3]

If anyone needed her nerves calmed at game time, it was the world's greatest high school girls' basketball player. "Denise used to drink a whole bottle of Pepto-Bismol before a game, she was so nervous," says Cyndy. The night Denise became the first player to score 1,600 points in one season, she was so nervous she brought two right-footed shoes to the district semifinal in Grundy Center and had to borrow a left shoe from the local boys' coach. She broke the record in the second half after going to the bench to get her own left shoe, retrieved after a fan's "quick trip" to Whitten. "I once made her pee her pants," says Cyndy. "She had a weak bladder and stomach. She was shooting a free throw, and I was blocking out and said, 'this girl sure has a big butt.' She peed her pants at the free-throw line. Part of her nervousness was that she had two, sometimes three, guards on her much of time."

They're gonna put us in the tourney.
They're gonna make big stars out of us.
The greatest team that ever hit the big time.
And all we got to do is play naturally!
——"Play Naturally," a rewrite of The Beatles' "Act Naturally," on the eve of Union-Whitten's state tournament berth

Win or lose, Paul Eckerman was cleaning his hog house at 6:30 the next morning. But caring for his new sow and eleven pigs— gifts of the Union-Whitten booster club for the coach's new acreage just outside of Whitten—would be a heck of a lot easier if he was scooping hog manure the morning after a Cobra victory, something Eckerman had failed to provide boosters in six trips to the district finals in eight years. That's *six straight losses* in the game to go to state, for which Union-Whitten has thus never qualified. Even the least cynical of observers might entertain the notion that those starter pigs might be a good career move for Eckerman should the Cobras lose yet another district final, particularly after the *New York Times* and *Chicago Tribune* had been badgering the Cobras at practice all week while limelighting Denise Long, who had merited a spot in *Sports Illustrated*'s heralded "Faces in the Crowd" feature seventeen games into the season.

So when Eckerman finally took Union-Whitten to state courtesy of an 83–77 win over Gladbrook, he was not about to sit Denise down. The Cobras had suffered their only loss that season when Eckerman withheld his top seven players in a meaningless game the night before sectionals began. The Long cousins packed their Beatles albums and record player for the trip to Des Moines—"Denise loved the Beatles," says Cyndy, "and we sang 'Play Naturally' on the bus." They and their teammates looked forward to spending one week in a city hotel, the Hotel Fort Des Moines. Cyndy kept a souvenir napkin from King's Food Host for her scrapbook. "Taboo for the team are greasy foods, pop, candy, popcorn and French fries," reported the Marshalltown newspaper in a profile of the Cobras at state. "Denise definitely doesn't drink milk before games because of 'cotton mouth.'" The *Times-Republican* also published the first-person account of Cobra player Mary Hammill. "Younkers was the host store to the team," wrote Mary. "Its display window was especially attractive and eye-catching with a miniature basketball court. It also contained a basketball girl dressed in one of the team suits, the Cobra bench blanket . . . , and the merchants of Des Moines gave charm bracelets to the players."[4]

Cyndy, forced to improvise, penned one of her state tournament poems on toilet paper, capturing the cacophonies and excitement a small-town teenager encountered in a city hotel—the bugs, the noise, the resident peepers, and the vigilance of the team chaperone, often the coach's wife:

> With Paglia writing her term
> paper, there wasn't much choice;
> and this is the only thing in
> our room that I have a voice.
> My bed is one place I can
> sleep in, if I can find my

way there;
But with Denise's underwear
strung clear from the door,
it's very rare.
So then I go in the bathroom
to take a warm shower;
And there in the bathtub the
clothes hamper with one
lonely flower.
Retreating to the closet for the
last place to go;
and there a centipede 9" long
crawling very slow.
By this time the "bong" of
the clock and the horns
and the fire trucks;
and Pam was snoring, Denise
started coughing—just my luck.
Mrs. Eckerman banging
frantically on her floor;
And the lobby boy trying
to peek through our door.

For its opening game against Bennett, Union-Whitten quickly
sold out its allotted six hundred tickets—two hundred short of the
combined population of the two communities. Denise Long, carry-
ing a national-record 61.6 points-per-game average into the game,
told reporters she had practiced two to three hours most summer
days in the Whitten town park to reach her goal set in seventh
grade: to play in the state tournament. "I have never worried about
the number of points I score," she told reporters. "All I have been
interested in is winning and getting to play in a state tournament."
In her first state appearance, Denise poured in 93 points, shattering
the tourney record of 74 set the night before by Everly's top-rated
Jeannette Olson. Long, firing in 32 of 46 field-goal attempts and
setting a tournament record with 29 free throws, passed Olson in

the third quarter of the 114–66 blowout for the Cobras. But Coach
Eckerman left Denise on the floor until the final minute. As the
Marshalltown newspaper reported, Eckerman incurred the wrath of
some Bennett fans, but he had "some logical answers for his critics."
"Sure I left her in there, but this girl has worked so hard she deserves
all the records she can get," Eckerman responded. "She's the one
who got us down here and I'm not about to sacrifice any records she
can get."[5]

"Long Sets Girls' Record: 93!" waxed the headline in the *Des
Moines Register*. But as expectations soared over the possibility that
Long would give fans an encore performance of her career-high-
scoring game—she had scored 111 points earlier in the season,
which merely tied the Iowa single-game record—and copyeditors
questioned the propriety of exclamation points in headlines, the
primary drama unfolded: all bets were on that top-rated Everly
and second-ranked Union-Whitten would clash on Saturday night,
unleashing the top two scorers in Iowa history in the title game.
Union-Whitten cruised into Saturday night with 19- and 28-point
victories over Pocahontas and Rockwell City in which Denise scored
64 and 61 points, respectively, prompting the *Register*'s headline on
March 16, 1968, "Olson Duels Long in Title Game." On Sunday morning, reporters dragged out the exclamation point again:
"Union-Whitten Wins It: 113–107!" Olson, averaging 58.7 points
per game going into the tournament and outscoring Long 76–64,
hit two free throws with three seconds left in regulation play to send
the game into overtime, but the Cobras finally won in the highest-
scoring game in Iowa state tournament history. "Jeanette Olson won
the battle, but Denise Long won the war—and what a great one
it was," reported the *Register*. "If the madcap struggle between the
state's two top-ranked teams wasn't the best title game in history, it
will do until someone figures out a better one." Everly coach Larry
Johnson remarked that "probably 11,000 fans" rooted against his
team. And Cyndy Long, who had scored a career-high 41 points,
seemed, poetically, to get in the last word: "I knew we couldn't get
beat," she told reporters. "Nobody can beat us. That's not bragging.
That's a fact."[6]

Following the Saturday night championship, the patriarchs of the game—IGHSAU director Wayne Cooley and tournament publicity director Jack North—as well as WHO radio and TV broadcaster Jim Zabel feted the Cobras at a victory dinner at the Hotel Kirkwood. Then there was a Sunday breakfast at the Hotel Fort Des Moines, where the team stayed, before the police escorted the Cobras and a caravan of cars out of Des Moines. They were headed toward Marshalltown, where the awaiting crowd of one thousand constituted, according to the local paper, "the largest gathering in that town since movie star Jean Seberg's homecoming." It was St. Patrick's Day, and Cobra green was the color of the day. The girls rode in and out of Marshalltown atop a fire engine bound, along with four hundred cars, for Whitten, twelve miles away. "Only a grass fire could slow down the victory celebration," reported the *Des Moines Register*, referring to the ten-minute stop the fire truck made to extinguish a grass fire alongside the road. The entourage ended up at the Union gym, where one thousand fans had gathered to hear each of the players speak and Cyndy Long read a poem. The championship trophy stood four and one-half feet tall and weighed thirty pounds.[7]

I started to write a poem in study hall,
When Debbie Calloway laughed at it and made me ball.
She said, "It doesn't make sense, and neither do you."
So I started over and she kept laughing, too.
But I don't care, for I know;
That everybody makes fun of me . . . so?
——January 22, 1968, vs. Dows; UW won 136–41

Cyndy Long wrote this poem for the game against Dows, when Denise Long pumped in 111 points, tying the all-time state scoring record set by Monona's Norma Schoulte in a 1952 tournament game. The poem reveals a state of self-knowledge and maturity uncommon for high school sophomores and shows that Cyndy reveled in her role as basketball court jester. Her self-described "free spirit" proved as uncontainable as Denise's prowess on the court.

Cyndy's mother registered her at a Des Moines business college in 1970, but she never attended; instead, she played briefly for *Look* magazine's women's team. In the heady early 1970s, when hitch-hiking was socially acceptable for young people but rarely done by single women, Cyndy Long hitchhiked throughout the West alone, supporting herself with odd jobs. She eventually bought a vw Beetle—the one she drove to French Lick, Indiana—and drove around America with a sleeping bag and basketball. She wound up in Newport Beach, California, where she lived with brothers Doug and Dwight for four years. The Long boys later returned to Iowa and operated a tavern in Eldora, where Cyndy worked, and since 1996 have operated a Marshalltown restaurant where Cyndy waits tables. She has never married.

> I'm a free spirit, and I don't have any regrets. I'm also glad I grew up when I did. People have no conscience anymore, and nothing is sacred. *Hoosiers* was like us; that was a major flashback. We never knew we were special, and I was never jealous of Denise. We were taught a work ethic and that sports teaches competition without hurting anyone. But today . . . look at Dennis Rodman. How can a kid admire someone who dresses as a woman?
>
> I love to rebound and fight for the ball. I didn't have any sisters and hung out with guys and started playing full-court when I was thirteen. Never thought about it being better than six-player at the time. But do I wish I could have played full-court? Yeah.

In 1993, when the 1968 Union-Whitten state champs held a twenty-five-year reunion, there wasn't much trouble finding the starters on the team: Pam Paglia Norman and Deb Calloway lived in Whitten, Carol Hanusch Gunderson in Union, Mary Hammill in Marshalltown, and Denise Long in Des Moines. Cyndy Long, of course, read a poem, and then, surrounded by the entire team nestled on a hayrack that carried a large green sign, "1968 State Basketball Champs," paraded down a Union main street lined with onlookers; she was the only player still able to wear her uniform.

Jean and Jo Langerman led three different high schools to the Iowa girls' state basketball tournament as they moved around the state with their mother, a beautician, during the Depression. Some fans and players resented the Langerman twins for their independence as well as for their talent, and after high school they joined a women's professional team that played "regular" basketball against men.

The players' mother, known as "Mama" Langerman, was a struggling single parent who, caught in the grips of the Great Depression and practicing a trade that permitted mobility, moved around every so often because she felt it was best for her two daughters. If the hairstyling business wasn't good in Whittemore, she could pick up her shop and move on to Parkersburg, and then to Hampton— which she did. Or perhaps looking forward to what opportunities basketball might provide for her talented twins, she believed that she needed to find the right community and coach who would help Jean and Jo polish their skills. In any case, Mama Langerman moved her family three consecutive years to three small Iowa towns, where Jean and Jo, as fourteen-year-old freshmen playing their fourth season of varsity basketball, led Whittemore to a third-place finish at the state tournament in 1931, followed by state championships in Parkersburg and Hampton in 1932 and 1933.

Divorced and characterized as strong-willed, Mama Langerman didn't allow her five-foot-eleven twins to play their senior season at Hampton because she fought with the coach. But that didn't hamper the careers of Jean and Jo, already known as "the first ladies of Iowa basketball." The twins ultimately wound up members of the Iowa Basketball Hall of Fame and received offers, which they declined, from Paramount Film Studios and the Bennett Studios of Dance in New York City. (Although I found no evidence that the twins ever danced, it is conceivable that their grace on the basketball floor was considered readily transferable to the dance floor.)

The Langerman twins soon starred on the nation's top amateur teams before playing professionally with a Missouri team called Olson's All-American Redheads. As a barnstorming attraction, the All-American Redheads were surpassed in popularity only by the Harlem Globetrotters, a celebrity status attained because the women played local men's amateur teams by five-player men's rules and won half of the two hundred games they played annually. "They weren't redheads, but their mother was a beautician. They could be anything they wanted," a former high school teammate said about the Langerman twins. "The mother was very domineering and the girls were not very social. At the state tournament they stayed apart from the rest of the team with their mother. . . . The twins caused friction."[8]

Although grade-school girls playing varsity basketball was not uncommon in the 1930s, playing for three different towns in three seasons was a rare and questionable practice. An Iowa sportswriter captured the public's disapproval: " 'Why,' you may be asking, 'didn't the Langermans play as seniors?' The flip answer heard over the years is: 'They ran out of towns.' Don't junk that as a possibility, at least of towns willing to go an extra mile to land a hair stylist accompanied by two tall daughters."[9]

The Langerman twins were characterized as "not very social," their mother was known to be domineering and strong-willed, and the family's nomadic ways met with flip criticism. The public response to their personalities and lifestyle shows the cultural restrictions that these women confronted. But the Langermans' history also reveals ways in which the women overcame these restrictions and shaped their own lives. The story is an important one. In the middle of the Depression, a divorced woman moves her daughters around the state to enable them to secure their future. Strong-willed, divorced women—let alone a woman who openly questioned the authority of male coaches—were socially unacceptable in a conservative cultural environment that fostered traditional gender roles.[10]

That the Langermans "could be anything they wanted" raises interesting questions about accepted social constructions and, specifically, about matters of agency and freedom for Iowa women, whose roles were allegedly restricted under the tropes of separate spheres and domesticity. The antiquated game of six-player girls' basketball, invented by educators whose concerns mirrored those of the Victorian Era, survived for one century because—at least partially—

of a conservative culture that ascribed traditional gender roles for women.[11]

The high school careers of the Langerman twins and Cyndy Long, occurring more than thirty years apart, show how gender informed and influenced Iowa six-player girls' basketball. Power relations in gender arrangements had shifted during the period separating the eras in which the Langerman sisters and Cyndy Long played high school basketball. Whereas the Langermans and their mother were castigated for questioning gender roles, Long was an admitted free spirit whose forward ways were more than simply acceptable—she was publicly celebrated. Announcing "Nobody can beat us" and traveling cross-country alone constituted behavior that ran counter to the "cookies-and-milk" ideology that had earlier served as the foundation for girls' basketball.

Cyndy Long's adoration of the professional player Larry Bird has profound meaning involving the intersection of gender, class, and race. Long called Bird the ultimate player because "he couldn't run or jump" but had a ferocious work ethic, and other Iowa players mention Bird as a hero as well. The former Celtic player was perceived as having to play well beyond his natural ability in order to survive in the NBA, a sometimes hostile world that seemed analogous in some ways to that of Iowa girls in the six-player game. Like Bird, a small-town midwesterner who overcame physical and cultural hardships to soar to greatness, Iowa girls had to fight a number of obstacles.

First, the fact that high school girls had to settle for a male role model because there were no women players to emulate offers proof for a sweeping indictment of the gendered nature of the sporting world. Second, because six-player basketball was the province of small, rural towns whose agricultural base was founded on a strong work ethic and its inherent values, the game was class governed in the sense that a blue-collar player like Larry Bird was chosen to project its worth because he was perceived to share its values. Finally, the statement about Bird's jumping ability has racial implications: he was sometimes a victim of the "white men can't jump" slur. Iowa high school girls thirty years ago and earlier may have chosen a white player as a role model for the same reason that they idolized a man: that's all that was available. Iowa small towns where girls' basketball flourished rarely had citizens of color. According to the 1990 census, Iowa was the third whitest state in the nation, a fact that remained steady throughout the twentieth century. African American players were sometimes found on college, industrial, and AAU basketball teams, but before Iowa cities started programs in the 1960s, African Americans were rarely seen on Iowa high school teams and almost never in the small towns. In 1970 southwest Iowa's Harrison County (population fifteen thousand) was home to *one* African American family. Many sources consider Colleen Bowser, who transferred her senior year from Wichita, Kansas, to Des Moines's Valley High School in 1965, the first great African American player in Iowa girls' basketball history. But even though race was a factor, the primary descriptor in Colleen Bowser's case was gender. "She was the closest thing to a boy player we'd ever seen in Iowa girls' ball," said her coach, Chuck Neubauer, revealing once more the standard to which girls of any color were held.[12]

Also notable in Cyndy Long's experience was the twenty-five-year reunion that gathered together her teammates from the 1968 championship squad. Such reunions were commonplace for former players of championship teams. And the teams that reunited shared a common characteristic: the individual players, more likely than not, settled in the vicinity of the town where earlier they had found glory on the court. Talented female players, after all, were unlike their male counterparts, who could convert their athletic prominence into college scholarships; and after attending college they were less likely to return to their hometowns or farms. All the starters on Cyndy Long's Union-Whitten team remained in central Iowa, and most of the members of the 1971 state champion Farragut Admiralettes, who staged a reunion in 1996, lived near that town. When the eleven members of the 1974 champion Manilla Hawkettes reunited in 1999, all but three still lived in Iowa. It is conceivable that the strength of Iowa rural culture—which manifested itself on the basketball floor—kept these players from moving away. The reunions, in any case, reveal a steely bond of camaraderie and loyalty among the women.[13] The shared experiences of Iowa six-player basketball veterans result in a litany of stories colored by the gendered nature of the game.

Rhea Wigg was in eighth grade when Treynor High School won the Class A Iowa high school girls' state basketball championship in 1994. Not only did this southwest Iowa school win a state crown in the first all-five-player tournament (from 1985 to 1993 schools chose between the five- and six-player games), but Treynor coach Gail Hartigan became the first woman to coach an Iowa state basketball championship team since 1937. When Wigg graduated from Treynor in 1998, she had played on four straight state-qualifying teams, earning a starting position as point guard her senior year. When she was in junior high and told to pick a position, she chose forward. "If we'd have stayed in six-player, I'd have been a guard," said the five-foot-four Wigg, "because of my quickness and size. But I was glad when they went to five—I liked it a lot better. You needed to be more well-rounded. I hated standing there at half court with nothing else to do but wait, then fight somebody at half court. I would rather dribble full court myself." Rhea Wigg would not have become one of the best three-point shooters in school history under the six-player rules, whose gender restrictions would have left her "standing there at half court"; short, quick girls were customarily placed in the guard court.[14]

The Depression-era Langerman twins were successful at carving their own path. Similarly, the efforts of Myrna Hauschildt Feekin to get ahead can be viewed as a matter of agency rather than restriction. A forward on Gladbrook's state championship teams in 1959 and 1960, Hauschildt got "a foot up" on other girls by playing on the varsity team as an eighth-grader; this was common among exceptional players. Like the Langermans, Hauschildt parlayed her basketball skills into a postsecondary career. "I was going to work in a feed mill because my parents couldn't afford college," she said. Instead she played six-player basketball for seven years for Commercial Extension School of Commerce, commonly known as "secretary school." And like Mama Langerman, Myrna Hauschildt's children played an important role in her decision to live where she did. She chose to settle in the state "for the benefit" of her athletic daughters, one of whom merited all-state selection in three sports: basketball, track, and volleyball.[15]

Sarah Allen White was an Iowa player who argues that the leadership skills and competitive experiences she gained from the basketball floor immeasurably influenced her lifelong pursuits—a career as naval commander. Allen was a five-foot-eleven jumping center at Ida Grove, an all-state player whose school won state championships in 1928 and 1929. She was a basketball mascot at age four and fourteen years younger than a sister whose only sporting opportunity was intramural basketball. Allen's father was a prominent western Iowa lawyer; her mother was a teacher. Allen, herself, was trained as an engineer at the University of Iowa and had worked for the FBI for six years at the time the United States entered World War II. After attending naval officers' training, she put her engineering background to work and designed weapons for the wartime U.S. Navy, retiring as a full commander in 1969. Allen White identified a team spirit in the navy that was similar to that of her basketball team: "Playing basketball was very important because I learned that you can't be out for yourself," she remarked. "And when you couldn't do things for yourself, the team would do it." Allen White also acknowledged that while still in high school she was chosen to be a "parade princess" at the Drake Relays, a nationally prominent spring track-and-field meet in Des Moines. The honor was consistent with the commonly displayed "apologetic behavior" of female athletes who strove to prove that girls could play sports and still be feminine.[16]

The Depression-era experiences of the Langerman twins displayed the gender arrangements in place for female athletes at that time. Similarly, the careers of another pair of northern Iowa sisters shed light on the gender complexities of six-player basketball over fifty years later, in the 1980s. When in their effort to make girls' basketball acceptable women physical educators adopted a "cookies-and-milk" strategy—a plan to make a competitive game seem noncompetitive by making it less physically demanding—they weren't

concerned with the consequences of girls playing five-player basketball in college after having played the less strenuous six-player
game in high school. Even exceptional and well-conditioned players unaccustomed to the rigor of playing full court risked physical injury. Also, in the post–Title IX era, colleges and universities
now faced the challenge of stocking five-player basketball programs
with women who had played the less demanding six-player game.
Such was the experience of thousands of Iowa girls, including sisters
Shawna and Stacey Paskert of Emmetsburg, who suffered physical
injuries when they played the five-player college game after switching from high school six-player basketball. Their experiences reveal
another effect of basketball having been gendered in the game's early
days, a concern that became much larger when the game switched
rules in 1993. Whereas the only girls who needed to adjust to the
five-player game before 1993 were those who played at the postsecondary level (and those players whose Iowa high schools opted for
five-player rules in 1985), now *all* Iowa girls played a considerably
tougher brand of basketball.

Shawna Paskert, a six-foot-four all-state athlete who averaged 38
points and 10 rebounds as a high school senior in the six-player
game, got a wake-up call when she toured Europe with an American
team in 1988. That fall she began a college basketball career at
Sioux City's Morningside College that was plagued with injuries;
after having never been hurt in high school, Paskert suffered knee
injuries three straight years playing the "new" five-player game. "It
was an instance of the conversion [to five-player ball] being more
physically taxing than we thought," Paskert says. "Neither my sister
nor I had any physical problems whatsoever until we played 'five.'"
Shawna Paskert, who became a high school basketball and volleyball
coach, was hurt badly enough and often enough that she played only
two seasons for her college team.[17]

Stacey Paskert, three years younger than Shawna, played forward
through her freshman season at Emmetsburg but was moved to
the guard court on the varsity team. Like so many players in that
predicament, she had little choice. "[Coach] Ted Bailey said, 'You'll
never play for me if you're a forward,'" says Stacey, "so he worked

and worked with me." All the hard work paid off because Stacey Paskert became a Hall-of-Fame guard whose 1991 Emmetsburg team went undefeated. The team won the state championship, and she set an all-time state tournament record for interceptions. Recruited by several Division I schools, Stacey chose Omaha's Creighton University, where coach Tony DiCecco, a former Iowa high school coach, led the program. "Tony knew Iowa girls had a good work ethic, and Creighton was nearly all six-player vets. And we were ranked from 1992 to 1994."[18]

But Stacey Paskert suffered injuries more disabling than sister Shawna's—and sooner. "On the second day of practice, I blew my knee out. So I red-shirted and had surgery," recalled Paskert. "When I came back, I was hurt in the third practice. I quit my junior year, but instead of having my scholarship taken away, I worked like a graduate assistant, doing the laundry and such." Stacey Paskert still runs and plays basketball, despite the fact that she has been diagnosed with arthritis and tendonitis. "I have no cartilage in my knee, and I walk down stairs one step at a time," she says. "I had never been hurt before in high school, and I had pads on everywhere playing 'five.'"

There were, of course, Iowa girls who were hurt playing *six-player* basketball. Sandy Van Cleave finished her high school career at Montezuma in 1971 as one of the most successful players in Iowa history, having led her team to an eighty-nine-game winning streak en route to two state championships and a 115-3 record over four years. Van Cleave was selected to play in the Pan-American Games and earned a basketball scholarship to Parsons College in Fairfield, Iowa. But as a high school freshman, Van Cleave suffered a knee injury on the court, and she claims that a doctor "bungled" his effort to help her and left scar tissue in the knee. "I was in pain all the time from then on," says Van Cleave, who relied on a personal toughness to continue playing.[19]

Sandy Van Cleave's perseverance and accomplishment of becoming an All-American years after suffering a painful knee injury as a fifteen-year-old freshman reveals the underlying deceit of apologetic behavior and cookies-and-milk strategies—such ideologies

were simply social constructions governed by existent societal gender arrangements. While some players might have given up basketball after suffering serious knee injuries, Van Cleave and the Paskerts
played in a more competitive climate, and their toughness—characteristic of good athletes, male or female—presupposed any gender
roles. Sandy Van Cleave and the Paskert sisters, like so many Iowa
girls raised on farms, detasseled corn in the summer, which was
strenuous physical labor. Van Cleave was a self-described "tomboy
who never washed dishes," the youngest of seven children whose sisters became cheerleaders because they were "sissies." "My brothers
would beat the pants off me in basketball, but if I cried they wouldn't
let me play," recalls Van Cleave. Thus some of the best six-player
athletes resisted any cookies-and-milk strategy.

One of the most visible results of gendered basketball was the overwhelming number of male coaches for girls' teams: not one state
championship team was coached by a woman between 1937 and
1994. Evidence of the gender imbalance can be found as well in the
list of men and women chosen for the Golden Plaque of Distinction
to the Superlative Iowa Coach, an award from the Iowa Girls High
School Athletic Union for state tournament success. From the late
1920s through the early 1990s, only 3 of the 52 coaches so honored
were women. But in order for women to win coaching awards, they
have to first get jobs and stay with them, an achievement—as Gail
Hartigan, a rare success story, reiterated—that is becoming increasingly rare. At the start of the twenty-first century (November 2000),
only 38 of the 393 head basketball coaches of Iowa high school girls'
teams were women, a number remarkable for several reasons. For
only the second time since the 1978–79 season (the first being in
1999), fewer than 10 percent of girls' coaches were women. And *38*
was exactly half the number of women who held coaching jobs only
twelve years before (1988–89)—and the smallest number of female
coaches since 1977–78.[20]

But the clearest understanding of the paucity of women coaches
is reached when viewing the numbers over time. While the annual
turnover for male coaches is 18 percent, more than 37 percent of

women coaching girls' basketball change jobs every year. The result is staggering: *only 3 Iowa women among the almost 400 head girls' coaches (men and women) have a tenure of more than ten years.* While the average tenure of the 355 male coaches in 2000–2001 was almost eight years, the average for women was four years. A likely reason for this statistic is that, as Hartigan argued, women coaches usually give first priority to familial responsibilities. But the shrinking number of women coaches is often attributed to conditions triggered by Title IX as well. At the time of its passage, male athletic directors, forced to start up girls' basketball programs, usually picked other men as coaches; in Iowa this situation occurred primarily in large schools, since the game was already in place in the small towns. "People hire people they know, people who look like them," argues Donna Lopiano, executive director of the Women's Sports Foundation. "When you're a minority or a woman, you're going to lose that deal."[21]

In the seventy-year span between the advent of the IGHSAU and the demise of six-player basketball, the few women who *did* coach often loomed large in state affairs. For example, Gail Hartigan and Connie Shafar were both prominent coaches and two of the first women board members of the IGHSAU. Often, women who pursued coaching careers left the state; among them was Ellen Mosher, a head coach at Whittier College, the University of Minnesota, and UCLA, where she coached all-time great Ann Meyers. Mosher was a second-generation player and one of six sisters who played at Allison-Bristow High School, where her coach, Dale Fogle, made a strong enough impression that he became her role model. Men like Fogle, Gene Klinge, Carroll Rugland, and Les Hueser thus became models of behavior on the basketball court for hundreds of young women, many of whom routinely ascribe their successes in the sport to their coaches' propensity for the discipline required of playing hard and playing to win. Hueser, whose Hubbard-Radcliffe team won the last six-player title in 1993 and who retired two years later with over seven hundred career victories, argues that competition has been diminished with the change to five-player. "I always thought I had girls who would go through walls," Hueser says. "It's not the same with five-player." Why the coach believes attitudes have changed is not clear, though the uniqueness of six-player basketball and a change in social and cultural values or a shift in authority are likely contributors. "Five-player will never have the same fan approval," according to Hueser. "The empty seats around me at the state tournament belong to ticket holders who don't come now."[22]

Rugland was a member of the male-only coaching staff that in July 1971 directed the first Union-sponsored girls' basketball clinic held in Iowa, the five-day camp in Ida Grove called the Iowa Girls Basketball Academy. The clinic provides evidence of the gender ideology in place just prior to the passage of Title IX: the girls practiced basketball with voracious spirit but then participated in activities earlier found in finishing schools for girls. Academy participants were given a steady fare of what can be described as apologetic behavior—programs given by Omaha's Patricia Stevens Career and Business School that focused on "proper etiquette, grace, and manners" and included "showing the girls the proper way to walk, sit and stand" as well as fashion shows that featured the players modeling clothes. "Play like boys on the court but act like ladies off it" was still the reigning paradigm in 1971. Earlier, similar training in etiquette had been required of the women who played in the All-American Girls Professional Baseball League, the wartime social experiment of chewing-gum mogul and Chicago Cubs owner Philip K. Wrigley. The league, which operated from 1943 to 1954 and was the focus of the film *A League of Their Own*, demanded in a "charm school guide" that its players, "rapidly becoming the heroines of youngsters," abide by rules of conduct that required women to wear lipstick at all times and forbade them to wear slacks or shorts in public.[23]

But almost thirty years after her participation in the Iowa Girls Basketball Academy, one player didn't remember the etiquette training, though she fondly recalled nightly steak dinners at a lakeside chalet and the warehouse that was converted into a basketball court. Another academy participant, West Central player Deb Kaune, diplomatically described the lessons in etiquette as "a unique opportunity to make mostly farm girls look professional." She more easily recalled other activities, like listening to speakers such as Bill Russell. These comments along with photographs from the academy program show that teaching etiquette to the best basketball players in Iowa was downright silly. In one picture players listen intently to a coach during practice, while in another, still dressed in basketball shorts and T-shirts, they giggle as a business school representative shows them "the proper way to walk."[24]

That the academy provided such traditionally feminine activities served to remind that Iowa six-player girls' basketball was a gendered business—on and off the basketball floor.

SIX

The Demise of the Six-Player Game

No person in the United States shall, on the basis of sex, be excluded from participation in, be denied the benefits of, or be subjected to discrimination under any education program or activity receiving federal financial assistance. – Sec. 901(a), Title IX, Education Amendments Act of 1972

Is it true you are pushing five-girl, full-court basketball? If so, why? Mr. Califano, have you ever seen an Iowa girls' basketball game? If not, what are you basing your convictions on? – Letter to Joseph Califano, September 27, 1978, signed by thirteen girls in a North Mahaska, Iowa, high school speech class

On November 8, 1969, eighty-three Iowa high school teachers and coaches each paid a fifty-cent registration fee to attend a girls' basketball clinic held at the Women's Gym at the University of Iowa in Iowa City. It was a *five-player* basketball clinic. Sponsored by the Iowa Division for Girls and Women's Sports (DGWS) of the American Association for Health, Physical Education, and Recreation (AHPER), an affiliate of the National Education Association, the half-day clinic showcased the "experimental" five-player game adopted only recently by the DGWS. It used the Iowa Wesleyan College women's basketball team to demonstrate. Conducted at a time shortly before city schools in Iowa had begun to initiate girls' basketball programs, the clinic promoted the five-player game. "We certainly would like to do everything we can to encourage the schools here to use DGWS rules whenever possible," the state DGWS basketball chairperson wrote to the woman, a Des Moines physical education teacher, who directed the clinic. That the DGWS sponsored the clinic was a stunning development in itself; until 1963 this group comprised a significant share of the women physical education teachers who opposed interscholastic competition of any stripe. But that year the DGWS revised its policy on competition in high school girls' sports and for the first time permitted "extramural participation arranged to augment a sound and inclusive instructional program in physical education." The DGWS explained the policy change as follows: "Periodically, it becomes necessary to review and revise these standards because of changes within our sport culture and because of research which reveals new understandings concerning the nature and direction of women's sports." That the DGWS now not only supported competition for girls but championed the five-player rules for basketball signaled a major shift for national educators who for years had fought against girls' competitive sports. Change was in the air.[1]

Within three years of the clinic, Title IX of the Education Amendments Act of 1972 was passed and was "about to do for women's athletics," wrote one commentator, "what the Nineteenth Amendment did for women's rights." It would make five-player girls' basketball inevitable in Iowa. In the 1970s Iowa six-player basketball became an unlikely political battleground, one concurrently serious and comically absurd. While *Sports Illustrated* reported that E. Wayne Cooley was the man responsible for "the best girls' athletic program in the U.S.," a state senator in Cooley's own backyard, Minnette Doderer of Iowa City, chided the IGHSAU's executive secretary for not including more women in the Union's administration. Soon, such groups as the Iowa Commission on the Status of Women, the Iowa Women's Political Caucus, and the Iowa Civil Liberties Union declared their opposition to six-player rules. Before the decade was over, Joseph Califano, secretary of the Department of Health, Education, and Welfare (HEW), the federal department charged with the regulation of Title IX, had entered the fray. The

journalist George Will declared that HEW's making Iowa girls' basketball a "human rights issue" was "beyond parody." Six-player basketball remained in the national spotlight even in the 1980s, when a
trio of junior high girls (with the support of parents and politicians)
threatened to have the game dragged into court. When the Union
finally dismantled six-player basketball in February 1993, almost a
quarter century had passed since that Iowa City five-player clinic
was held in 1969.[2]

The fact that objections to the six-player rules and to the male
administration of the Union occurred almost simultaneously was
hardly surprising: the passage of Title IX encouraged consideration
of the first matter, while a half century of men's governance of the
only girls' athletic association in America forced change concerning
the latter. There wasn't a female board member with full voting
rights in the IGHSAU until *after* Title IX.

Girls' state basketball tournaments were held in various Iowa
cities and towns for five years prior to the formation of the Union
in 1925. According to a three-inch news story buried deep in the
sports section of the *Des Moines Register*, Drake University invited
twenty-seven teams to participate in 1920, and twenty-four showed
up. "Only ten-minute halves will be played so that the players will
not be overworked," reported the *Register*, a statement echoing the
popular cookies-and-milk ideology constructed for the game. Also
noteworthy was the roster of teams: although girls' basketball had
been introduced in Iowa in the 1890s in cities like Dubuque, the first
state tournament was comprised entirely of teams from small towns,
most with populations well under one thousand. This was a trend
that would continue when the tourney came under the purview of
the Union a few years later. By week's end, the first Drake tourney,
won by northwest Iowa's Correctionville, was the lead sports story
in the Sunday edition of the *Des Moines Register*, which, as "The
Newspaper Iowa Depends On," started a century-long practice of
showcasing the state tournament. In 1926 the first state tournament
under the sanction of the newly formed Iowa Girls High School
Athletic Union was a round-robin that held its final in the north-
central town of Hampton, whose team won the title under coach Ju-

lia Hemenway. Correctionville, Iowa's first state tournament champion, and Hampton, the Union's first tournament winner six years later, were both coached by women, as were most of the state's high school girls' teams during that era.[3]

But after the advent of the IGHSAU, a woman-coached state championship team quickly became a rarity for many reasons. Because of gender arrangements in the public school system (discussed throughout chapter 5), superintendents and principals were almost exclusively men, and these male administrators often coached girls' basketball in the small towns. Administrators rarely accommodated female coaches who were raising children, forcing the women to choose between coaching and a family. Denied the opportunity of having had women coaches, Iowa high school girls, in a 1949 Union survey of more than two hundred players, overwhelmingly preferred male over female coaches. The lasting result was that the percentage of girls' basketball coaches who were women fell to an all-time low of 1.5 in 1972 (when Title IX was enacted). Women's coaching never regained the numbers it had seen in the early twentieth century; since 1971 only 30 of the 610 coaches who qualified for the state tournament—fewer than 5 percent—were women. At the 2001 state tournament, only one of the thirty-two teams that qualified for state in four classes had a woman as its head coach; statewide, 38 of the 293 girls' basketball coaches—13 percent—were women.[4]

The Union was formed in 1925 when twenty-five small-town educators disagreed with the Iowa High School Athletic Association's decision to quit sponsoring the girls' state tournament. The Iowa High School Athletic Association (IHSAA), started just two years earlier, had conducted both boys' and girls' activities from 1923 through 1925, when the organization sided with the growing national movement to suppress female varsity sports. The IHSAA agreed with such groups as the Committee on Women's Athletics (CWA) that, from a moral and health perspective, intramural play was best for girls; the anti-competition educators, including female physical education teachers as well as male groups like the IHSAA, believed, too, that it would be better to offer all girls some athletic activity rather than provide basketball to just a few, which might occur, they argued, in larger schools, where enrollments were high and gym time was at a premium. The gym issue was critical to the IHSAA, for boys' basketball was growing in popularity and, in addition to these other arguments against varsity girls' basketball, sharing facilities wasn't a popular option with the group.

The problems of a lack of facilities and scheduling conflicts tended to appear more often in larger schools and were major reasons why the schools led the movement to restrict girls' basketball to intramurals in Iowa and across the nation. In small-town high schools the number of students was so low that intramurals frequently weren't possible even though half the girls, and usually more, might play basketball. In any case, these issues were at the heart of the debate that would rage for over a half century and were concerns that compelled the IHSAA to stop sponsoring girls' tournaments. The same questions and issues were debated among the general Iowa populace as well. "The whole gamut of arguments involving intramural versus interscholastic competitive sports," a former superintendent of the State Historical Society of Iowa wrote, "was discussed by citizens, educators, and students."[5]

Not only were the twenty-five educators who broke with the IHSAA all men, but nearly all of them were school administrators from small towns who understood that girls' basketball was important to community life. None of the fifteen directors on the Union board who represented the four districts in Iowa—northeast, northwest, southwest, and southeast—during the Union's first twenty-five years (1926–1950) came from a town larger than five thousand. From the onset the lifeblood of the Iowa Girls High School Athletic Union was found in the state's smallest communities.[6]

The men who founded the only autonomous association dedicated to high school girls' sports in America soon made it explicit in their bylaws that only school administrators—superintendents and principals like themselves—would be allowed to direct the Union. Their thinking followed the line that they, and *only they*, were fit to direct the sporting activities of young girls. The Iowa High School Athletic Association had a similar requirement that its board members be administrators, but the IHSAA, of course, directed boys' activities. Because only rarely was a woman hired as an Iowa school administrator, the founders of the Iowa Girls Athletic Union thus installed a gendered superstructure that effectively barred women from serving on its board of directors. The "school administrators only" bylaw of the IGHSAU constitution was used by apologists throughout the twentieth century; whenever the paucity of women members was borne out, apologists rebutted that, as the Union's E. Wayne Cooley has stressed, "if there are not enough women superintendents and principals, that's not our fault."[7]

Accompanying the gender-biased administrative structure of the Union from the outset was this distinction: in the Union's first year of sanctioning schools, 159 of them created girls' basketball teams, and nearly all of them hailed from small towns. The larger schools, located in cities where girls' basketball had little importance to community life, aligned with the likes of the Committee on Women's Athletics, which was battling interscholastic athletic competition among girls. Despite rules changes—the game changed from a three-court to a two-court format in 1934—Iowa basketball grew in popularity, reaching the highest participation level for any American schoolgirl sport in 1950, when 70 percent of Iowa high school girls played the game.

In 1954 the Union hired as its executive director E. Wayne Cooley, a young assistant to the president of Grinnell College. Cooley, who was a 1938 graduate of tiny Coon Rapids High School in western Iowa and a naval officer in World War II, agreed to take the job with two stipulations: that he be permitted to add sports to the Union's current offerings (which consisted of basketball only) and that he return to Grinnell after accomplishing his goals at the IGHSAU. "The [Union] board came to me and said they were in trouble. I told them, 'I must have your agreement that I have a free hand to add programs, modeling this expansion as we did the liberal arts programs at Grinnell,'" said Cooley. "The first thing was softball. I told [Grinnell president] Sam Stevens I'd return in five years, but I couldn't leave the new girls' programs hanging."[8]

Cooley, a high school sports official and sometimes musician, also decided that the entertainment value of the state basketball tournament needed improvement. Acknowledging the vast pool of high school talent statewide, Cooley injected a formerly listless half-time on championship night with polished musical extravaganzas and dance and gymnastic performances. Later he would add a parade of champions, individuals and teams, from various other sports. And sharp young men in tuxedos always swept the floor of Veterans Auditorium. These participants and others were caught by television cameras that brought the tournament to nine midwestern states and that were paid for by a burgeoning list of corporate sponsors that Cooley recruited. The emphasis on pageantry was part of an increasingly acceptable corporate mentality that accompanied postwar affluence. Cooley was lionized by some sports journalists as the "John Ringling of girls' basketball" and "Cecil B. deCooley."[9]

By 1973, when *Sports Illustrated* published the most comprehensive series on women's sports in its twenty-year history, Cooley had used his "free hand" to expand the number of Union-sanctioned girls sports to include, among others, softball (added in 1955), golf and tennis (1956), track and field (1962), and swimming (1967). That year 488 Iowa high schools belonged to the Union, which sponsored 17 championships in 13 sports: basketball (438 participating schools), track (423), softball (302), golf (247), tennis (86), distance running (82), coed golf (77), volleyball (65), gymnastics (49), swimming (46), coed tennis (26), synchronized swimming (9), and field hockey (6). Cooley and the Union also readily expanded other activities that strengthened the culture of girls' sport in Iowa. There was the Iowa Girls Basketball Academy in Ida Grove, after which many of the staff coaches reconvened at the Union's coaching school, where educators could earn a coaching endorsement and the Union's advisory committees assessed their various sports.[10]

But the showcase for the Union was undisputedly the state basketball tournament, where politicians found free publicity, and celebrities of various sorts attracted crowds (after he had won an Olympic gold medal, screaming teenagers greeted Bruce Jenner in the halls of Veterans Auditorium on a 1977 tournament night). "Every year I think it is impossible to improve on this tournament and the pageantry that goes with it, but every year it seems to get better,"

Iowa governor Robert D. Ray, a tournament mainstay, wrote in March 1974 to Eugene Evans, the Lo-Ma basketball coach who served as president of the IGHSAU Board of Directors that year. Tournament week provided millions of dollars in sales revenue for city merchants, so in show of appreciation the Greater Des Moines Chamber of Commerce hosted an annual breakfast at which the Sweet Sixteen teams were introduced to their hosts. For example, Montgomery Ward was the host merchant for the girls' team from Hubbard, whose players received such gift souvenirs as a rain bonnet, a purse mirror, hand lotion, Chanel cologne, and eyebrow pencil—all items appropriate for young women. The tournament queen in 1974 received a cookbook from the Meredith Corporation (publishers of *Life*, *Look*, and other magazines) and, for her and her court, a watch and pearl necklace from a local store.[11]

In its three-part series, *Sports Illustrated* devoted five pages to the Iowa program, gushing in particular over Cooley. "The Iowa girls' sports program has developed in the past 20 years. Prior to that, things in Iowa were the same as elsewhere—that is, bad and unequal. The man responsible for the change is Wayne Cooley," reported the magazine. Calling Iowa a "utopia for girls' athletics" and a locale that "can offer conclusive proof of the viability and rewards of female athletic equality," *Sports Illustrated* reported to a national audience what Iowans already knew: "All those dire warnings of the medical, moral, and financial disasters that would follow if girls were granted athletic parity are considered hogwash in Iowa. . . . In fact, there may be no place in the U.S. where sport is so healthy and enjoys such a good reputation."[12]

For Cooley the article confirmed that his decision to expand the sporting options for Iowa girls was the right one. "*Sports Illustrated* sent two reporters out here to see what effect Title IX would have on Iowa," Cooley said. "The result was that [Title IX] barely caused a ripple, because equal sharing was already in place in Iowa."[13]

Events soon appeared on the horizon, however, that cast a pall on that glowing health and good reputation.

The resistance to five-player basketball involved more than gender issues and the cultural connections between the six-player game and rural Iowa. There were significant financial factors contributing to the perpetuation of six-player basketball, one being that its dissolution could threaten vested interests the Union held in the sport. In the watershed year of 1972—when Congress passed Title IX—revenue generated solely by girls' basketball represented almost three-fourths of the gross income for the IGHSAU and bankrolled the dozen other Union-sponsored sports. Even as late as 1993, when six-player basketball was dispensed with and volleyball continued to grow in popularity, basketball revenue provided for 50 percent of the Union's $1.5 million budget; volleyball accounted for just 18 percent. The Iowa Girls Athletic Union was organized with the solitary purpose of providing competitive basketball, and even though a dozen sports have been added since 1925, the Union's showcase in 1993 was still basketball.[14]

While the Union administers girls' sports for all Iowa high schools—regulating the playing seasons, setting schedules, determining the number of games, enforcing bylaws, and monitoring officials and protests, among other activities—it collects only a paltry annual fee—ten dollars per school in 2001. Instead of drawing its resources from the schools, the Union historically has garnered the lion's share of its income from the state basketball tournament, which lasts more than one month—from sectionals through districts through regionals. Its lengthiness was the result of there being three teams advancing through the first-round sectionals. More teams meant more games, which meant more income. "Why do you think we had so many teams advancing?" remarked Eugene Evans, the president of the Union board for 1977. From the tournament that year the Union shows the following figures: sectionals, $232,051; districts, $188,190; regionals, $52,942; and state, $247,576, providing a total income of $720,759, a 127 percent increase of gross basketball revenues since 1969. In comparison, Iowa high school softball (which similarly held a lengthy statewide tournament) made just over $125,000 for the Union in 1977, and it was the only other sport with an income greater than $13,000. And in Oklahoma, the only other state to play six-player basketball longer than Iowa, girls' basketball contributed $150,000 to the state athletic association in 1977—approximately one-fifth of the sport's total contribution in Iowa. The Oklahoma Secondary School Activities Association administers both boys' and girls' sports, of which there were but eight—more evidence that the IGHSAU had strengthened the state's athletic programs for females.[15]

When the income from basketball was figured in with the other sports' revenues and income from television and program advertising, program sales, official fees, and merchandise sales, the total income for the Iowa Girls High School Athletic Union in 1977 was $980,017. But total expenses amounted to $949,465, leaving a net income of $30,552. The state basketball tournament alone cost $253,850, almost two-thirds of which paid for the travel and tournament lodging and meals for each of the sixteen teams as well as their coaches and managers' costs. There were such incidentals, too, as trophies and banquets, and expenses for officials throughout the entire tournament—early February through mid-March—which wound up just over $36,000. The rent and expenses for Des Moines's Veterans Memorial Auditorium for the 1975 tournament alone had surpassed $21,000.[16]

It didn't take a financial wizard to understand why the Union, or anyone conversant in Iowa girls' athletics and partial to this peculiar style of basketball, turned squeamish when its cash cow was threatened.

In late August 1971 Ruth Johnson, a physical education instructor at West High School in Davenport, joined Mason City's Alice Phillips as Iowa's representatives to the first National Conference on Girls' Sports Programs for the Secondary Schools, sponsored by the Division For Girls and Women's Sports and held in Estes Park, Colorado. The conference, while acknowledging the national trend toward providing girls with expanded opportunities to participate in sports, gathered physical education leaders from across the country to choose future directions for secondary athletic programs. Not only did the Iowa educators, whose state's provision of thirteen interscholastic sports made it a national leader, share their success stories with the other conferees, but the DGWS adopted resolutions that, for the first time, promoted competition at the secondary level and, according to Johnson, became the impetus for the Title IX legislation. The fact that national leaders listened to Johnson and Phillips showed how much respect Iowa girls' sports were given—Iowa, having its own athletic association, was the only state whose girls' prep sports were not under the jurisdiction of the American Association for Health, Physical Education, and Recreation (AHPER).[17]

At the time of the Estes Park conference, the Iowa DGWS and the Iowa Girls High School Athletic Union were working together in the best interest of girls' sports; and Ruth Johnson, a state chairman of DGWS but representing the Union in Colorado, was a primary reason. Johnson's concurrent service to both organizations had noteworthy ramifications: the DGWS was an offshoot of the National Section for Girls and Women's Sports, the powerful group of physical education teachers who had fought against interscholastic sports, and now it was aligned with the most successful organization at *promoting* girls' athletic competition. And the IGHSAU was the only institution in America strong enough to stand up to the national forces, like the DGWS, that had formerly made opposing girls' competitive sports their crusade.

In the early 1970s, the crusade against competition was replaced by the promotion of competition, and the irony of this overwhelming change in attitude by the formerly anti-competition leaders was not lost on seasoned observers of the Iowa sporting and educational landscape. "The same educational leaders now screaming for equality were writing and publicly declaring the evils of girls participating in any form of competitive athletics earlier," Eugene Evans, former president and two-term board member of the Union, wrote in 1978. Indeed, a women's movement comprised of Progressive Era reformers had denounced *any* form of competitive girls' basketball, five- or six-player, early in the twentieth century. The women's movement that gained momentum in the Title IX era, however, made the five-player rules a political issue that often served as a litmus test for feminism.[18]

In Iowa a visible sign that the anti-competition leaders had changed their beliefs was a stirring among city school officials, who began talking in the late 1960s about implementing high school girls' sports programs. "Dr. John McCaw has a hearing set and is interested in obtaining people, women especially, that could reflect on the possibility of the five-player system," Judith Bischoff, a Drake University physical education instructor, wrote to a high school teacher. McCaw was a Drake colleague who organized support for the five-player game in Des Moines, which was starting up basketball in the schools in 1972. Hearings such as these provided the setting for the complex debate over five- and six-player basketball that soon evolved, a debate that was new in Iowa because its citizens had rarely criticized the six-player game. In this new political context, however, the game's value was now questioned. "It is obvious it [five-player] could be an unfavorable position to take, but the idea of implantation will start wheels turning even though it may not be adopted," Bischoff continued, capturing the uncertainty that the ensuing debate was likely to produce.[19]

When during the 1960s Iowa physical education leaders who had formerly opposed competition changed their minds, their first forays into the sporting world were conducted by the DGWS, which sponsored track, golf, gymnastics, and tennis in the large schools. "The larger schools didn't like the Union, but the small schools did," said Johnson, who coached swimming, field hockey, soccer, and gymnastics at Davenport West—a city school aligned with the DGWS. "And the Union was not knowledgeable about these sports I coached." In the late 1960s, Johnson introduced competitive swimming, field hockey, and gymnastics into the Davenport schools, and the results were often published in the widely read IGHSAU bulletin. The DGWS continued to introduce "new" sports—bowling, synchronized swimming, and, of course, basketball—to the city schools until 1975, when the large schools finally joined the Union, and it assumed sponsorship for most girls' athletic activities. Thus Ruth Johnson, already a revered leader in state athletic administration and the current chairperson of the Iowa DGWS, was chosen by the Iowa Girls High School Athletic Union to serve as a liaison and an "advisory" board member in the fall of 1969. Five years later she gained a voting position in the Union when she was named the board's first woman at-large member. "We in IDGWS have worked long and hard for the constitutional change which would permit a lady to vote on this important board," the chairperson for the IDGWS had written to women physical educators to encourage them to get their school administrators to endorse Johnson for the board. The letter obviously worked.[20]

Ruth Johnson's emergence as the preeminent female sports promoter in Iowa in her time can be traced to the women's sporting culture in which she was raised. Johnson's mother, Gladys Brooker Aston, was a swimming champion at the University of Iowa, where she then taught physical education until Ruth enrolled in the early 1950s. At Iowa Gladys Aston worked under women's physical education director Elizabeth Halsey, a nationally prominent reformist late in the Progressive Era who was educated at the University of Chicago and Wellesley College, where she taught in the hygiene department. According to Johnson, Halsey was opposed to competition for women at the college level and below, a philosophy consistent with the beliefs of most women physical educators during that era. "Halsey was anti-competition, except for field hockey, and my mother was a competitive swimmer and taught competition," said Johnson. "The women's 'I' Club, which sponsored swimming, was started when my mother taught at Iowa, then disappeared when she left."[21]

After graduating from Iowa in 1955, Johnson wasted little time before promoting girls' athletic competition from her Davenport teaching position. She became politically involved on state and national levels with the American Red Cross, the AAU, and the DGWS. "Competitive athletics are an essential part of education," she wrote in 1972 to an Iowa college women's physical education instructor. "Is it really wrong to encourage spectators to attend girls' competition? Does anyone really want to work to excel in a vacuum?" In the 1960s she began introducing various sports to girls in the Davenport schools, usually working by herself and with little or no money. "We started gymnastics for nothing, and I worked for free. It didn't last—there were accidents and insurance problems. Synchronized swimming didn't last, either. There was no broad-based support because these [sports] were just in a few large schools," Johnson explained. Despite their initial difficulties, however, these two sports subsequently became established activities with their own advising committees under Union sponsorship.[22]

So when Johnson was selected as an advisor to the Union board, the all-male administration was bringing aboard an assertive woman who had changed the athletic landscape for Iowa girls but had stepped on some toes along the way. Fortunately for the Union—and perhaps one of the reasons Johnson was selected for the role—Ruth Johnson was an adamant supporter of six-player basketball. "I loved the six-player game, and it was a fact that grandmothers, mothers, and daughters had all played, and everyone came to support them," Johnson said. "You can't compare five and six—the following is not the same. I wept when I couldn't play basketball."[23]

Even though Johnson taught in a city school system—the schools that were starting up basketball programs and clamoring for the five-player game—she was vocal about her support for six-player basketball. By 1972 six-player proponents viewed the increasing criticism of the game as a real threat to the best schoolgirl sports program in America, and Johnson fought back with a vengeance. She wrote to Bischoff, the Drake instructor:

> Iowa has the best, most complete program for girls of any state in the Union. It is best because its organization is totally committed to making an excellent program for girls. It finances this total program basically through its basketball structure. Is a set of rules worth destroying all the other participation opportunities? . . . When and if gymnastics and volleyball can take some of the financial load that basketball and softball now carry, then and only then can the Union as it is now structured afford to experiment with their basketball rules. . . . The educational values of competitive basketball are there whether the girls are allowed to dribble two times or twenty times.[24]

Not only was Johnson concerned that fiddling with six-player basketball, which bankrolled all other girls' interscholastic sports, would endanger the status of those activities, but she also recognized that some city schools were biting the hand that fed them. While the large schools, particularly those in Des Moines, became increasingly vocal about playing five-player basketball as they initiated programs, they continued to receive Union funding for participation in such sports as golf, tennis, swimming, gymnastics, and volleyball—and most of these city schools were not yet members of the Union. "The larger schools have done nothing but take," claimed Johnson, who, as a Davenport West coach, taught in a "large" school herself. "They have received travel allowances for state competition upwards to thousands of dollars over the years. All of this without any return to the Union in any of these programs to date. Yet these same schools now seek to destroy the foundation of these gifts."

Furthermore, the city school educators' and DGWS's questioning of the propriety of six-player basketball was perceived as nothing less than a threat to the survival of the Union itself, whose sole reason for existence was, at least initially, to support and promote girls' basketball. Ruth Johnson was convinced that many male administrators and athletic directors in Iowa wished to combine the IGHSAU with the Iowa High School Athletic Association (IHSAA), and undermining the six-player game was the first step in accomplishing that. There was some support for merging those two interscholastic organizations. "The boys and girls state athletic associations keep trying to outdo each other in pushing more games, more holiday tournaments and playoffs, anything which might bring more money into their coffers in the true tradition of the pro sports promoters," broadcast Oelwein's KOEL Radio in December 1972. Curiously, the station was located in the heart of northeast Iowa's girls' basketball stronghold. "We urge consideration of a plan to put all types of extracurricular activities, both girls and boys, under a single state board made up of teachers, principals, and superintendents . . . to operate under the state Department of Public Instruction, which is answerable to the legislature." Johnson, however, rejected such talk about dissolving the IGHSAU. "The athletic directors wish there to be only one athletic association as all the other states have. It would make their job so much easier," Johnson wrote to Bischoff. "Of course, you know there are no women athletic directors in Iowa—and, of course, the boys association would maintain control. When this happens, I wonder how well our girls' programs will be managed."[25]

Detractors argued that because the girls' Union *already* was run solely by men, risking the demise of the IGHSAU for regular basketball was worth the gamble. But the Union had recently announced its first female board member—albeit a nonvoting member—and Ruth Johnson advised Wayne Cooley to stand his ground. "I hope you are not running scared from the big schools," she told the Union leader in her advisory capacity on the board. "Don't be afraid of battles when you are right. . . . There is no need to attempt to structure our system after the boys'. I would suggest to you that once again, we are way ahead offering educational opportunities."[26]

Two years after the 1972 passage of Title IX, the IGHSAU provided for the first time a constitutional provision for a female board member with voting privileges. The likeliest candidate for the first "Lady Board of Directors Member—At Large" was Ruth Johnson, who, having served five years already as an ex-officio member, was elected by Union member schools in October 1974. Once on the board in a voting position, Ruth Johnson wasn't prepared for her fellow members' change in attitude toward her. "When I had no vote, I had more power. As soon as I got the vote, they were no longer gentlemanly," she recalled. Whereas the board sought her opinion when she was simply an ex-officio member, its value now seemed somewhat diminished. "Their attitude was, 'well, you have a vote,'" Johnson said. "My power went to zero." She served a four-year term, from 1974 through 1978, then declined when Cooley suggested she run for election again. Ruth Johnson's perception that she received diminished respect from men was eerily similar to what would transpire twenty years later—when Iowa girls began playing five-player basketball.[27]

Many of the public school systems in Iowa's cities, including those in the state's capital and largest community of Des Moines, started up high school girls' basketball in 1972, the same year that Title IX was passed. The debate over which game to play had started years earlier, however, evidenced by the five-player clinic in Iowa City in 1969. And while this discussion began in the cities, it eventually engaged all corners of the state and beyond, as proponents of six-player basketball felt compelled to defend their game.

The parameters of this debate were the result of convergent historical facts and cultural events: national organizations for the physical education of women and girls, like the DGWS, had become supportive of varsity competition; city school districts, as a result, introduced several sports for girls, including basketball; and the impending passage of Title IX not only provided the promise of a more level playing field for girls but also fostered a climate of equity that pervaded all walks of life. Perhaps the overarching factor in the debate over basketball rules was this impulse for equality that an increasingly broad-based, middle-class women's movement had introduced and made acceptable to the larger culture, the American middle class. This transformation of gender arrangements was the best explanation for the quantum leap taken by women physical education leaders like the DGWS, who had gone from barring varsity competition to supporting the most rigorous form of basketball, sidestepping the tamer middle ground of the six-player game. There were some Progressive Era reformers, especially those who advocated higher education for women, who endorsed physical education for girls. But it was the Progressive Era reformers who had dismissed *any* sort of competitive basketball as too strenuous for girls, and the Title IX–era proponents of the five-player rules who comprised middle-class women's movements, that represented *and* transformed the operative gender arrangements of their time.

The eagerness with which some members of the physical education community embraced Title IX reflects, at least to some degree, changes in Iowans' attitudes about women. "An examination of Iowa Poll results over the years does confirm a sea change in public opinion sometime in the 1960s," the *Des Moines Register* noted in 1993, fifty years after the inception of its prominent public-opinion poll. The Iowa Poll's questions revealed as much about contemporary gender arrangements as did its published findings. "The Iowa Poll won't win any sexual equality awards for the questions it was asking in the '40s and '50s," the newspaper admitted. "At that time, [the poll] took great interest in a woman's component parts—her brains being a notable exception." Whereas polls in 1951 revealed that 81 percent of women and 69 percent of men favored a requirement that girls take housekeeping in school, and that farmers believed farm girls made better wives than did city girls, by the 1960s the Iowa Poll was asking about equal pay for women and abortion. Not all of the early Iowa Polls reflected a conservative attitude about women, however. The 1947 poll showed strong support for high school girls' basketball, a finding that probably surprised no one.[28]

When Title IX of the Education Amendments Act of 1972 radically transformed the structure of American sport without even using the word "athletics," more than a hint of the ensuing climate of equity, as E. Wayne Cooley claimed, was already visible in Iowa. But a law that could possibly require schools to provide the same number of sports for women and men and funding proportionate to the ratio of female to male athletes was inevitably bound for venomous attack. "If the truth were known, I dislike all of that title except the very last part," the executive secretary of Washington's prep association began his speech, entitled "Title IX, ERA's, 14th Amendment and Sex-Separated Programs," at the annual conference of the National Federation of State High School Associations in 1977. At the same meeting the director of Wisconsin's prep athletic association couldn't have been clearer about his attitude toward the legislation: "As for girls' basketball, if anyone deserves credit for promoting it, it has to be that monster called HEW and its big stick called Title IX. This three-letter noun that attracts four-letter adjectives from many of us has done an unbelievable amount of promoting sports for girls in schools."[29]

Fortunately for Iowa girls, the state hadn't the need for outside promotion. In 1971–72, the school year immediately preceding federal enactment of Title IX, 1,960 teams competed across the state in softball, volleyball, cross-country, track and field, golf, tennis, gymnastics, swimming, and six-player basketball. But it was this last sport—basketball—on which Title IX would have the most effect in Iowa. Because colleges and universities now risked losing funding if they did not expand women's athletic programs, for the first time ever girls' participation in high school athletics translated into economic benefits in the same way that boys' did. Postsecondary institutions would now provide roughly the same number of athletic scholarships for girls and boys, so it was incumbent upon the high schools to provide the athletes. Title IX created a demand for female high school athletes, and in Iowa that meant that college basketball programs, which played the five-player game, would be forced to draw on girls who had played only the six-player rules. There were unintended and even pernicious consequences from Title IX, including a nearly 50 percent decrease in the number of women's collegiate teams coached by women (see chapter 5). But the effect of the legislation on Iowa high school basketball was self-evident; the argument that six-player basketball hampered guards' postsecondary athletic opportunities was legitimate.[30]

In 1972 there were still smaller towns without girls' basketball, though most rural communities with populations of two thousand or less offered six-player girls' basketball in their high schools. There were exceptions, however. "I am interested in getting a girls' basketball team started here. Thus I would like a rule-book for the Iowa High School Girls' Basketball," a female physical education instructor from Williamsburg, a town of two thousand, requested of the Union in 1969. Similarly, the urge to play five-player ball was not confined to the cities. "For a long time I've been wondering why Iowa girls do not play basketball using AAU-DGWS rules. Our school does not play competitively so we do use these rules in our P.E. classes," a female instructor from Sutherland (population seven hundred) in northwest Iowa asked Cooley. "I would like to urge adoption of these rules both for the girls' sake and the spectators'." Cooley wrote in reply that he would be "deeply opposed to a severe change in playing rules when it is quite evident the superior game is associated with our state."[31]

In the words of E. Wayne Cooley, the 1970s were a "trying pe-

riod," and before the decade was over, Cooley was regularly ap-
plauded in some quarters for providing unparalleled sporting opportunities for girls and demonized in others because the organization
that provided those opportunities was directed almost completely
by men.

The ink with which the Education Amendments Act of 1972 was
etched into law had barely dried when the statewide media in Iowa
began addressing the value of six-player basketball. What ignited
the discussion was the October decision by the Des Moines School
Board to permit competitive girls' basketball in the city's six public
high schools, starting on a limited basis the winter of 1972–73 and
expanding to a full schedule of games the following season. Des
Moines's initial foray into competitive girls' basketball was modeled
after a recently established interscholastic league playing six-player
rules in Cedar Rapids whose policies aimed to provide parity with
boys' programs. Girls' games were to be played in the same gyms
where boys played, identical admissions were charged, and coaching
salaries for girls' and boys' teams were made equal. Sharing gyms
and charging the same ticket prices were common practices among
schools with established six-player programs, but one obvious difference between the new city programs and those in the rural school
districts was the scheduling of girls' and boys' games on different
nights. The girls' game almost always preceded the boys' in small
towns, a cultural tradition that seemed to preserve and promote
parity as well as encourage community cohesion. Scheduling girls'
and boys' games on different nights, as was done in the cities, served
to accentuate differences and de-emphasize school spirit.[32]

But the Des Moines school board hesitated to commit to state
tournament play, which would require the schools to play six-player
basketball. Among the school board members was Dr. John McCaw,
the Drake University professor who solicited support for the five-
player game with a public hearing in November 1972. As a result, in
part, of vigorous support displayed at the hearing and with other
members joining McCaw in support of the five-player game, the
school board tried to force the Union's hand. The future competition of Des Moines high school teams in the tournament that the

city had hosted regularly for fifty years was contingent upon the girls' game being made more equal to the boys'. Specifically, this equality would be achieved by adopting the DGWS (or AAU) rules of full-court play and the unlimited dribble—five-player basketball. The change in rules, according to proponents of the five-player game, would ostensibly permit girls to expand their skills and thus earn college scholarships previously denied to them because of the restrictive nature of the old game. The Union, of course, provided evidence otherwise, and the question of whether girls had limited opportunities for college scholarships after playing six-player basketball in high school was a focal point of the debate—and, finally, the legal point on which the future of the game turned.[33]

For the most part, the state media supported the six-player tradition, exemplified by the editorials broadcast on Des Moines's WHO-TV and WHO radio: "To radically change the game of girls' basketball at the high school level, as it has evolved over the past fifty years, in the interest of 'equality,' would be doing a disservice to the girls and could turn an exciting sport of feminine skill into one that emphasizes basic weaknesses." The editorial, entitled "Girls' Basketball: What Price 'Equality'?" was a direct response to the Des Moines school board's action, and it captured the prevalent anxiety over Title IX and made explicit the gendered nature of the six-player game. "The girls' weaknesses, as compared to boys'," the editorial declared, "is in jumping ability, speed afoot, and stamina. Which is understandable because, to coin a phrase, they just aren't built that way." Twenty-two years earlier WHO-TV had broadcast the first prep sporting event televised in Iowa—the girls' state basketball tournament—and was part of the current nine-state telecast. But the Des Moines radio station's editorial directly opposed the city school board's action to consider playing five- instead of six-player basketball. Earlier in 1972, when Cedar Rapids, the second largest city in Iowa, had started a six-player program and committed to the state tournament, school systems in the cities of Waterloo and Council Bluffs, both with populations of about sixty thousand, did the same. "Why should the Girls' Union tamper with a successful commodity?" wrote a Waterloo sportswriter, reflecting a popular opinion among media in the cities, other than Des Moines, that were opening their arms to six-player girls' basketball.[34]

The decision by the Des Moines school board to explore the possibility of its schools playing five-player basketball had ignited discussion among the state's citizens, educators, media, and politicians. On the side of the six-player traditionalists was the sweeping history of having provided Iowa girls with the most popular, enduring high school game in America. Whenever critics pointed out that six-player basketball failed to provide a future for its players, its defendants readily noted that 20 percent of AAU All-Americans at midcentury had played in Iowa high schools. If such numbers as well as the cultural baggage that six-player basketball carried as a principal element of rural Iowa life weren't enough, there was always the argument that the game financed the other dozen sports in which thousands of girls participated throughout the year. But eclipsing even the financial well-being of Iowa girls' sport was its *cultural* well-being, which included a sense of security that was critical to many parents. The father of a high school player wrote this to Ruth Johnson in 1974:

> I think I told you that my daughter is planning on attending Luther [College] and, hopefully, playing some basketball. We witnessed a game at Luther last winter, and I had an opportunity to talk with some of the players who had previously attended our summer clinic as players in the games held during those clinics. The girls were uniformly pleased to have an opportunity to participate even though they did not appear to be sold on the five player rules. However, they accepted the rules as an accomplished fact. When I asked them the main problems that they encountered, there appeared to be two. The first was the lack of status on the campus that they had been used to in high school. This will come as time passes if the program improves and becomes more attractive. The second was the officiating. One of the players described it as "atrocious" and the other girls nodded their agreement. They further stated that they simply had to grit their teeth and learn to

live with it. They indicated that it was especially difficult since they had been used to top-notch officiating in high school. I have since found that girls in several other colleges expressed the same general feeling.[35]

According to this parent, Iowa players were used to a higher status and good officiating in their high school careers. "As a class they [Iowa female players] tend to be the most popular girls, enjoying more status in the eyes of other students, their teachers and townspeople," *Sports Illustrated* had written in its 1973 series. It was an observation that didn't hold true in other states. The fact that Iowa basketball players were spoiled by top-notch officiating might be expected: in 1974 the IGHSAU spent just under thirty thousand dollars on officials for the tournament alone.[36]

While supporters of six-girl basketball expressed their concerns about switching to the five-girl game, the five-player proponents were setting up a legal foundation for their argument. Bolstered by the passage of Title IX, these people stood behind a belief best articulated by Peggy Burke, a University of Iowa physical education professor who led the charge against the six-player rules:

> The basic issue is not whether girls and boys must play the same rules but whether each is being provided with the basic information and skills which will enable them to develop their talents and progress in that area of expertise beyond their high school years. . . . Boys are given instruction and coaching in essentially the same game that is played in colleges, recreational leagues, and national and international competition. On the other hand, girls are confined by the rules to a dead-end game that is played no where else in the world except in the high schools of four other states, some of whom are in the process of changing.[37]

Burke dismissed the Union's defense that basketball supported the entire girls' program as "a double irony for the Iowa basketball player in that her talents are being used in a game that lessens her chances for future success while she generates the funds that provides programs and potential success for swimmers, softball players, golfers and track and field performers."[38]

Dr. John McCaw, the Drake professor who served as president of the Des Moines school board, stressed the more "active" nature of the full-court game when he convinced his colleagues to refrain from endorsing six-player basketball for their system. His comment raised the ire of six-player supporters. "I was amazed to read that . . . Dr. John McCaw, board president, suggested exploring changes for his country cousin's game to make it more active," read a letter to the editor of the *Des Moines Register*. "I hope Dr. McCaw and others . . . join us at Veterans Auditorium in March for the state tourney. Order your tickets now, however, because these 'inactive' games are sellouts months in advance every year." Board president McCaw was widely criticized for his stance. "The change of the rules . . . would be a deterrent at this time. It is girls' basketball that the girls are participating in," wrote a former Iowa high school coach, O. E. Lester, to McCaw. Lester, who doubled as superintendent at Oakland High School (enrollment of less than two hundred), coached more state-basketball qualifying teams between 1934 and 1956 than anyone in Iowa history. He had been coaching in California for twelve years when he wrote McCaw: "The California schools don't have a fine sports program like Iowa." Similarly, E. Wayne Cooley and the Union received the support of small-town school administrators who felt threatened by the city once more. "We in the rural area and those who represent the smaller school districts in Iowa feel that too often the larger schools try and impose upon us their wishes," wrote a superintendent to Cooley.[39]

But the Union executive secretary was also receiving letters of a different perspective. In August 1973 Cooley was asked to meet with the Iowa Commission on the Status of Women, which was intent on discussing its "general concerns in the area of athletics." The Iowa Women's Political Caucus also began examining the gender gap in the Union's board of directors as well as the propriety of continuing six-player basketball.[40]

The remarks of college professors McCaw and Burke, especially regarding the more active nature of five-player basketball and the opportunities it might provide female athletes beyond high school, exemplified the increasingly instrumental utilitarian values attributed to sports. The positions of McCaw and Burke reflect the commercialized and commodified realities of modern sports, whereas many of the individuals who wrote the Union supported "the country cousin's game"—pastoral six-player basketball.[41]

By the mid-1970s the convergence of several events—the passage of Title IX, introduction of girls' basketball into Iowa cities, examination of the Union structure, and increasing debate in the media over basketball rules—had catapulted the Iowa girls' game onto the national stage. A wire-service story that appeared in the *Miami Herald* as well as many other newspapers across the nation, typified the media attention focused on the controversy over Iowa six-player basketball. In the United Press International (UPI) report in March 1975—two days before the start of the fiftieth Union-sponsored girls' state tournament—E. Wayne Cooley admitted that groups outside Iowa were pressing for a changeover to five-player basketball. Cooley was steadfast in his support of the old game, noting "women physically cannot compete with the men . . . and they wind up playing poor second cousins to the men's game full court." At the same time Cooley argued, somewhat contradictorily, that Iowa players had no trouble adapting to the full-court college game, citing as evidence that nine of the twelve members of the American team that had played in China in 1974 were Iowans and *every* starter on the U.S.A. team that had recently competed in the World University Games were Iowans.[42]

Further evidence that six-player basketball was a long way from vanishing was Cooley's bizarre position of being able to turn down a national television contract. "It just didn't work out. We [the IGHSAU] demand that we have complete control over the announcers, cameramen, and crew, and we just couldn't get together on it this year," said Cooley after he rejected a contract with ABC to televise the girls' tournament for the *Wide World of Sports* weekly series. Cooley's rejection of the ABC bid because of "control" issues showed how tightly he still held sway over the sport and how sophisticated the

Union had become regarding media. The Iowa Girls High School Athletic Union had produced most, if not all, of its telecasts, and it had employed a television producer since 1966.[43]

By 1976 the pressure to change had also intensified *within* the state. "I am concerned about possible violations of Title IX in regards to differences in the operation of the girls athletic union and boys athletic union," the superintendent of a *small* school district wrote to Cooley as well as to the state superintendent of schools. "Of course this happens when you have two organizations, two administrators, two boards of control, etc." In the hypersensitive atmosphere surrounding Title IX compliance, any mention of "possible violations" quickly raised a red flag with educators, and Cooley was no exception. "Be assured we have confidence at this time that we are in a position of being free of critical review,'" Cooley shot back to the superintendent. "Further, on many occasions I have heard Ms. Gwen Gregory [a HEW Title IX interpreter] speak from a podium indicating 'Iowa is one state that is relieved from being suspect in discrimination against girls.'" High school girls' coaches in Tennessee, where the six-player game had recently been dragged into court and ruled noncompliant with Title IX, sent letters of support to Cooley in late 1976.[44]

As critics inside the state and out made a confrontation seemingly inevitable, advocates of six-player basketball had numbers and tradition on their side. "I played guard and loved every minute of it," wrote a former player to Cooley in 1977. "I especially hope a change is not made because some *parent* wants a daughter to play college ball." This letter brought up a problem whose resolution would become paramount before the ordeal was over: Was it adults or players who wanted the change, who stood to benefit from it? And what *were* the benefits—that is, what were the criteria to be used in determining "benefits"?[45]

In the late 1970s the battle over girls' basketball was fought mostly on adult turf. In June 1977 several prominent women leaders presented a debate in Des Moines to review the respective merits of five- and six-player basketball. The Iowa Women's Conference pitted veteran girls' coach Louis "Bud" McCrea, who had won state championships in 1975 and 1976, against Dr. Peggy Burke, a professor and chair of the Department of Physical Education and Dance at the University of Iowa and past president of the Association of Intercollegiate Athletics for Women. McCrea noted that sixty-three Iowa six-player veterans were presently on college scholarships to compete in five-player basketball, ostensibly showing that the best athletes will earn college athletic scholarships regardless of the game they played in high school. But McCrea also focused on financial concerns. "Our girl athletes are currently held in high esteem, so why leave the financially secure six-player game?" the coach argued. "Basketball supports all the other sports, providing 72 percent of the gross income [from girls' athletics]." In contrast, Burke focused on the "basketball court" and gender issues and ignored the financial aspects. "It is an emotional issue, but we must deal in facts. The game is not for the fans, entertainment, or moneymaking," the physical education professor said. "I personally was limited to playing the six-player game. I was a guard, and I resented someone else shooting my free throws." Burke also commented on the male domination of the IGHSAU board of directors, alluding to possible legal action when she mentioned that HEW had recently forced the Alabama prep association to include women on its board. "The game will change, whether voluntarily or by judicial or legislative action," concluded Burke.

Afterward, Minnette Doderer, the state senator from Iowa City, questioned McCrea on how the game helped develop girls into becoming young ladies—in other words, she questioned the long-held ideological comportment of girls' basketball. She made two resolutions that the 1977 Iowa Women's Conference passed, although neither by a unanimous vote. The first insisted that the more rigorous, five-player basketball be adopted. Conference leaders considered five-player basketball more progressive than the other "dead-end game" because it, as Burke had argued, would enable girls as well as boys to be "given instruction and coaching in essentially the same game that is played in colleges, recreational leagues, and national and international competition." The second resolution demanded that the Iowa Girls High School Athletic Union and the Iowa High

School Athletic Association (the boys' group) have equal representation of women on their boards of directors.[46]

The remarks of both women evoked the criticism that physical education leaders who rallied *against* competition had been leveling for a half century: "The game is not for the fans, entertainment, or moneymaking," Burke avowed, and that was the exact charge of the Progressive Era reformers and later critics. And Doderer's caustic comment about developing "young ladies" questioned the propriety of the six-player game itself—designed to accommodate contemporary gender arrangements—just as the earlier critics had. The difference was that for many middle-class female leaders in 1900 the development of young ladies was a noble pursuit (and a rationalization for special, six-player basketball rules), while seventy-five years later, such an activity—particularly when directed by men— was highly questionable for Doderer and others.

Six-player advocates had not heard the last of either Doderer or Burke. In September 1977 in a committee session of the Iowa legislature over rules with officials of both the IGHSAU and IHSAA, Doderer strongly criticized Cooley for the administrative gender gap in the Union, and she wouldn't accept his response that the by-laws were to blame. "I say all the brains in governance of athletics aren't confined to male school superintendents and principals," Doderer said. "There is only one woman school superintendent in Iowa and only about half a dozen women principals. I still think women should be on the board of governance instead of limiting it to a group of employees who are not women." In October Cooley was invited to discuss these matters at the fifth annual convention of the Iowa Women's Political Caucus, which was sponsoring a debate over girls' basketball that was similar to the one held at the earlier Iowa Women's Conference. And almost one year later, the Iowa Commission on the Status of Women voted to go on record in support of five-player basketball, contending that "it is the belief of the Commission that the present six-player divided court basketball game currently played in Iowa high schools represents a denial of equal educational opportunity and violates the intent of Title IX."[47]

But the commission itself was divided on the issue: Phyllis Howlett, the commission's chair, wrote E. Wayne Cooley a personal letter that showed the divisive nature of the controversy and castigated her peers for declaring six-player in violation of Title IX "without study or recommendation of a committee." "I want it made clear to you and the Board that I did not support the position," Howlett wrote to Cooley, "and I have spoken with the Governor's office expressing this. . . . With the magnitude of some problems facing our country and its women, it is most disquieting to me to see the Commission and the federal government spending time and energy in pursuit of amending the rules by which we play games." The commission's declaration that six-player basketball was in violation of Title IX "without study or recommendation of a committee" was a remarkable event in itself; the game, no matter how it was played and how it appealed to the participants and the fans who followed their teams, had become the focus and vehicle for a broader debate about gender equity. It had become a litmus test.[48]

The remarks of Howlett and letters to HEW secretary Joseph Califano from Dr. Burke and a North Mahaska High School speech class—letters expressing contrasting opinions in the debate over Iowa girls' basketball—found their way into a commentary in October 1978 by George Will, the widely read, conservative columnist who is also a nationally popular pundit on sporting issues. In a newspaper piece titled "Is Iowa Girls' Basketball a Human Rights Issue?" Will belittled HEW for expending effort on seemingly trivial matters like basketball rules, basing his views in part on an essay by Burke, whose title, "Six-Player Basketball From a Human Rights Viewpoint," Will declared "beyond parody." Burke had included the essay with her letter to Califano, advised him that six-player basketball "seriously discriminates against those girls who play it," and asked that Title IX be rigorously enforced. At about the same time Califano had received the letter from the high school speech class *supporting* six-player rules and asking him a question few had bothered to ask: Why not ask the girls who play the game? The Iowa students also wondered why the federal government didn't concentrate on more important problems, such as foreign affairs and the national budget." It was a comment similar to Howlett's, whose remark about the government spending time and energy in pursuit of amending the rules by which we play games was repeated by Will and captured the tone of his essay. "If a 'human rights' campaign is impotent against the Gulag Archipelago," wrote Will, tongue firmly in cheek, "try it against Iowa."[49]

Whether or not Iowa girls' basketball was a "human rights issue" had not yet been decided in 1978, but the game remained prominent in the national spotlight. At that time observers who believed that resolution of the problem lay with the players themselves would prove to be prescient. What would surprise everyone is how long the resolution took in coming.

SEVEN

All Dressed Up but Nowhere to Go

We have let tradition hold us back. Now Iowa girls have less opportunity to develop their athletic talents than do girls in other states. And they are denied opportunities that are available to Iowa boys. – Bill Russell, *Des Moines Register* op-ed, "Iowa Girls Handicapped by Old-Style Basketball"

Lamoni, Iowa, was an unlikely site for disaffection with gender arrangements in the sporting arena. Located five miles north of the Missouri border and nearly one hundred miles due south of Des Moines, Lamoni—with its two thousand residents—was the largest town in rural Decatur County in the early 1980s. Lamoni was the site of Graceland College, a tiny liberal arts school with strong ties to the Church of Jesus Christ of Latter Day Saints, a denomination that held steadfastly to conservative and traditional beliefs about women's roles. Among the students who attended Graceland in the 1970s was Bruce Jenner, who won the gold medal in the decathlon in the 1976 Olympics and was thus conferred, in some circles, with the title of "the world's greatest athlete." Seven of the track-and-field records that Jenner set at Graceland College had belonged previously to Bill Russell, a social sciences professor at the school he had attended in the 1950s. It was Bill Russell's fourteen-year-old daughter, Shauna, who, in August 1983, joined two other Iowa girls in filing a class-action lawsuit in federal district court, contending that six-player basketball violated the Equal Protection Clause of the U.S. Constitution. The *New York Times* reported that the suit claimed Iowa girls were victims of discrimination because they simply did not get "the full benefit and experience of the game of basketball available to Iowa boys."[1]

Previous efforts to have six-player basketball declared unconstitutional in the few states where it was still played had met with mixed results. In November 1976 a federal judge in United States district court in Tennessee ruled that the six-player girls' game played there violated the Equal Protection Clause of the Fourteenth Amendment and exhibited an obsolete notion that girls are "weak and awkward." The ruling was in response to a suit filed the summer before by a sixteen-year-old high school girl who argued that half-court basketball prevented her from earning a college scholarship. But an appellate court reversed that decision, concluding that there was no evidence of any intent to discriminate between the sexes. Similarly, a sixteen-year-old Oklahoma girl filed suit, claiming that "girls' " rules violated her civil rights; but a federal judge in the United States district court in 1977 allowed 834 girls who opposed playing the five-player game to intervene and ruled that he "had no jurisdiction to consider a challenge to Oklahoma's high school girls' basketball rules." A motion filed by several Oklahoma coaches failed to get a reversal, but the affidavits submitted in the case shed light on conflicting opinions about the experiences of six-player veterans playing five-player basketball in college. Despite the favorable court ruling in Tennessee, six-player basketball soon disappeared in that state. It was played until 1995 in Oklahoma, the last state in America to convert.[2]

Kathy Rush, coach of the U.S. women's basketball team at the 1976 Olympics, said "little or no consideration" was given to girls who played six-player basketball when the Olympic team was chosen. But perhaps the most startling affidavit came from University of Iowa women's coach Lark Birdsong, who said, "I do not recruit guards [who played in the six-player game]—ever." These remarks contrasted with the defense that the IGHSAU continued to offer: talented girls who played six-player basketball easily converted to the five-player game in college. In 1978 the Union released a bulletin that included a list of thirty-five high school guards who had received basketball scholarships for that fall.[3]

Five-player proponents in Iowa eventually found a legal hook on which to hang their hats that fell somewhere in between those seen previously in Tennessee and Oklahoma. In April 1979 Diana Lee Dodson, a ninth-grade girls' basketball player in Arkadelphia, Arkansas, sued her school district and superintendent as well as the Arkansas Activities Association, alleging that six-player basketball deprived girls of equal protection of the law. Unlike the Oklahoma court, the Arkansas federal district court ruled that girls forced to play by six-player rules "were improperly being denied the full experience and benefit of the game of basketball." Moreover, a legal scholar on the Dodson case remarked that the evidence presented at the trial in support of six-player rules showed that *tradition* was the only real reason for these rules: "Today, experience in those states in which females play full-court basketball demonstrates that there are no physiological or anatomical reasons why females are any less able than males to play full-court basketball. In addition, since half-court basketball remains a vestige of the days when females were considered physically incapable of strenuous activity and deserving of an inferior position in society, it cannot be continued no matter how traditional and popular it may be among the fans of a particular state."[4]

Regardless of the Arkansas court ruling, Shauna Russell faced a chilly legal climate. The U.S. Department of Health, Education, and Welfare, the agency in charge of enforcing Title IX before the Department of Education was given the responsibility, had already ruled that Iowa six-player basketball did not violate this law. On December 27, 1978, HEW helped to prolong girls' basketball when Secretary Joseph Califano, who had discussed the rules problem thoroughly with E. Wayne Cooley, disclosed the department's interpretation of Title IX as it applied to the game: "Whether a school has six-player, half-court basketball is entirely up to it, if its overall athletic program is non-discriminating. The regulation does not require that any particular sport be offered or that the same sport be offered to boys and girls. It does not require schools to offer versions of the same sport."[5]

Moreover, while it took time for the law to improve opportunities for women, enforcement was rare in the law's first decade. Two years after Title IX's passage, there were still fewer than fifty women on athletic scholarships throughout the country, compared with about fifty thousand men. In 1984 the U.S. Supreme Court effectively gutted Title IX in *Grove City v. Bell*, ruling that it applied only to educational programs that received federal funds, rather than to entire institutions. Discrimination on the basis of gender was thus legal if programs, including athletics, did not get federal money. But Congress overrode a veto by President Reagan and nullified *Grove City* four years later with the Civil Rights Restoration Act of 1988. This act ruled that Title IX was applicable to the entire institution if *any* part of the institution received federal monies. Such was the national climate that served as a backdrop for three Iowa girls and their class-action lawsuit.[6]

In January 1982 Bill Russell penned a fifty-word memo to E. Wayne Cooley. "Why do we retain the old rules after virtually all other states have moved to the more demanding full-court game?" the Graceland professor asked. In a typically endearing yet truncated bureaucratic response, Cooley replied: "At this point I offer solely personal opinion and [am] in no way reflecting opinion or attitude of school persons across the state nor of our Board of Directors; my answer not being an ipso facto reflection of school people, rather one of my own. I am of the opinion the economics of extracurricular activity programs enter strongly into a position adopted by school people of the state. . . . Iowa is the one island where the girl supports totally her own competitive athletic program."[7]

One year later, the tone of Russell's correspondence had shifted from one of inquiry to one of action. "I am very interested in changing the rules of girls 'basketball' in Iowa to real basketball," Russell informed a Des Moines group calling itself "5 on 5 Inc." The group met in February 1983 and drew sixteen men, women, and junior high girls. Among the latter was Shauna Russell, who had read an advertisement for the meeting in the *Des Moines Register*. "I told them I'd join," said Shauna Russell. "They were looking for plaintiffs." Among the adults attending the meeting was Dr. Peter Wirtz, a Des Moines orthopedic surgeon who disclosed his study showing that girls who played six-player basketball suffered significantly more knee injuries than those who played full-court ball. In his survey of male and female varsity players at twenty-two schools, there were sixteen ligament ruptures in fifteen girls and only one in a boy. Half of the girls' injuries occurred while "jump-stopping," which occurred often in the half-court game that required abrupt stops at the center line. "This is the main reason I would promote a change," Wirtz told the group.[8]

In fall 1982 a group of parents, players, and fans had formed 5 on 5 Inc. to promote the revision of girls' basketball rules. Wirtz became the president and chairman of its steering committee; its treasurer was a Des Moines man named Lauren Madden, whose eighth-grade stepdaughter, Kari Wolf, would join Shauna Russell and another eight-grader, Joleen Enslow of Indianola, as lawsuit plaintiffs; the three girls wanted to play what Bill Russell had called "real basketball." Officials of the nonprofit organization estimated early on that a lawsuit would cost approximately fifteen thousand dollars, and in 1983 Bill Russell, a longtime political activist and a recent Decatur County Democratic chairperson, suggested the following sources for funds: university and college women's basketball coaches in Iowa, the National Organization for Women (NOW), Iowa Women's Political Caucus, Graceland liberals, the Democratic Party, and "personal friends."[9]

According to *Des Moines Register* polls, most Iowans did not share 5 on 5 Inc.'s enthusiasm for a change. In a 1977 poll, 48 percent of Iowans preferred six-player girls' basketball; 27 percent preferred five-player ball. In 1984, shortly before the five-player option was permitted, slightly more than half of the state's citizens still favored the six-player game. And just three months before the lawsuit was filed, 71 percent of the members of the Iowa High School Athletic Directors Association favored the then-current six-player rules. Not surprisingly, the strongest support came from the smaller schools: 76 percent of the athletic directors at schools with fewer than three hundred students preferred six-player basketball.[10]

Nevertheless, on August 20, 1983, a class-action civil rights suit was filed in the United States District Court for the Southern District of Iowa on behalf of Shauna Russell, age fourteen, of Lamoni; Kari Wolf, age twelve, of Des Moines; and Joleen Enslow, age thirteen, of Indianola. Defendants in the lawsuit were the IGHSAU, its board of directors, members of the State Board of Public Instruction, the Iowa Department of Public Instruction, and its superintendent, Robert Benton. Like its unsuccessful counterparts in Tennessee and Oklahoma, this lawsuit contended that six-player girls' basketball constituted sexual discrimination and was in violation of the Equal Protection Clause of the Fourteenth Amendment, which guarantees that states must apply laws equally to everyone. If it weren't formidable enough that other lawsuits had failed, these plaintiffs had to face E. Wayne Cooley and the only girls' athletic union in America. "Friendly persuasion would not be the way to solve the problem," said the 5 on 5 Inc. treasurer, Lauren Madden, Kari Wolf's stepfather.[11]

And Bill Russell acknowledged the uphill legal struggle:

> The defendants will have going for them the reluctance courts generally have for handing down decisions that declare actions of the state to be unconstitutional, particularly when the action seems to enjoy popular support. Judges fear that respect for the judicial system will decline if they render unpopular decisions. . . . The plaintiffs will have the argument that the half-court game does not allow them to develop their athletic skills and reap the physical benefits that the more demanding game allows. They will further argue that the more skilled athletes are seriously hampered in their chances of getting a scholarship to play college basketball because they have not played the more demanding game.[12]

Indeed, all three plaintiffs said separately that they wanted to earn college basketball scholarships. "These three young girls stepped forward and said they would like to do this on behalf of other girls in the state of Iowa," Lauren Madden told the press shortly after the lawsuit was filed. From most indications the teenagers *did* appear to "step forward," though such statements are best considered along with the facts that Bill Russell and Lauren Madden—two of the primary leaders of 5 on 5 Inc.—were parents of two of the plaintiffs. But the teenagers claimed to have attended the first 5 on 5 Inc. meetings on their own volition. And on at least one occasion Kari Wolf and Shauna Russell wrote each other. "Do the kids bother you about the suit? They were bothering me, but not anymore," Kari wrote, just days after the lawsuit was filed. "We had some people call wanting to get involved. Almost all of the people at [Des Moines] Dowling [High School] want 5 on 5." "I've been lucky and haven't really gotten any negative opinions," Shauna wrote back. "Most of my friends prefer 5 on 5 and we had talked about it a lot before the suit."[13]

Just as Ruth Johnson's growing up in a culture of women's sport directed her to a career in physical education, Shauna Russell's family history partially explains her actions as a fourteen-year-old. Her father was a legal scholar and department chair as well as a former college track champion; her mother, Val Russell, became a law librarian after teaching physical education early in her career. Shauna Russell became an attorney herself, and fifteen years after the lawsuit, she practiced law in Osceola, a Clarke County community about fifty miles north of Lamoni. She identifies the Russell family's interest in law as having more to do with her becoming an attorney than the experience of the lawsuit itself. "It didn't hurt that I was a feminist in fourth grade, though," she said. Shauna Russell grew up playing full-court basketball; having to play six-player when she reached high school was a major disappointment. The decision to sue, she claimed, was hers:

> I grew up playing basketball with boys. Two of my dad's col-
> league's sons were my age, and we played regular rules during
> open gym. I didn't know there were different rules until fifth
> grade, and when my sister and Dad talked about six-player

rules, I didn't believe them. The underlying message was that girls were not as capable as boys, and that issue might have been batted around in family discussions.

At the time of the lawsuit, there might have been criticism out there, but I didn't hear it. I did have a sense that the townspeople thought Dad was behind it [the suit]. But Mom made sure that it was my decision.[14]

On a midweek afternoon in early March 1984, as the customary fifteen thousand fans flocked to Veterans Memorial Auditorium in Des Moines for the state tournament, the attorneys involved in the lawsuit gathered just a few blocks away before U.S. District Judge Donald O'Brien. "We were pleased O'Brien was the judge," said Shauna Russell. "He was a Democrat, and my dad knew him." Surrounded by two attorneys for the Union and an assistant attorney general who favored the six-player game, Faith O'Reilly, attorney for the three girls, labeled the Iowa game "a dual system with unequal benefits" before using a civil rights analogy. According to O'Reilly, some girls may want to "sit in the back of the bus—that's certainly their choice." It was unconstitutional, however, for the state to make them submit to unequal opportunities. In April O'Brien confirmed Shauna Russell's belief that he wasn't about to drop the suit: the judge rejected requests to dismiss the lawsuit by the defendants, the IGHSAU and the Iowa Department of Public Instruction, who argued that the three Iowa girls had no right to challenge the existing basketball rules in federal court. Equally foreboding for six-player traditionalists was that in citing precedents for his ruling, Judge O'Brien ignored the Tennessee and Oklahoma suits and referred only to the Arkansas case, which declared that girls and boys must play under the same rules. "This case clearly involves conscious acts by state and local officials to treat female basketball players differently than male basketball players, thus bringing the Equal Protection Clause of the U.S. Constitution into question," O'Brien ruled.[15]

Considering that the trial was set for summer and its likely outcome would be to dismiss six-player rules, the Des Moines school board directed administrators to implement five-player basketball in all physical education classes starting in the fall of 1984. The Des Moines board was indeed prescient: three days later—on May 18, just two days after Judge O'Brien set July 11 as the trial date for the lawsuit—the Union made the startling announcement that, beginning that fall, Iowa girls would be permitted to play five-player basketball and there would be a five-player state tournament in 1985. The IGHSAU's seven-member board voted unanimously to allow local schools to choose either set of rules or, ostensibly, both: "This resolution will allow the Iowa Girls High School Athletic Union to provide an equal opportunity to young women who desire to compete in the five-on-five game, while still offering to those who so desire the opportunity to continue to compete in the six-on-six game. . . . By this procedure, it is also the intent [of the Union] to allow a decision on the local level as to which form of competition will be played. A school may have teams playing five-on-five, six-on-six, or both."[16]

Ironically, the decision to allow the *schools* to choose which game they wanted to play was viewed widely as a victory for six-player advocates. "A stroke of genius and more than a touch of fiscal reality," wrote basketball historian Jan Beran about the action. "A brilliant tactical move by Field Marshal E. Wayne Cooley," argued an Iowa sportswriter, who believed that the Union secretary delayed the five-on-five takeover for a good year or two: "While the other side works out the tangles, the six-girl game will chug contentedly along for a few more years than it would have otherwise." "We covered the waterfront," Cooley remarked fifteen years after the 1984 *Union* action. "I stayed up all one night thinking what to do and walked into our attorney's office the next day and told him we would offer both five and six. That was the key to the whole thing: offer both. The battleground then became the individual schools'. Local choice was the answer."[17]

Of course it was improbable that, considering the logistics, any school—large or small—would be able to put both five *and* six-player basketball teams on the court. Unlikely, too, was a fast changeover to the five-girl game, even for those city schools clamoring for the switch; the Des Moines school board, when it ordered all its schools to abide by five-player rules, resolved that it wouldn't play the game competitively until there were enough other schools that had switched from six-player "to allow for a competitive season of play and a meaningful state tournament experience." School boards in the cities of Muscatine and Davenport recommended plans that "phased in" five-player basketball over five years, which meant that varsity competition would begin with the 1988–89 school year.

One remaining point of contention was Cooley's remark that "the resolution was not developed in response to the lawsuit," which the plaintiffs and their supporters viewed as arrogant and untruthful. The remark was one of several factors that made this a lawsuit that wouldn't go away. 5 on 5 Inc. wrote in a letter to "friends of girls' basketball," soliciting financial support for their cause: "First, it's great that the Iowa Girls High School Athletic Union has finally recognized that our girls should be allowed to play five-player ball by amending its rules to allow local schools to offer the five-player game as well as the six-player game. What it did was attempt to take the monkey off its back and place it on local schools officials. (Incidentally, Union officials say their action has nothing to do with impending litigation!). . . . We continue to pursue our case in Federal Court."[18]

A primary reason to push forward with the lawsuit, according to the plaintiffs' supporters, was the problem that the Des Moines school board had confronted: if a school's athletic opponent, usually a conference team, didn't choose to play the same game, then the changeover would result in an incomplete or abbreviated schedule. And the plaintiffs' supporters knew that six-player basketball and the Union remained so strong in the small towns that those districts would surely stay with the game, and the bifurcation of the state's basketball program might create havoc. U.S. District Judge Donald O'Brien sensed as much when in late September he denied the Union's request to dismiss the lawsuit on the basis that it had amended its rules and that local schools now decided which rules they followed. O'Brien acknowledged the change, but he also noted that the IGHSAU had a tremendous influence over how the game of girls' basketball was played in Iowa. Thus 5 on 5 Inc. continued to raise funds, realizing that a court victory—the kind won in a courthouse—would likely force the defendants to pay some or all of the winners' attorney fees. "If we win," Bill Russell wrote in a fundraising effort, "there is a good chance the judge will order our legal fees paid by the defendants."[19]

Fundraising for the five-player effort certainly created strange bedfellows. "One faculty member here is an officer in the Iowa chapter of the NOW [National Organization for Women]," Bill Russell wrote to Lauren Madden. "She thinks they could help in some way. . . . Many [Democratic] Party activists are quite friendly toward our suit." At the same time, Mary Louise Smith, former chair of the Republican National Committee, endorsed the lawsuit, as did several other political and civic leaders whose support was enlisted by a Des Moines women's rights activist, Joanne Fine. "She [Fine] and a group of women she works with agreed to join us and help raise funds," Madden said. Along with Smith, the list of supporters included several state senators and representatives—Republicans *and* Democrats—as well as a member of the state Board of Regents, a former attorney for the Iowa Civil Rights Commission, a Des Moines city councilwoman, and the Iowa division of the American Association of University Women.[20]

Pressing on with the lawsuit soon created much stranger bedfellows. The original July trial date was moved back to November when the Indianola and Lamoni school districts—where plaintiffs Joleen Enslow and Shauna Russell attended—were added as defendants. Threatening to sue her own school had immediate but possibly unfavorable consequences for Russell. In August the Lamoni Board of Education approved a resolution to change to five-player basketball and to petition the Bluegrass Conference (Lamoni's athletic league) to begin full-court play during the 1985–86 school year. By suing her school, Shauna Russell was suing her father, a member of the Lamoni school board and, of course, perhaps the lawsuit's strongest proponent. "As a member of the school board I am now in a very awkward position with my daughter suing the board. My main concern is financial," Bill Russell wrote to the plaintiffs' attorney. "I appreciate your promise not to seek attorney's fees from the Lamoni school."[21]

The Russells' primary problem was neither the Lamoni school district nor that Shauna was suing her father; it was that Lamoni had no opponents with whom to play five-player basketball. That is why the school board petitioned the *entire* conference to play full-court. Bill Russell then took the fight one step farther. "It seems to me that as the plaintiffs' attorney you ought to name the conferences as well as the member schools as defendants," he wrote to Mark Bennett. "A school cannot make a change to 5 on 5 without other schools to play. Getting a conference to make the shift is about the only practical way for a single school to begin the change for itself."[22]

The threat of suing entire conferences worked. After several conferences voted to play full-court basketball and despite U.S. District Judge Donald O'Brien's denial of the Union's request to dismiss the suit, a joint written statement issued by the plaintiffs and defendants on October 24, 1984, dismissed the federal lawsuit. "Since schools are currently making decisions on the local level whether to participate in five-on-five, six-on-six, or both, the parties agree that it is in the best interest of girls' high school interscholastic athletics to end the court action," the statement said. For the first time the Union acknowledged that the suit was a factor in its May decision to change the rules. The IGHSAU also pledged that it would not rescind the rule change, and that in the matter of which game girls would play, it would "remain neutral in the decision by local school districts." Financial considerations were a largely unspoken factor in 5 on 5 Inc.'s decision to drop the lawsuit, and in the settlement the Union agreed to pay the plaintiffs' fees. "While schools around Lamoni are still playing the half-court game, our ability to raise the needed money seemed to be greatly limited by the fact that our best support is in Des Moines, Davenport, and other large population areas where the schools are already making the switch," Russell wrote to a prospective supporter after the case was dropped. Once more, the tension between city and country was palpable: large schools were opting for the five-player game, while the small towns stuck with tradition. "The settlement saved a significant amount in anticipated legal fees and, consequently, we are able to return 100 percent of your contribution," the 5 on 5 treasurer Madden reported as he returned money to supporters, whose contributions were promised to be returned if the lawsuit were won.[23]

The only problem remaining was that Shauna Russell was all dressed up and had nowhere to go. Following the example of nearly all rural schools in 1984, the seven members of the Bluegrass Conference, with the exception of Lamoni, chose to stay with six-player girls' basketball. "We couldn't find any opponents—we even looked into scheduling Missouri schools. But there was no one to play," Shauna Russell said. "So it was either play six-player or not play at all." Thus, ironically, the Lamoni school board reverted to the old rules. "So Shauna, a sophomore, may not get to play the real game before she graduates here, but the logs are beginning to roll and we think the half-loaf we have won will turn into a full loaf before long," Bill Russell wrote soon after the suit was dismissed.[24]

A four-year starter at Lamoni who played in both the forward and guard courts, Shauna Russell never played the "real game" or saw "the full loaf" before graduating in 1987. Nor did she earn the college basketball scholarship that she had dreamed about. "By the time I was a senior," she said, "I had lost my skill for dribbling. There was an absence of self-confidence engrained in six-player. . . . I understand why they [the IGHSAU] wanted to keep it. There were the economic reasons, and that fabulous tourney was a good thing. But there was also the fear that people wouldn't support five-player. Iowa had this fabulous tradition, but it's too bad they weren't on the forefront, going forward instead of always looking backward."[25]

Lawsuit or not, Bill Russell refused to give up fighting six-player rules. In November 1985, nearly one year to the day of the lawsuit's trial date, Russell published an essay on the *Des Moines Register*'s op-ed page entitled, "Iowa Girls Handicapped by Old-Style Basketball." Once again Russell outlined the argument against the traditional game: "Years ago, Iowa girls were divided into three courts for basketball. Those in the center court neither shot the ball nor had the chance to garner a rebound off either backboard. The two-court game was a real step forward. Now is the time to take that final step and let the girls play basketball."[26]

"The final step," when the half loaf turned into a full loaf, was still several years down the road. Bill Russell was right: it *was* time to let the girls play basketball. But earlier, farther back on the road to full-court basketball, Ruth Lang and Cyndy Long, the Nicholson sisters and the Langerman twins played in a world that was, in many ways, *fuller* than what was to follow. Numbers provide the evidence: When the Nicholsons played six-player basketball, seven of ten Iowa high school girls played the game. In 2001 fewer than one in four did, and that was in the *small* schools. In 4A districts (the large-district classification in which schools average over one thousand students), one in twenty-three girls played basketball. The high status of the game is gone and not coming back.[27]

In 1980 the Iowa Civil Rights Commission declined to approve a proposal that would have disallowed high school six-player basketball on the basis that players were not given an equal chance to win college athletic scholarships. Although guards playing the six-player game couldn't shoot and neither guards nor forwards could dribble more than twice, research confirmed that six-player veterans who later played full-court college basketball still looked favorably upon the old game. In a study that questioned 132 former Iowa high school players, including 90 (68 percent) former forwards, who were now playing the five-on-five game at Iowa colleges and universities, 79 (60 percent) believed that the six-player game offered more girls an opportunity to play than did the five-player game. In the same study, 75 of the 132 players questioned (57 percent) believed the game should not be changed to full-court.

Even when the IGHSAU permitted individual school districts to choose between the two games in 1984, research showed no significant difference in postsecondary opportunities for basketball scholarships. In a poll of more than 250 high school coaches, one researcher concluded that "the change of rules virtually had no impact on either the six or five-player competitors in relationship to collegiate playing opportunities." "Because the larger schools made the transition to five-player ball while the smaller schools retained the six-player style, this researcher believes that the number of better athletes available at larger schools would dictate more candidates for intercollegiate ball. The numbers, not the rules, favor the five-player game."[28]

Even the National Organization for Women, which would support the 1984 lawsuit aimed at banning six-player basketball, released a study that showed Iowa girls' athletics in a highly favorable light. A 1979 report by NOW's Project for Equal Education Rights revealed that slightly more than *half* (50.6 percent) of Iowa's high school athletes were female, which meant that the state led the nation in the percentage of high school girls' athletic participation. The reason NOW joined the anti-six-player forces after publishing this study can be interpreted in various ways. The organization might have believed that Iowa girls' athletics was so strong that a change to five-player basketball would not diminish participation but perhaps even increase it. But it was more likely that NOW supported the fight against six-player rules because switching to the five-player game had become a political issue, one now included on a feminist agenda supporting the belief that equality implied sameness. In other words, athletic opportunities for girls and boys would be equal only when they played the same games.[29]

In response to the NOW study as well as to a *Chicago Tribune* survey that tracked the college-level athletic opportunities for Chicago area high school graduates, the Iowa Girls High School Athletic Union queried the state's athletic directors in 1981 "to see whether this record for interscholastic participation carried on into intercollegiate opportunity." The Union asked 337 Iowa athletic directors about the plans of seniors to participate in college basketball in Iowa after their high school graduation. The survey revealed that there were five girls for every four boys playing college basketball in Iowa, and that female players outnumbered males 32 to 29 in the number of graduates competing at the collegiate level in other states in 1981. Across the Mississippi River in Illinois, where five-player girls' basketball was the game, there were four times as many boys as girls who had graduated from the state's high schools participating in college-level programs.[30]

A sex-equity consultant with the Iowa Department of Public Instruction remarked in 1982 that Iowa's heralded girls' basketball tradition had "done wonders as far as expanding opportunities for women." And in the summer of 1984—at the same time that the Union was preparing to defend the venerable game in a court of law—a periodical entitled *Title IX Line*, which reported on sex equity in schools, used Iowa's program as an example for other states to follow.[31]

If finances were any indication of the overall health of six-player basketball, then the game reached unparalleled success in the late 1970s. For most years in the ten-year period beginning 1967, Iowa high school boys' basketball produced a considerably higher gross income than the girls—at least $100,000 more until 1974, when the gap closed. By 1977 girls' basketball income had risen to close to $721,000, less than $27,000 shy of the boys' total, and the 1978 figure of $748,000 represented an increase of more than 135 percent from the previous decade. In 1978 six-on-six girls' basketball provided the lion's share of income for the IGHSAU: the figure for softball that year was $193,000, and the gross income drawn from track and field was less that $15,000. Twelve years later, in 1990, basketball provided barely 50 percent of the IGHSAU income; volleyball and softball combined for 34 percent. Also, in the mid-1970s, the girls' state basketball tournament continued to average higher attendance at each session than the boys'. The figures for 1975 show total attendance at more than 86,000 and averages per two-game sessions of nearly 11,000 fans. "The high point for basketball came in 1978, when we had our last sellout championship game," said Cooley. "It was six years after Title IX, and six-player was just sailing." To better accommodate the full-time staff of ten, the Union moved in the summer of 1977 into a neo-Georgian-style home in Des Moines that formerly had been the residence of Iowa's governors. It was purchased from the state for $140,000. The coronation of the basketball player as queen of Iowa was complete.[32]

The implied threat of the law, however, proved stronger than any mitigating factors and led directly to the rule change of 1984. As was expected, most schools that changed to the five-player game were from Iowa cities that hadn't offered high school basketball before Title IX; the smaller schools with strong basketball traditions retained the six-player rules. Only 21 schools changed during that first season (1984–85). Another 51 switched the following year, and by 1989, just 82 out of 449 Iowa high schools offering girls' basketball played the full-court game. Cooley, an adamant six-player advocate, had reluctantly offered the five-player option after a survey of high school girls showed their preference for full-court basketball. He anticipated that the demise of the old game would be gradual but inevitable: "We diversified, we changed gears, but we lost players when we went to five," Cooley said. "I knew that would happen, so I didn't want the conversion to happen overnight. So it took nine years [1984–1993] to get accustomed. We offended many adult spectators because we had huge support [for six-player]. We took the position that, no, we're not obligated to switch, but how long can we fight off the federal government?"[33]

Nine years of "getting accustomed" came to a stunning halt on Wednesday, February 3, 1993, when the Union board voted unanimously to end six-player basketball after the 1993–94 state tournament. "The queen is dead. Long live the queen," opened the lead story in the *Des Moines Register* the following morning. "It's not the end of the world," E. Wayne Cooley told the media. "It's been a very romantic time, at least for the 39 years I've been here. . . . The [six-player] tournament was the grande dame of the whole nation as far as women and girls' basketball tournaments are concerned," said Cooley, couching his message in gendered language that undoubtedly caused some women to wince, though happily so, for the grande dame's era was indeed *complete*. The irony of changes in attitudes was not lost on Cooley. "The same people who in 1926 complained about girls' basketball and dropped it were, in the late 1960s, wanting it back again," Cooley said years later, omitting that the game the recalcitrants usually wanted was the five-player one.[34]

While it wasn't the end of the world, the decision to discontinue six-player basketball, as the *Des Moines Register* reported the day after the Union's bombshell, "was met with shock and disappointment," particularly in Iowa's smallest communities. "It was a stake driven right into the heart of small town tradition," read a news story in the *Woodbine Twiner*. "Few people that are natives of cities like Des Moines, or live outside the state, realize the tie between six-player girls' basketball and the small towns where it has flourished." "When my wife told me the news, it was like someone close to me had died," said Rick Reinking, girls' coach at southwest Iowa's consolidated Irwin-Kirkman-Manilla High School. Lynne Lorenzen, the national all-time leading basketball scorer from Ventura, was concerned that the switch was a sign of the future, foreshadowing the disappearance of small-town customs. And coach Gail Hartigan, a member of the board that made the decision, was even surprised herself. "I knew it was coming, but I never, ever dreamed it would come this fast. It was one of the most difficult decisions that we've ever had to make," she said.[35]

The decision was made after four months of Union research indicated that there would be a significant number of schools changing from six-player to five-player basketball within the next two years. A primary reason for the lengthy conversion to full-court basketball after 1984 was due in part to the absence of an enrollment classification system, the result of there being so few five-player teams and the ensuing geographical problems. In other words, a high school with an enrollment of one hundred that played five-player ball, though such situations were rare, would have to compete against schools with one thousand students or more.

So when the Union began its research in the fall of 1992, fifty member schools quickly jumped to full-court basketball. An avalanche, of sorts, was in effect, and by January 1993 it appeared that the annual total of 275 six-player schools and 135 five-player schools would be reversed by the 1994–95 basketball season. The Union even predicted "the possibility of fewer than 100 schools playing six-player basketball by that time." Regardless, the IGHSAU made grand plans for one last six-player tournament in 1994, a proper escort out the door for the grande dame. "One of the things that came into the board's thinking is that there's no way that we could let that six-player tournament die as a second-class citizen after what it had done for the girl athletes in the states," said Mike Henderson, the Union's longtime information director.[36]

As it turned out, the Union had severely miscalculated. "There were twenty-seven schools still playing six-player that fall. There was an avalanche to five-player, and it was a voluntary, local issue," said Cooley, sounding eerily but understandably similar to Guy Ghan, the state official who had supervised hundreds of Iowa school mergers (see chapter 2). As with consolidation, the switch to five-player basketball began with outside pressure and ended with local decisions, situations that were not entirely "voluntary." When the 1993–94 basketball season opened, the avalanche had ended. In November 1993 the Union, while unveiling a four-class structure that would crown four champions in March, sent to all member schools a memorandum with the "new" basketball adaptations: "All 401 schools in the state have entered the five-player basketball tournament next spring, so this marks the first time in history no six-player tournament series will be held. As a result, the rules of the game are new to nearly two-thirds of our schools. It is quite important to be familiar with the new rules of five-player basketball."[37]

The long period of "getting accustomed" was over, and, as usual, E. Wayne Cooley appeared to know all along what he was doing. While the Union's unexpected, midwinter decision provided plenty to talk about—"Iowans Pick Sides on Six-Girl Game," read the *Des Moines Register*'s lead headline two days following the change—the IGHSAU was apparently responding to the wishes of most Iowans. In 1991, for the first time ever, a *Register* poll showed that a slight majority of Iowans, who had had six years already to get familiar with full-court girls' basketball, favored the five-player over the six-player game. "I started to spread the word and slowly began to win converts," Donald Kaul, the *Register* columnist who had bashed six-player for decades, wrote upon its demise. "First, big-city people, then suburbanites and, finally, the little people in the little towns that make up the disappearing backbone of this state came over to my side." Cooley, who had known what the endgame would be and was able to forestall it back in 1984, was philosophical and a little rueful when I interviewed him in 2000, seven years after the demise of six-player basketball. "We were center stage back when it [six-player] was controversial, and the networks covered the tourney," Cooley said. "*Sports Illustrated* called us a 'grand and glorious place.' When they bury someone, people usually show up. But they [the media] haven't been back since."[38]

While the number of Iowa girls playing basketball eventually dissi-pated after the game changed entirely to five-player in 1993, female athletic participation fostered by Title IX exploded in other states. In 2000 nearly 2.8 million high school girls competed in athletics, ten times the number in 1972; NCAA-sanctioned sports counted al-most 151,000 female athletes, five times as many college participants than before the law's enactment. But "the great untold story of suc-cess" that resulted from Title IX, according to education secretary Richard W. Riley on the legislation's twenty-fifth anniversary in 1997, was the progress made in education: women now made up the majority of American college students. By 2003 women rivaled or surpassed the number of men in medical and law schools as well as doctoral degree programs in American universities.[39]

Although Title IX fostered enormous changes in education for women, the American public most often identifies the legislation with its ties to athletics. This has occurred because of two question-able beliefs: (1) that Title IX is to blame for the disappearance of hundreds of men's athletic programs, an opinion that its critics have prominently and successfully placed in the media, and (2) that Title IX has succeeded in leveling the playing field for women. Though women comprise 55 percent of the undergraduate population, they make up only 42 percent of collegiate athletes and receive just 32 percent of recruiting funds, causing some Title IX supporters to question whether American women are not more readily accepted as doctors and lawyers than as point guards.[40]

Among the 4,571 complaints received in 2001 by the Depart-ment of Education's Office for Civil Rights, which is responsible for Title IX enforcement, only 99 dealt with college, high school, or elementary school athletics. The department reports that most complaints concern such issues as the unavailability of openings in academic courses and sexual harassment in schools. Amazingly, in Title IX's thirty years of existence, no school has ever been denied federal funding for noncompliance, though schools have often been threatened with such penalties. The fact that only a fraction of Title IX complaints deal with athletics and that no school has lost federal funding in thirty years help explain why the playing field is still far from level. That the law is poorly enforced is one of the few facts upon which supporters and critics alike can agree.[41]

In spring 2003 two events raised age-old questions surrounding women and sports that had not drawn such public scrutiny in a quarter century. The appearance of a woman golfer in an all-men's Professional Golf Association (PGA) tour event and another possible governmental weakening of Title IX dragged out issues that were seemingly settled. Annika Sorenstam's decision to play a "boys" game and a national commission's consideration of limiting scholarships to female athletes proved this wasn't the case.

Often considered the best woman golfer ever, Sorenstam competed in May 2003 in Texas's Colonial Tournament, becoming the first female to appear in a PGA event since Babe Didrickson in 1945. Many of Sorenstam's supporters were rankled by critical remarks similar to those hurled thirty years earlier when Billie Jean King threatened the male-dominated game of tennis by challenging and defeating Bobby Riggs in an exhibition match. PGA golfer Vijay Singh remarked: "She doesn't belong. . . . We have our tour for men, and they [women] have their tour. She's taking a spot from someone in the field."[42]

But the appearance of the Commission on Opportunity in Athletics, created by the Bush administration, held far wider implications for women and athletics. Title IX supporters feared that the Bush administration would change compliance regulations, resulting in the law being gutted once more and fewer opportunities and less funding for women's and girls' athletics. Title IX supporters pointed to several indicators of revision: Bush addressed possible changes to the legislation during his presidential campaign; he appointed a known opponent of bias-free laws to run the Office for Civil Rights; and the fifteen-member Commission on Opportunity in Athletics, which represented only Division I programs (there were no representatives of Division II and III institutions, community colleges, or high schools), was, according to critics, stacked with opponents of Title IX.[43]

The point of contention with Title IX regulations was the "substantial proportionality" section of the three-part test with which an institution must comply. In order to be in compliance, a school needs to pass only one part; the other two prongs include "history and continuing practice of developing interests and abilities of the underrepresented sex" and "effectively accommodating those interests and abilities." The proportionality component requires that participation opportunities for men and women are proportionate to their respective undergraduate enrollments; if women comprise half of a school's student enrollment, then half of its athletes should be women.

Critics of the proportionality prong, including President Bush, who campaigned against it, claim that it is simply a quota that has resulted in the destruction of many "minor," nonrevenue men's programs across the country. One critic called it "a feminist form of sex discrimination." Supporters argue that proportionality is not a quota because there are two other ways a school can comply with the legislation. In fact, two-thirds of schools about which complaints were filed claimed compliance under the "effective accommodation of interests and abilities" section—a fact that some would say proves the number of athletes by sex is not proportional to the student enrollment in those schools.[44] "You can have an enrollment of 55 percent women where only 35 percent of the athletes are women and still be in compliance as long as you can show you've met the interests and abilities," the manager of a consulting firm on Title IX issues said.[45] But critics who argue that men's athletics have suffered because of a gender quota system resulting from the rule of proportionality point to the fact that more than four hundred men's sports programs, including wrestling, tennis, swimming, and track, have been lost. Wrestling in particular has suffered heavy losses in the Title IX era, losing about 170 teams during the last thirty years. While wrestling is a rapidly growing sport in high schools, there were 37 percent fewer NCAA wrestling teams and nearly two thousand fewer college wrestlers in 2001 than twenty years earlier.[46]

Not surprisingly, a consortium of coaches from the National Wrestling Coaches Association filed a lawsuit that challenged the way Title IX is enforced. In May 2002 the Justice Department filed a motion asking that a federal court dismiss the lawsuit, contending that only individual schools can correct the wrongs claimed by the plaintiffs. Even though the lawsuit was dismissed, Title IX proponents did not necessarily regard the action as an endorsement of Title IX regulations. In fact, when the Education Department announced that it would strive to expand opportunities for women in a way that does not diminish existing men's teams, an attorney who specializes in Title IX interpreted the statement as a suggestion that the Bush administration was considering the revision of Title IX regulations.[47]

Indeed in June 2002, less than one month after the department stated its intention, Secretary of Education Roderick Paige created the Commission on Opportunity in Athletics to study reform of Title IX. On February 26, 2003, the commission released its report. Among its twenty-four proposals was a recommendation that would permit colleges to give only 47 percent of their participation opportunities to women, regardless of how many females were in their undergraduate population. Other proposals changed the ways schools counted male and female athletes—"walk on" athletes, nearly always male, wouldn't be included in the final count, which would serve to benefit men. Another recommendation provided that "non-traditional" students (those not between the ages of eighteen and twenty-four and students with children) not be included in an institution's undergraduate population when the school was demonstrating compliance with the proportionality prong of the three-part test. Most non-traditional students are women.[48]

On the same day that the commission released its study, two of its members, Julie Foudy and Donna de Varona, argued in a minority report that many of the recommendations made by the majority

would "seriously weaken Title IX's protections and substantially reduce the opportunities to which women and girls are entitled under
current law." Commissioner de Varona herself had had some experience with reduced opportunities: after earning two gold medals
in the 1964 Olympics, there was no college swimming scholarship,
anywhere, awaiting her. According to the Women's Sports Foundation, the commission's proposals would result in high school girls
losing 305,000 participation opportunities and female college athletes losing 50,000 as well as $122 million in athletic scholarships.
Education Secretary Paige refused to include the minority report
in the official majority report but did state that he would act on
only those recommendations in the latter that received unanimous
approval.[49]

In spring 2003 the criticism of golfer Annika Sorenstam's appearance in a PGA event and the release of a commission's report to
change Title IX were seemingly unrelated events. But both sprang
from the same impulse: in an America that has been radically transformed for the better by a civil rights law that has achieved unprece-
dented gender equality, athletics remain the last turf that many men
refuse to share. They seem to say that permitting women to work in
courtrooms and corporate offices is okay, but at least leave men the
golf course.

In 1993, more than twenty years after the passage of Title IX,
42 percent of participants in Iowa high school sports were female—
the same percentage of women who compete nationally in college
athletics today. But only a few decades earlier, 70 percent of Iowa
girls had played one sport alone: basketball. Statistically speaking,
Iowa and the rest of the country were finally equal.[50]

Epilogue

The final act was played out this week when the Iowa Girls High School Athletic Union voted to give up the six-player game in 1994. I'm proud. It shows that if you curse the candles long enough, sometimes you can blow one out. – Donald Kaul, *"At Long Last My Mission Accomplished"*

Understanding Iowa six-player girls' basketball entails acknowledging its contradictions. It was an activity that was simultaneously conservative and progressive, and its extraordinary appeal and survival occurred precisely *because* of these contradictions. The contradictions that marked girls' basketball similarly characterized the larger Iowa culture.

During a century in which rural America became increasingly less populated, visible, and important in the national consciousness, Iowans constructed in basketball a story they told themselves and others that reinforced the beliefs that held their culture together and made their lives meaningful. Through basketball they showed the world stubbornness and art, toughness and diplomacy. Through basketball, Iowans showed the rest of the world what women were capable of. The elaborate basketball culture that evolved as the story was told was filled with unsuspected mutations, both delightful and debilitating. Many women contended that their lives had been deeply affected by their basketball experiences during their teenage years—that often treacherous period when lifelong habits are learned. Many reported that qualities they cultivated on the basketball floor—discipline, self-confidence, peer respect, perseverance, *joy*—shaped their futures and, later on, defined their pasts.[1]

But in basketball, too, Iowans learned that permitting men to govern high school girls' sports proved almost irreversible, especially considering the gender bias that was built into the Union's bylaws. The "healthy" game for girls was, at least partially, for men.

The fact was that Iowa girls *were* capable of doing more with a basketball than dribbling it twice in half a court. Six-player basketball wasn't as demanding as full-court, but the wildly successful and elaborate culture that evolved eclipsed that fact for many years. Only a few years after five-player basketball was introduced in high schools, Iowa girls had proven they adapted well and quickly: in March 1998 more than twenty Iowa high school seniors had accepted NCAA Division I basketball scholarships. During the 1999–2000 season, half of the women's basketball scholarships offered at Iowa's four Division I universities—Iowa, Iowa State, Northern Iowa, and Drake—were held by Iowa graduates who had played only full-court ball in high school.[2]

Unfortunately the emphasis on high school sport as a prelude to college athletic scholarships led to increasing elitism in and commodification of the game—and a decline in overall participation. A Union survey in 2001 showed that for every ten Iowa girls who play basketball in seventh grade, only two were still playing as seniors. Fifty-six percent of the girls who play basketball their freshman year in high school will quit before their senior year.[3]

In the end, Iowans publicly displayed in basketball their comfort with contradiction. Six-player girls' basketball, like the rural culture in which it flourished, had been rife with conflicting meanings.

In January 2001, late in the second half of a girls' basketball game between two run-of-the-mill southwest Iowa teams, rivals Boyer Valley and Woodbine, the most recent of a flurry of turnovers by both squads caused a Woodbine fan to lean back against the wall on the upper row of the bleachers and sigh. "You know, if you put these two teams together, you might have a decent team," groaned the man. The circle of fans around him let loose soft chuckles, but further commentaries died in their throats. The implication of "putting these two teams together" was unspeakable. The already-consolidated Boyer Valley Community School was in Dunlap, a sleepy Irish-Catholic town with a reputation for having never emphasized education; in contrast, the Protestant, more conservative Woodbine was so hypersensitive about education that its school board elections often drew the longest list of candidates for any district its size in Iowa. Within less than two months both school districts, located in communities nine miles apart, would put before their voters more than $5 million each in school bonds. In a state with severe teacher shortages on the horizon, in a county (Harrison) whose population of fifteen thousand comprised some of Iowa's poorest residents, two school districts with high school enrollments averaging two hundred students were asking their citizens for over $10 million for new buildings nine miles apart.

Woodbine had warded off every consolidation movement the state had presented in the twentieth century. But Boyer Valley had been formed when Dunlap consolidated with another previously reorganized district, Dow City–Arion, and later added students on a whole-grade sharing basis from East Monona. A few well-meaning Boyer Valley residents had once broached the subject of consolidating with Woodbine, but they were met with icy silence. Woodbine wanted no part of its neighbors to the north. There were cultural differences between these two communities.

During the seven years that had passed between the switch to five-player basketball in the fall of 1993 to this midseason game in 2001, the Woodbine girls had had little success on the court. The banners hanging from the gymnasium ceiling were indicative of their struggles. Six of them had been hung since 1993, but they were all for the glory of boys: three basketball banners, two football, and one wrestling. The Lady Tigers had weathered several coaches since Bob Jasper, and in 2001 a local man was the head coach. Homegrown coaches must overachieve just to survive, and this coach, having not yet exceeded expectations, had parents and fans talking, just as they had about Jasper seven years earlier. Some things never change. Some Woodbine men still sit together in a corner of the gym, their wives nowhere to be seen. Their attendance at the game predates five-player basketball, and the commentary in that corner is markedly different from what is heard on the other side of the court, where couples and families sit.

But among the things unchanged in the Woodbine gym there is one thing strikingly different in 2001. It's the poem entitled "Don't Curse the Players" printed on the back page of the program. It reads:

> Please don't curse the girl down there,
> She's my daughter, you see;
> She's only just a girl you know,
> And means a lot to me.
> I did not raise my daughter, sports fans,
> For you to call her names;
> She may not be a superstar
> But it's just a high school game.

The poem, its author unknown, is often printed on high school programs to remind adults to practice the good sportsmanship they expect of their children on the court. In the twenty-first century, the dissipation of public civility can be seen in the audiences of sporting events. Before the switch to five-player girls' basketball, the first line of the poem usually read, "Please don't curse the boy down there." To curse a girl was unthinkable, a culturally defined boundary that was rarely crossed. Apparently, some fans now cursed female players as readily as males. In at least that quarter, girls and boys were finally equal.[4]

Two months before the aforementioned five-player game, in another southwest Iowa gym, twenty women age twenty-five through fifty gathered in the town of Atlantic, where they worked as faculty or staff in the local school district. Among the women were several who had played college basketball and four who had played on Iowa state tournament teams. On this night, these women would reprise six-player basketball, taking on the local high school team. Ironically, none of players on the high school team were even teenagers when the six-player game was discontinued in 1993. Although the exhibition was an early-season fundraiser to send girls to leadership conferences, the most notable feature of the game was the enthusiasm with which the mostly middle-aged women returned to the game of their youth. And in a salute to a state tournament tradition, a half dozen men dressed in tuxedos swept the court at half-time. The Atlantic High School girls' team, which would qualify for the state tournament at season's end, easily whipped the elders at their own six-player game, but nobody cared about the score. More notable was the comment of the six-player veteran who wondered afterward whether there would be any interest in thirty years in watching twenty middle-aged women play five-player basketball. The prospects appeared slim. In terms of cultural elaboration, complexity, and ritual, the move from six- to five-player basketball for Iowa girls was like returning to black-and-white from color television.[5]

Nineteenth-century gender ideology dictated that girls play a different form of basketball than boys. While physical educators fine-tuned the new game for boys, making minor adjustments once the essential rules were in place, no such stability awaited female players. Throughout the twentieth century, the game that girls and women played was always in flux. They played with nine, eight, six, and five on a side, sometimes full-court, sometimes in two courts, and—early on—sometimes in three. They played with ribbons in their hair and stockings covering their legs, then skirts and bare midriffs. As rules and rituals shifted to accommodate the gender arrangements of the time, the only stability in American high school girls' basketball was found in Iowa. There, an amalgamation of historical events, cultural inclinations, and institutional strengths shielded the state from the national decline of the sport at midcentury.

The preeminent event that served as the foundation for Iowa six-player girls' basketball was the insistence of twenty-five male administrators in 1925 that a separate athletic union for high school female athletes be started. The formation of the Iowa Girls High School Athletic Union was monumental in part because it provided the state's girls with institutional support not found anywhere else in

America. In addition, the fact that only men were involved in its initial governance is crucial because seventy-five years later the Union is still male-dominated. This contradiction characterizes the game itself and why it survived and prospered. If the game hadn't been conservative, its popularity would have diminished much earlier, for the outdated gender beliefs that dictated a special, less strenuous game had already disappeared elsewhere; if the game hadn't been simultaneously progressive, the unusual community support for female participation in an intensely competitive sport would not have ensured the game's survival.

The contradictory nature of Iowa basketball worked in its favor because Iowa culture itself contained contradictions; it was hardly the conformist and dreary place presented by many educators, politicians, artists, and media throughout much of the twentieth century. Gender roles were rarely static in rural Iowa, where women worked alongside men to handle challenging agricultural chores. What gendered arrangements existed were often the result of national forces, such as the Progressive Era notion to create gender-specific studies, which resulted in home economics classes for girls. Iowans were used to physically and emotionally strong females, far removed from the Victorian ideals from which six-player basketball emerged. So when Iowa girls and basketball proved to be a good fit, boys in the state, unlike their peers nationally, were rarely intimidated by the girls' game. Iowa six-player basketball developed traditions so early and so firmly in the state that even though the game's administrators felt compelled to defend its virtues, the players rarely believed that they were intruding upon a "masculine" game. "Gender" had been invisible. But when the curtain came down on six-player basketball, gender suddenly became everything.

Here lay a defective game. Opponents of six-player girls' basketball can easily argue that disallowing half a team of girls from shooting is hardly basketball, and the two-dribble rule helped nobody when it came to finding the scholarships that legislative and judicial edicts had made available. Half the players stood gawking at the other half at least half the time—sometimes more if the other half court was filled with either particularly polished or highly unskilled players. And while the herky-jerky flow of six-player and its sudden stops could result in knee problems, those athletes who left behind the defective game sometimes suffered gruesome injuries that came from the pounding unfamiliarity of running up and down a whole basketball court.

Critics can have their fun with it, but they will be hard-pressed to find a more successful athletic activity for high school females in American history than Iowa six-player girls' basketball.

Initially constructed as a less strenuous, more mannerly "female" activity, girls' basketball took on the shape of its host culture in Iowa. The game took flight in a state that prided itself in a stubbornness that surfaced against outside forces, most prominently fights concerning educational matters. The game settled in the countryside and small towns, where physical prowess on the basketball court constituted an acceptable accomplishment for Iowa girls. Small-town schools shaped the game, and the rural Iowans who adopted it saw their own resplendence on the court. In a world that was increasingly removed or simply inaccessible for rural Iowans, basketball—a game—became far more than a game. The girls on the floor were tough and resilient, just like their parents and fans in the stands, and Iowans didn't bend when the federal authorities came calling to tell them, of all things, how they were to play basketball. It was the most successful sports program for girls in the United States of America, and the government wanted to dicker with it? It resembled too closely the so-called "progressive" education leaders' complaints about Iowa's country schools when the state produced throughout the twentieth century the most literate citizenry in all fifty states. Iowans decided when it was time to close the country schools. Then they decided when it was time to close down six-player basketball. And after they did and looked down at the court, they no longer found it resplendent.

Iowa High School Girls Participating in Basketball, 2001 (by Class)

Class (Average student enrollment)	% of girls playing	Total no. playing statewide
4A (1,061)	4.25	1,895
3A (422)	8.33	1,964
2A (215)	13.3	2,960
1A (113)	22.2	2,879

Data source: IGHSAU

Sex of Head Coaches for Iowa Girls' High School Teams, 1971–2001

Years	Women coaches	Men coaches	total
1971–72	6	360	366
1972–73	11	371	382
1973–74	19	424	443
1974–75	26	447	473
1975–76	32	459	491
1976–77	28	467	495
1977–78	34	461	495
1978–79	47	447	494
1979–80	50	443	493
1980–81	50	441	491
1981–82	59	428	487
1982–83	63	422	485
1983–84	70	416	486
1984–85	61	425	486
1985–86	59	421	480
1986–87	63	412	475
1987–88	67	394	461
1988–89	76	366	442
1989–90	63	363	426
1990–91	71	348	419
1991–92	75	338	413
1992–93	75	330	405
1993–94	67	335	402

(*cont.*)

Years	Women coaches	Men coaches	total
1994–95	62	336	398
1995–96	58	340	398
1996–97	51	347	398
1997–98	41	357	398
1998–99	40	356	396
1999–2000	37	358	395
2000–01	38	355	393

Data source: IGHSAU

Number of 7th-Grade versus 12th-Grade Girls Playing Basketball (1999–2000)

For every 10 Iowa girls playing basketball in 7th grade . . .

in 8th grade	8.7 were playing
in 9th grade	5 were playing
in 10th grade	3.5 were playing
in 11th grade	2.7 were playing
in 12th grade	2.2 were playing

. . . fewer than three are still playing as seniors.

Data source: IGHSAU

All-Time Leaders among Six-Player Teams
Qualifying for the State Tournament

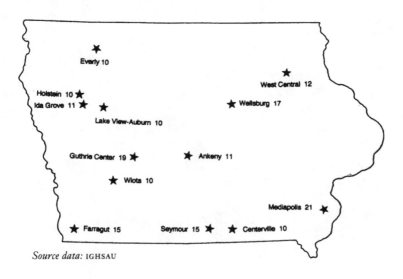

Source data: IGHSAU

Notes

Full bibliographic details are unavailable for some citations, as newspaper clippings from individuals' personal archives were frequently used as a source of information.

INTRODUCTION

1. In 1968 Boone was also midway through his first four-year term as the Southwest Iowa representative elected to the board of directors of the Iowa Girls High School Athletic Union. Two years later, Boone served a one-year stint as president of the Union, then was reelected by member schools of the Southwest District to serve on the board for a second term before announcing his retirement in 1971. Boone served as the Woodbine superintendent for almost thirty years, and the athletic complex in the town bears his name.

2. See Eitzen and Zinn, "The De-athleticization of Women," 362–70. For a feminist overview of women's basketball that discusses the dilemma between being a "lady" and "athlete" in America, see Ford, *Lady Hoopsters.*

3. T. L. Henion, "Clock Winding Down on 6-on-6 Basketball," *Omaha Sunday World-Herald*, February 7, 1993, p. 1A.

4. Berenson, *Line Basketball*, 12.

5. Vertinsky, *The Eternally Wounded Woman*, 21. For other works that examine the role of physical education for women during the Progressive Era and help to put Iowa girls' basketball into historical context, see Cahn, *Coming On Strong*; Banner, *American Beauty*; and

Messner, *Power at Play*. The message was clear, writes Messner, that "women were biologically destined to tend to the business of housework, childbearing, and childrearing," and playing sports diminished their ability to perform these tasks. As a result, girls' competitive basketball was phased out in most American states, and when girls did play, they did so "at a much reduced level"—what critics and advocates alike considered the six-player game that thrived in Iowa and a few other states (17).

6. Cahn, *Coming On Strong*, 61.

7. Quoted in Beran, *From Six-on-Six*, 30.

8. Beran, *From Six-on-Six*, 33.

9. Chisholm, *1949 Yearbook*, 126; Beran, *From Six-on-Six*, 50. For a colorful and thorough historical description of Iowa six-player girls' basketball, see Beran, *From Six-on-Six*. Beran contends that there were several interacting social, political, and economic factors that accounted for the success and duration of the Iowa game: male advocacy for girls' basketball; an absence of women physical educators who opposed competition among girls; less demand on gym space than in city schools; and acknowledgement that basketball was not too physically taxing for rural girls, whose nineteenth-century immigrant ancestors brought with them a tradition of physical activity. Other factors attributing to the success of the sport in the state, Beran argues, were that female attractiveness was not jeopardized by athletics, and basketball filled an entertainment void in small towns, becoming a source of community pride (xiv, xv).

10. Beran, *From Six-on-Six*, 155.

11. Chisholm, *1949 Yearbook*, 143.

12. Beran, *From Six-on-Six*, 100.

13. Beran, *From Six-on-Six*, 103; Bauer, "Girls Win, Boys Lose," 36.

14. "If there is a universal popular religion in America, it is to be found within the institution of sport," Harry Edwards wrote in his 1973 classic, *Sociology of Sport*. For an extended discussion of the relationship of the Protestant ethic to other spheres of social life, such as sport, see Prebish, *Religion and Sport*, 86–103, and Oriard, *Sporting with the Gods*.

For an account that shows how the paradox of play is rooted in a larger cultural question concerning the contemporary degradation of human endeavor, see Morgan, *Leftist Theories*, 129. Morgan claims that a group of social critics as diverse as John Dewey, Jurgen Habermas, and Robert Bellah share the view that advanced capitalist society has no use for "everything else it is that people do that might be properly described as noneconomic." For more on the function of play in America, including a discussion of how the muddled moral climate of early college football represented the conflicted values of the larger culture, see Oriard's *Reading Football* and *Sporting with the Gods*.

15. Shortridge, *Atlas of American Women*, 73.

16. Beran, *From Six-on-Six*, 83.

17. Bauer, "Girls Win, Boys Lose," 35.

18. Beran, *From Six-on-Six*, 101. For an insightful account of sports cultures, see Rooney, *A Geography of American Sport*. Rooney considers such factors as level of participation, local monetary support, game attendance, and press coverage in the designation of a "sports region."

19. See Fuller, *The Old Country School*, 25–41.

20. I have depended heavily on the network of coaches, educators, and former players whom I met as a sportswriter covering girls athletics in Iowa for more than a decade as well as known informants with whom I worked as a journalist reporting on such community matters as school boards and city councils. For a discussion of the use of journalistic techniques as one form of interviewing informants in ethnographic enterprises, see Agar, *The Professional Stranger*, 92. I also located informants through nonrandom (convenience or "snowball") sampling, designed to elicit new ideas and points of view. For more on this standard ethnographic practice, see Sanjek, *Fieldnotes*, 399. As for using the literary story or essay, which, according to Geertz, *Interpretation of Cultures*, 3–30, is perhaps the best form in which to present cultural analysis, compelling arguments can be found in Goodall, *Casing a Promised Land*; Shank, *Dissonant Identities*; and Van Maanen, *Tales of the Field*.

21. For an illuminating treatment of how metropolitan daily

newspapers and news magazines constructed college football as a spectacle at the turn of the century, see Oriard, *Reading Football.*

22. For a detailed, intriguing description of how players had to "convince people that women could somehow participate in sports and still be feminine," see Festle, *Playing Nice*, 32–52. This was accomplished through "apologetic behavior," defined by Festle as "behavior intended to reinforce the socially acceptable aspects of sports while minimizing the perceived violation of social norms." Apologetic behavior compelled some girls to wear ribbons in their hair when they played and coaches and officials to require opposing teams to share cookies and milk following games. "In essence, female athletes compensated for their lack of femininity on the court by making up for it in their language, looks, and behavior." Accompanying the growth of women's sports has been an emerging historical and social science literature that uses gender—the social organization of sexual difference—as an analytical tool for the study of sport and women. Cheska, *Proceedings of the Annual Meeting*, suggests that equality for women's sports will occur only when male and female traits are equally valued on the playing field. Messner, *Power at Play*, contends that throughout the twentieth century, organized sports have bolstered a "challenged and faltering ideology of male superiority" that forbade coeducational sports and resulted in the female athlete serving as contested ideological terrain (16). For a comprehensive study of how the campaign to suppress women's basketball was the "centerpiece" in the fight to control women's sports, which itself became the battleground for broader societal and cultural gender conflicts, see Cahn, *Coming On Strong.*

23. Beran, *From Six-on-Six*, 122. See also Eitzen for his exhaustive 1976 study of sport in secondary schools, "Sport and Social Status," 110–18. Eitzen found that, in spite of the opportunities Title IX provided for females, interschool sports programs continue to stress overwhelmingly the importance of boys and men and the disregard for girls and women.

24. IGHSAU *Constitution*, 1998–1999, 99–102. While most public school administrators in Iowa are men, 223 of 1,180 superintendents

and principals in the state—almost 19 percent—in the academic year 1998–99 were women according to the Iowa Department of Education. However, only 10 of the 292 full-time superintendents were women, fewer than 3.5 percent, a number not significantly different from the 1982 national figure showing that only 1.8 percent of superintendents were women.

25. The dominant metaphor regarding six-player basketball isn't dance; instead, the history of the game has turned on the metaphor and trope of "separate spheres." For a fascinating definition of this metaphor—"the figure of speech, the trope, on which historians came to rely when they described women's part in American culture" in the late nineteenth century—see Kerber, "Separate Spheres," 10. Nowhere was the language of separate spheres more metaphorical than on the basketball court, where girls literally played in two separate spheres. Guards, who weren't permitted to shoot, were confined to the defensive court, and forwards were restricted to the offensive court; neither position was allowed to cross center court. Because the game was adapted in the 1890s by women educators for whom domesticity was a major concern, the history of the Iowa game has been interpreted through the metaphor of separate spheres. For further discussion on how historians have used the trope of separate spheres to describe the domestication of basketball, see Chepko, "The Domestication of Basketball," 113–16.

1. The Curtain Is Raised on a New Game

1. Joe Monsen and Fred Monsen are pseudonyms. I have used pseudonyms for the players, their family members, coaches, teachers, and administrators associated with the Woodbine team during the 1993–94 season. All other names found in this chapter, including citizens of the community and former players and coaches, are the given names of the persons presented.

2. In the realm of sports and ethnography, there have been recent, notable works. See Adler and Adler, *Backboards and Blackboards: College Athletes and Role Engulfment* (1994), a study of a southwestern university's basketball environment in the 1980s; Bissinger, *Friday Night Lights: A Town, a Team, and a Dream* (1990), an analysis of

high school football in Odessa, Texas; and Blais, *In These Girls, Hope Is a Muscle* (1995), the description of a Massachusetts high school girls' basketball team and its community. See also Douglas Bauer's *Prairie City, Iowa: Three Seasons at Home* (1979), which does not focus on sports but captures particularly well the spiritual locus of the author's Iowa hometown.

3. Esser, who graduated from Woodbine in 1975, blazed to an American record performance of 57.3 seconds in the 400-meter hurdles that summer in the national AAU meet, a performance that stood for nearly ten years as the national high school record for the event. A quarter century later, 57.3 is still an exceptional time for a high school girl in the *open* 400-meter dash, and no Iowa prep hurdler has come within 3.8 seconds of Esser's record in the 400-meter hurdles. The 400-meter hurdles didn't become an Iowa high school event until 1979 or an Olympic event until 1984, by which time Esser had retired from competitive running. During her career, Debbie Esser won thirteen high school state track titles (still an Iowa record), captured four consecutive national collegiate titles at Iowa State University, and finished third in the 1980 World Cup competition in Montreal. (Marc Hansen, "Esser Does Three-Step Hurdles into Hall of Fame," *Des Moines Sunday Register*, July 28, 1991, 1D, 12D).

4. Unidentified coach quoted in Beran, *From Six-on-Six*, 36.

5. According to a survey completed by six history professors in Iowa, the state's high school coaches most often teach history. A survey of public high schools revealed that 57 percent of the respondents were coaches, and almost 40 percent of all Iowa history teachers coached a sport. Also, 58 percent of superintendents who responded wrote that they sometimes found it necessary to hire history and social studies teachers with coaching interests or experience over more competent noncoaching candidates. "The need to supply coaches for the wide variety of sports is a formidable influence on the hiring of teachers of history and, therefore, on the state of historical instruction in Iowa," reported the scholars conducting the survey. "Iowa is rapidly approaching the condition—if not already there— in which the ability and willingness to coach a sport are essential

qualifications for anyone who wishes to embark upon a career as a high school teacher. . . . Surely the student can learn a great deal from participating in sports. Yet the wholesale commitment to inter-scholastic athletics which pervades the schools of Iowa has had, we fear, a deleterious effect not only on historical instruction, but on all areas of high school life" (Carroll and Fitch, et al., "The Teaching of History," 13–15).

6. For a discussion of how weight training is a rationalized component of modern sport, see Guttmann, *A Whole New Ball Game*, 5–6.

7. The fact that Iowa high school boys began basketball practice one week later than girls has no lasting implications except that, unlike in other states, two separate prep sports organizations are in charge of such scheduling.

8. I gleaned this information from one of the previous season's weekly press releases from the Iowa Girls High School Athletic Union, six pages—front and back—of agate type that includes every current statistic imaginable. The release is a work of art so exhaustive that it must put similar ventures by professional and college associations to shame.

9. Jack and Mary Menken's letter was published in the *Woodbine Twiner* on February 24, 1993. The Menkens also noted how disappointed they were when told by the head coach that he had forgotten their daughter was still on the bench and had no reason for not playing her. The letter ended with this caustic remark: "Maybe when Woodbine switches to five on five girls basketball, the coach won't have to count so high and can remember who has and hasn't participated, but don't look for us in the stands if the same coach is still coaching." The problem with Franny Menken's playing time was resolved the following season when, as BJ had projected, she saw more court time in the five-player game.

10. Donald Kaul, "At Long Last, My Mission Accomplished," *Des Moines Register*, February 5, 1993, pp. 1A, 3A.

11. During the 1998–99 academic year, the same number of Iowa high schools offered girls' basketball and girls' volleyball—399 (*IGHSAU Newsletter* [Spring/Summer, 1999]). The popularity of vol-

leyball, introduced in Iowa schools in 1970, is a recent phenomenon, and its ascension parallels the demise of six-player basketball. During the 1983–84 academic year (one year before the state ruled that schools could choose between five- and six-player basketball), 365 schools offered volleyball, which was 125 fewer than those offering basketball. But as a percentage of overall high school girls' sports participation, volleyball in Iowa in 1983 ranked between 1.7 percent and 7.2 percent. Compared with the national average of 15.4 percent, Iowa ranked among the *bottom* five states for volleyball participation (Shortridge, *Atlas of American Women*, map 6.6).

2. RURAL EDUCATION AND GIRLS' BASKETBALL

1. Sarah Allen White, interview with author, Omaha NE, May 11, 1996; Betty, Carolyn, Glenda, and Ruth Nicholson, interview with author, Maynard IA, June 19, 1997; Cyndy Long, interview with author, Marshalltown IA, June 11, 1997.

2. See Reynolds, *There Goes the Neighborhood*, 4–5. In 1956 one out of every twenty high school districts in the nation was in Iowa, but this changed quickly. From 1955 to 1959, Iowa led the country in reducing the number of state school districts; it eliminated high schools with inadequate programs, decreasing the number of one-room schools (Smith, *Development of Public Instruction*, 113). From 1922, when the unsuccessful first consolidation movement ended, until 1974, Iowa's farm population dropped by more than 50 percent (from 1,005,000 to 452,000). Nevertheless, when the 1959–60 school year began, southwest Iowa's Harrison County, with a population of barely twelve thousand, still had nine high school districts and thirty-six one-room rural schools ("A Design for Educational Organization in Iowa," State of Iowa Department of Public Instruction, 1968).

3. See Alford, "School District Reorganization," 350–71.

4. See Fuller, *The Old Country School*. Fuller believes that "if there was a common Midwestern mind, it was surely shaped in large measure by the country school" (26).

5. Fuller, *The Old Country School*, 25–41. These laws permitted settlers to build schoolhouses and to tax themselves, but there was

no compulsion to do so. The system implemented charged parents a specified rate for each day their children attended school and put farmers' property in jeopardy if those bills weren't paid; thus it's easy to understand why few children attended school.

6. See Reynolds, *There Goes the Neighborhood*. "[The agrarian myth] has long involved an idealization of rural life and living and a sentimental attachment to the rural as somehow more 'natural' and moral," Reynolds writes (30).

7. See Fuller, *The Old Country School*, 45. The first Iowa school was built in 1830 in Lee County in the state's far southeastern corner, near Keokuk on the Mississippi River. Iowa was still an unorganized section of Michigan Territory. When Iowa became a state in 1846, there were already 416 schools in operation ("A Design for Educational Organization in Iowa," Iowa Department of Education, 1986, 1–2.)

8. Reynolds, *There Goes the Neighborhood*, 4–5. For detailed accounts of the effects of Progressive Era educational ideology, see also Robert and Helen Lynd's classic *Middletown in Transition*, and Cremin, *American Education*.

9. See Theobald, *Teaching the Commons*; Bryant and Grady, "Community Factors"; and Reynolds, *There Goes the Neighborhood*, 27. Theobold notes that rural schools historically engendered community allegiance, generating what scholars have identified as *centripetalism*—the tendency of various social and economic forces to centralize.

10. Fuller, *The Old Country School*, 245.

11. A spate of prominent writers in the early twentieth century, including Sinclair Lewis, Sherwood Anderson, Hamlin Garland, Ruth Suckow, and Edgar Lee Masters, confirmed that the Midwest was far from the idyllic garden romanticized in the nineteenth century. Their negative chronicles of the Midwest earned them inclusion in a literary movement, "the revolt from the village." More recently, Liahna Babener, in her essay "Bitter Nostalgia," demonstrates that one finds "bitter nostalgia" in the autobiographies of common midwesterners as well as the region's better-known chroniclers. Such ambivalence is rarely directed at midwestern education,

though, where the one-room schoolhouse in the late nineteenth century produced disproportionate numbers of national leaders in all walks of life—including those writers whose "revolt from the village" was apparently boosted by their early education. "We are so smug and complacent with our better buildings, and teachers colleges and organizations," wrote one unidentified memoirist, who progressed from a country school to an Ivy League education, "that we almost forget that learning is a personal matter like dying and that each one in the last analysis has to do it for himself" (Babener, "Bitter Nostalgia," 4).

In 1998 the National Adult Literacy Study listed Iowa as one of the top eight states in literacy, having only an estimated 13 percent of the adult population at the lowest literacy level (defined in the study as "adults displaying difficulty using certain reading, writing, and computational skills considered necessary for functioning in everyday life"). Iowa was tied with Colorado, Idaho, Minnesota, Montana, and Nebraska; only Alaska (11 percent) and New Hampshire (12 percent) fared better (*The Annual Condition Of Education Report* [Des Moines: Iowa Department of Education, 1998], xxii).

12. The biennial report of the Iowa state superintendent in 1901 listed sixteen common arguments against consolidation, with the first five as follows: 1) bad roads; 2) fear of greater expenses; 3) children "are kept too long on the road and too long from home"; 4) "careless drivers may be employed who will not attend to the comfort of the children"; 5) "people object to the removal of the little schoolhouse from the neighborhood, since it furnishes in many places, the only public meeting house. They say it will break up the Sunday school, the literary society and other neighborhood gatherings. *There is a sentiment concerning the little schoolhouse that objects to its obliteration from rural life*" (italics mine; Smith, *Development of the Iowa Department of Public Instruction*, 106.

13. The Iowa Department of Education has identified these three distinct patterns of school reorganization as having covered the following periods: consolidated school movement, 1900–22; community school movement, 1953–66; and school restructuring movement, 1985–95. According to the department, with the enactment

of the Consolidated School Law of 1906, "a statewide pattern of consolidation was intended but never fully realized. During the next 14 years, school districts which had been created on a township basis and in sub-divided townships joined with small towns and villages across the state . . . but the movement was slow in developing." Four years after the law had been passed, only ten such consolidated districts had been created, and the consolidated movement was completely halted with the agricultural recession of 1921–22 (*Annual School District Restructuring Report* [Des Moines: Iowa Department of Education, January 1990]).

14. Loren Keller, "Grand Valley School District To Be No More," *Omaha World-Herald*, March 20, 1998. The Boone Valley District near Humboldt in north-central Iowa was dissolved in 1988, and the Grand Valley District, which included Kellerton and Grand River in Ringgold and Decatur Counties on the Missouri border, was dissolved in 1997. The reason that so few districts are dissolved (or voluntarily closed by school district voters) is that districts usually choose to reorganize by one merging with another (consolidating). But Grand Valley officials, after considering that one-third of its 186 students, elementary through high school, were open-enrolled in other school districts, chose to dissolve. Control was an important factor in the decision; only the Grand Valley district voted on the question of dissolution. For reorganization, the other merging district would have also voted, and both would have had to approve the measure. And when reorganization measures fail, the state resolves the issue. "Our board wanted to maintain control over what happened to our students," said a Grand Valley official.

15. Guy Ghan, interview with author, Des Moines IA, September 8, 1997. Forty-five of Iowa's counties are expected to lose population in the twenty-five-year period from 1990 to 2015, during which time the state has a projected growth rate of 7.8 percent compared with the projected national figure of 24.7 percent (*Annual Condition of Education Report*, vii). "We don't need 950 towns in Iowa," Ghan says. For Ghan, small schools and small towns, like Iowa girls' six-player basketball, should be relegated to history as quickly as possible. "If

Russell [a southern Iowa town, population 531] were a private operation, you'd have to be foolish to invest in it," he says. "It's the same
thing with small schools. The people who opposed consolidation
were my age—they wanted a school in their town, but it wasn't going
to be for their kids. Girls' basketball was a small-town, rural Iowa
thing. And small schools have served their purpose."

16. See Kemis et al., "Perceptions of Educational Quality." The
study also revealed that parents in districts that closed a high school
held less positive perceptions of quality than did those in districts
that had not closed a high school.

17. See Priscilla Salant and Anita Waller, "What Difference Do
Local Schools Make? A Literature Review and Bibliography," prepared for Annenberg Rural Trust Policy Program, September 25,
1998; Bryant and Grady, "Community Factors," 21–26; W. H.
Dreier, "What Happens When the High School Leaves the Community?" paper presented at the Annual National Conference of
People United for Rural Education, Des Moines IA, February 5–
6, 1982; W. H. Dreier and W. Goudy, "Is There Life in Town
after the Death of the High School?" paper presented at the Annual Rural and Small Schools Conference, Manhattan KS, October
24, 1994; and Marjorie Coeyman, "Changing Times and Budgets
Put the Squeeze on Small-Town Schools," *Christian Science Monitor*,
November 24, 1998, p. 15s.

18. Catherine Burris, "Moneta, Population 26, Moves to Disincorporate," *Sioux City Journal*, November 11, 1996, p. 1.

19. See Scott Johnson, " 'Not Altogether Ladylike': The Prema-
ture Demise of Girls' Interscholastic Basketball in Illinois," paper
presented at meeting of the National Agency for the Advancement
of Sports and Health (NAASH), Chicago, 1991; Grundy, *Learning to
Win*, 114.

20. Lacher, "The *Register* Regroups," 1–2.

21. McElwain, *Profiles in Communication*, 4, 43–44.

22. Lacher, "The *Register* Regroups," 2.

23. Maury White, "North: He Was Reporter and Referee," *Des
Moines Register*, June 30, 1996, pp. 4D, 8D; luncheon program,
Fourth Annual Honors Luncheon of the Iowa Girls High School

Athletic Union, March 11, 1972, Veterans Memorial Auditorium, Des Moines IA.

24. Chuck Offenburger, "Old Pen Pals Finally Meet," *Des Moines Register*, February 12, 1998, p. 1T; Chisholm, "Girls' Basketball in Iowa," 143.

25. IGHSAU, "The Cover Girl," *1970 Iowa Girls' State Basketball Championship Program*; IGHSAU, "The Cover Girl," *1968 Iowa Girls' State Basketball Championship Program*; IGHSAU, "The Cover Girl," *1969 Iowa Girls' State Basketball Championship Program*.

26. IGHSAU, "1992 E. Wayne Cooley Scholarship Award," *1992 Iowa Girls' State Basketball Championship Program*.

27. Kaul, "At Long Last, My Mission Accomplished."

28. Kaul, "At Long Last, My Mission Accomplished."

29. Jane Schorer Meisner, "Final Season: High School Senior Learns Valuable Lessons on the Sidelines," *Des Moines Register*, March 7, 1993, pp. 2E, 3E, 5E.

30. Stephen Buttry, "Belles of the Ball: The Legacy of the '71 Farragut Adettes," *Omaha World-Herald*, four-part series, March 3, 1996, pp. 1A, 18A; March 4, pp. 1A, 8A; March 5, pp. 1A, 2A; March 6, pp. 1A, 8A.

31. Dan Johnson, "Remember Six-Player?" *Des Moines Register*, November 8, 1997, pp. 1S, 4S; Laura Murray, "Rallying behind Team," *Des Moines Register*, March 5, 1998, pp. 1A, 3A; Doug Thomas, "Recognition Comes with Basketball Titles," *Omaha World-Herald*, January 19, 1998, pp. 1A, 2A.

32. Iowa schools that offered both girls' and boys' basketball almost uniformly scheduled the high school varsity girls' game before the boys' contest, a practice that continues today in many small districts. "West Siders Win Athletic Contests: They Have Everything But the Good Looks," *Woodbine Twiner*, September 9, 1920, pp. 1, 4.

33. *Spencer Daily Reporter*, June 28, 1980, pp. 1–4A; Rothenberg, "Is It a Peep Show or a Sport?" *Wall Street Journal* (1969), 1.

34. *Hawkeye*, 1944, University of Iowa yearbook (Iowa City: University of Iowa, 1944), 264–68.

35. *Shipmates*, 1947, Woodbine High School yearbook (Lincoln NE: Seright Publication Bureau, 1947).

36. *Shipmates*, 1961, Woodbine High School yearbook (Lincoln
NE: Seright Publication Bureau, 1961).

3. REDHEADS AND BLUE DEVILS

1. An inspection of one small Iowa community helps reveal how
girls' basketball functions in the local culture. Maynard (population
500) is more typical of the state's small towns than atypical, and there
are other similar, consolidated school districts whose success in girls'
basketball matched that of West Central High School.

2. All quotes from Deb Kaune in this chapter are taken from a
telephone interview with the author, June 13, 1997.

3. Just how seriously area residents took basketball in the West
Central Community School District was evident in a 1973 letter
directed to Wayne Cooley and signed by the superintendent and
entire West Central school board. School officials in other states
likely did not concern themselves with such matters, but the West
Central board complained to Cooley about the performance of a
basketball official—a Marshalltown elementary teacher—who, according to these fans, whistled an inordinate number of fouls on
the Blue Devils in a regional tournament game. The board urged
Cooley "to remove the license" of the official (West Central Community School District Board to E. Wayne Cooley, March 2, 1973,
Ruth Johnson personal archives).

4. Almost thirty years later, Cooley recalled the controversy over
the Kaune transfer. "The transfer of student Deb Kaune from Starmont to West Central of Maynard was cleared of questionable recruiting. There was no ineligibility nor that of penalty associated
with the transfer from one member school to another" (E. Wayne
Cooley, correspondence with author, September 29, 1997).

5. Gene Klinge quotes are taken from a telephone interview on
June 13, 1997, and a personal interview on November 15, 1997.

6. Tension between the arch rivals over the Kaune affair lingered
more than a decade later. In 1985 one thousand fans ignored a blizzard and jammed the Maynard gym to watch the two teams play, but
an electrical outage shut the lights out in the fourth quarter, causing
no small consternation for West Central coach Gene Klinge. "We

had turned the corner and had maybe an eight-point lead when the lights went out," he recalls. "It was pitch black—no security lights—and we had a heated rivalry with Starmont, partially because of the Deb Kaune situation. The lights were off for maybe forty-five minutes, and [Starmont coach] Darrell Severson and I took our girls to the locker rooms. The crowd was really hot; both sides had such tremendous followings. Darrell said, 'We're gonna finish this damned game tonight,' and we did." With Klinge's son, the West Central mascot, donning a Blue Devil head and leading cheers, tension was diffused when the opposing fans engaged in a yelling match until electricity was returned. (Gene Klinge, telephone interview with author, June 13, 1997.)

7. All quotes from Gail Meyer in this chapter are taken from an interview with the author, Maynard IA, June 17, 1997.

8. After coaching West Central to the state tournament again in 1975, 1983, and 1989, Klinge closed the books on six-player basketball by taking the Blue Devils to the tourney in the game's last season in 1993. His team then qualified for state the first three years of the five-player game. Gene Klinge didn't miss a step when the game changed, and following the 1997–98 season, when his 735 career victories—all at West Central over thirty-six years—led all active Iowa girls' basketball coaches, the National High School Athletics Coaches Association honored him as the national coach of the year in girls' basketball. "I've got to feel good because a lot of coaches got out," he says. "And a lot of girls quit. The biggest problem was that kids were caught who were guards. Shooting is an art, and you don't learn it in one year. Several of them saw the handwriting on the wall. Six-player was such a family affair, but you couldn't get a book to read up on it. With five, I had to go to school on it. It concerned me, and I did a lot of talking to other coaches. But basketball is still basketball, and those first three years of five[-player], when we went to state, we had kids who could run the court" (Gene Klinge, telephone interview with author, June 13, 1997.)

9. All quotes from Glenda Poock in this chapter are taken from an interview with the author, Maynard IA, June 17, 1997.

10. Rich Holm, "Montezuma Draft Prompts Change," *Oelwein*

Daily Register, March 8, 1972, p. 2; Carroll Rugland, interview with author, Hampton IA, June 18, 1997.

11. Rich Holm, "Jennings, Koufax in Same Boat," *Oelwein Daily Register*, March 10, 1972, p. 2.

12. Holm, "Jennings, Koufax in Same Boat."

13. Buster and Juanita Parsons, interview with author, Maynard IA, June 19, 1997.

14. For this particular passage—a backyard, summer afternoon's conversation between an elderly woman and her daughters—I have chosen to represent it in the form of dramatic script (that is, a simple, verbatim transcription). The conversation would lose something in translation were it presented in another form.

15. While Maynard was losing the 1959 championship game to Gladbrook, 76–60, a blizzard dumped seven inches of snow on Des Moines and forced five thousand fans to spend the night at Vets Auditorium. The blizzard earned a place in tournament folklore after a disc jockey for Des Moines' KIOA radio, Forrest "Frosty" Mitchell, stuck in his own driveway, walked six miles in the snow to the station, grabbed a handful of records, and took them to the auditorium, where he provided the music for an impromptu sock hop for thousands. Mitchell became a popular sports announcer and is still broadcasting the tournament forty years later (Beran, *From Six-on-Six*, 76–77).

16. Les Hueser, interview with author, Hubbard IA, June 11, 1997.

17. "Officers Named to Head School Reorganization," *Logan Herald-Observer*, March 26, 1959, p. 1; "Give Enrollment for County Schools," *Logan Herald-Observer*, December 29, 1960, p. 1; "Reorganization Petitions Filed for West Part of County," *Logan Herald-Observer*, April 6, 1961, p. 1; Ila Wohlers, "Just Observations," *Logan Herald-Observer*, June 1, 1961, p. 2; Sharon Elkins, interview with author, Council Bluffs IA, November 18, 1998.

18. "Hold Meeting on Reorganization," *Logan Herald-Observer*, October 6, 1960, p. 1; "Petitions Filed for Logan-Magnolia School District; Hearing Is April 24th," *Logan Herald-Observer*, March 30, 1961, p. 1; "Hearing Held Monday for Proposed New Community

School District," *Logan Herald-Observer*, April 27, 1961, p. 1; "Voters Approve Logan-Magnolia Community School District Tuesday," *Logan Herald-Observer*, May 25, 1961, p. 1.

19. Eugene Evans, interview with author, Logan IA, November 12, 2000.

20. Betty Emrich, interview with author, Davenport IA, August 5, 1999.

21. John Carlson, "Team Inspired by Voices from Past," *Des Moines Register*, March 8, 1998, pp. 1A, 4A.

22. Chuck Offenburger, "Those Old Small-Town Sports Wars," *Des Moines Register*, January 18, 1998, p. 1B.

23. Fuller, *The Old Country School*, and West, *Growing Up with the Country*.

24. Guttmann, *A Whole New Ball Game*, 5–6. Guttmann has distinguished modern sports from primitive, ancient, medieval, and Renaissance sports by certain characteristics that, while not unique to the modern world, "taken together . . . clearly distinguished modern sports from those of the past." Those characteristics include secularism, equality, bureaucratization, specialization, rationalization, quantification, and an obsession with records.

25. Reynolds, *There Goes the Neighborhood*, 14, 42, and Shortridge, *The Middle West*. The cultural geographer James R. Shortridge casts the "middle landscape" as that juncture of culture and landscape achieved in Iowa, which he locates as "the true center of the Midwest" due, in part, to its "conservative, moral, solid culture."

26. Grundy, "From Amazons to Glamazons," 139–40. Nowhere does the "clear testimony to the power local institutions could wield" provide a sharper contrast than between the North Carolina and Iowa girls' athletic associations. Whereas E. Wayne Cooley was "the great compromiser" at the Iowa Girls High School Athletic Union, which kept the six-player rules but built the nation's greatest girls' state tournament, a primary organizer of the North Carolina Girls High School Athletic Association was Mary Channing Coleman, a fierce opponent of varsity competition for girls and the educator, according to Grundy, most responsible for the decline of North Carolina girls' basketball (Grundy, *Learning to Win*, 127).

27. "Fewest Farms since before the Civil War," *Woodbine Twiner*, November 16, 1994, p. 8; Robert Wolf, "Iowa: Living in the Third World," *Des Moines Register*, July 16, 1995, p. 3C; Bill Sheldon, "A Bolt of Hope for Dying Towns: Wes Jackson Hopes to Revive an Economy," *Kansas City Star*, January 1, 1995, p. 4B; Sam Roberts, "Yes, a Small Town Is Different," *New York Times*, August 27, 1995, sec. 4, p. 1.

28. The historian John Bodnar, in examining the divergent memories of respective generations, observes that Americans of the Depression generation (for him, born between 1902 and 1924), believed that the primary institutions and authorities that ruled their lives and pulled them through hard times "would never need to be changed." But the baby boomers (born between 1946 and 1964) "challenged virtually all the social mores and political values that had come before." They concentrated on self-realization while the older generation focused on accommodating authority (Bodnar, "Generational Memory"). Maynard's Nicholson sisters are "tweeners," born between the Depression and the baby boom, but their submission to authority and other personality traits make them allies with the older generation, as are women who played basketball into the early 1970s. The fact that Title IX was passed in 1972 is no coincidence— among the sweeping changes resulting from this legislation was the subversion of social and cultural paradigms.

29. Fuller, *The Old Country School*, 47.

30. IGHSAU, "The Cover Girl," *1978 Iowa Girls' State Basketball Championship Program*, 34; IGHSAU, "The Cover Girl," *1974 Iowa Girls' State Basketball Championship Program*, 7.

4. HARLOTS AND LADIES

1. All quotes from Ruth Lang in this chapter are taken from an interview with the author, Sumner IA, November 15, 1997.

2. Les Teeling (retired Sumner coach and English teacher), telephone interview with author, December 5, 1997.

3. Cahn, *Coming On Strong*, viii, and Brumberg, *The Body Project*, 6–7, 91.

4. See Cahn, *Coming On Strong*, 84, and "Pretty Virginia Harris." Virginia "Ginny" Harris Mango received between 150 and 200 letters from readers after the *Life* article appeared in 1940. "It was fun, but I didn't get a big head," she said. "I didn't have time to answer them, so I threw them out. I got just one nasty letter." After high school, Harris, a four-year starter at guard, played basketball for Mason City's Hamilton Business College and Davenport's American Institute of Commerce before marrying and settling in Waverly (Iowa). The absence of local girls' basketball in Waverly until after Title IX prevented her daughter from competing. "My mother had played the earlier, three-court game," said Harris Mango. "I would liked to have played five-player" (Ginny Mango, interview with author, Waverly IA, June 12, 1997).

5. Les Hueser, interview with author, Hubbard IA, June 11, 1997; Gene Klinge, interview with author, Cedar Falls IA, November 15, 1997.

6. Bloom, *A Pictorial History of Harrison County, Iowa*, 50, 60, 69, 73.

7. *Iowa Educational Directory* (Des Moines: Department of Public Instruction), for school years 1935–36, 1940–41, 1945–56, 1950–51, 1955–56, 1960–61, 1965–55, 1970–71, and 1975–76.

8. *Report of the Department of Public Instruction* (Des Moines: Department of Public Instruction), for school years 1930–31, 1935–36, 1940–41, 1944–45, 1950–51, and 1953–54. The number of women teachers during those academic years compared with the total number of Iowa teachers (both elementary and high school) are as follows: 13,212 of 16,418 (1930–31); 21,687 of 26,027 (1935–36); 19,989 of 25,047 (1940–41); 20,250 of 23,120 (1944–45); 17,576 of 23,450 (1950–51); and 18,008 of 24,535 (1953–54). The percentage of male teachers fell to 12 percent (20,250 of 23,120) in 1944–45, during World War II.

9. IGHSAU, *1948 Iowa Girls' State Basketball Championship Program*.

10. Messner, *Power At Play*, 17, and Festle, *Playing Nice*, 45. For an account of how women had to manage the contradiction between their role as athlete and as female, and how leaders managed the athletes, see Cahn, *Coming On Strong*, 100–101, 208.

11. IGHSAU, "The Cover Girl," *1969 Iowa Girls' State Basketball Championship Program*.

12. Powers, The "*Girl Question*," 2; Tyack and Hansot, *Learning Together*, 136–37.

13. From "Looking Back, 40 Years Ago," *Woodbine Twiner*, September 13, 2000, p. 4.

14. "Commercial Awards," *Shipmates*, 1947; "FHA," *Shipmates 1961*; "FCSC," *Woodbine Tigers*, 1994, Woodbine High School yearbook (n.p.); *Quintessence*, 1969, Missouri Valley High School yearbook (n.p.), 30, 32, 34.

15. MHS *Claw*, 1970–76, Manilla High School yearbook (n.p.).

16. Steve Padilla, interview with author, Council Bluffs IA, October 27, 2000.

17. Bauer, *Prairie City, Iowa*, 39.

18. See Eitzen, "Sport and Social Status"; Feltz and Weiss, "Impact of Girls' Interscholastic Sport Participation"; and Thirer and Wright, "Sport and Social Status."

19. Cahn, *Coming On Strong*, 24.

20. For a compelling analysis of cheerleading in North Carolina, see Grundy, *Learning to Win*. The cheerleading model "took on enormous force, coming to seem for many a timeless reflection of gender roles and expectations, a physical embodiment of a supposedly natural order" (114).

21. Bob Shields, director, World Cheerleader Council, "Programs for Cheerleaders and Drill Teams," speech delivered at the National Federation of State High School Associations annual meeting, Milwaukee WI, July 8, 1977; Ruth Johnson to Joe Deines, November 5, 1974, Ruth Johnson personal archives.

22. Stephen Buttry, "Coach's Lessons Lasted Long after Final Buzzer," *Omaha World-Herald*, March 5, 1996, pp. 1A, 2A.

23. Carroll Rugland, interview with author, Hampton IA, June 18, 1997; Gene Klinge, interview with author, Cedar Falls IA, November 15, 1997.

24. Tom Ramsey, interview with author, Farragut IA, November 21, 2000; Buttry, "Coach's Lessons," 2.

25. Eugene Evans, interview with author, Logan IA, November 12, 2000.

26. All quotes from Vadonna Hall in this chapter are taken from an interview with the author, Atlantic IA, November 9, 2000.

27. Colleen Kenney, "No Slam Dunk for Coaches As Girls' Motivations Differ," *Omaha World-Herald*, January 16, 2000, p. 1C.

28. Kenney, "No Slam Dunk for Coaches," p. 1C.

29. Gail Hartigan, interview with author, Treynor IA, November 17, 2000.

30. Ruth Johnson, interview with author, Davenport IA, August 16, 1999.

31. Grundy, *Learning to Win*, 116–18, and Cahn, *Coming On Strong*, 100.

32. *Shipmates*, 1958, Woodbine High School yearbook.

33. Published in "Here and There in Dunlap," *Dunlap Reporter*, September 2, 1999, p. 3.

34. Beran, *From Six-on-Six*, 18–22, 34–38, 71.

35. Beran, *From Six-on-Six*, 18–22, 34–38, 71.

36. Bloom, *A Pictorial History of Harrison County, Iowa*, 88.

37. Eitzen and Zinn, "The De-athleticization of Women," 362–70, and *Iowa Girls' State Basketball Championship Program* for 1968, 1969, 1970, 1973, 1974, 1975, 1978, 1992, 1999. Using Eitzen and Zinn's criteria (use of the feminine suffix *-ette* or the prefix *lady*), thirty of the forty-eight state tournament teams from 1968 through 1970 had sexist names; a similar analysis of the state qualifiers from 1973 through 1975—just after Title IX passed—reveals nearly the same figures, twenty-nine of forty-eight. Only after competitive basketball programs were started in Iowa's larger towns and cities and these teams began qualifying for the state tournament did sexist team names begin to dwindle. Many of the larger schools introduced basketball programs the same year that Title IX was passed (1972) and were sensitive to the gender issues implicit in the legislation; these school districts, more often than not, avoided sexist titles. Consequently, the 1978 tournament included more teams with non-sexist names (nine) than with sexist titles (seven), the predictable re-

sult of having teams qualify from cities like Dubuque, Cedar Rapids, Ames, and Fort Dodge. The difference in the number of city versus rural Iowa teams with sexist names was evident at the 1992 state tournament: eleven of the sixteen six-player teams used the feminine suffix *-ette* or prefix *lady* in their names, while the same held true for only three of the eight five-player teams, all from larger schools (recall that from 1985 through 1993 both games were played). By the 1999 tournament, the use of sexist team names had diminished considerably; only eight of the thirty-two qualifying teams (25 percent) contained *-ette* or *lady*. The small towns apparently had been less offended than their city cousins by the supposed violation, and they moved more slowly to correct it—just as they had with the game as a whole.

5. The Longs and the Langerman Twins

1. All quotes from Cyndy Long in this chapter are taken from an interview with the author, Marshalltown IA, June 5, 1997. The poems of Cyndy Long are collected in her scrapbooks, which also contain clippings from local newspapers that are mentioned.

2. According to Cyndy Long, Warriors owner Frank Muehle drafted Denise Long because he was trying to start a professional women's league and he considered the Iowa star a good player with whom to begin.

3. Lois Jacobs, "Denise Sets Big Goal—She Makes It," *Marshalltown Times-Republican*, March 7, 1968.

4. Jacobs, "Denise Sets Big Goal"; Mary Hammill, "Union-Whitten Packed, Ready for Tourney," *Marshalltown Times-Republican*, March 9, 1968.

5. Quoted in Jacobs, "Denise Sets Big Goal"; Dearrel Bates, "Cobras to Face Pocahontas in Quarterfinals," *Marshalltown Times-Republican*, March 14, 1968.

6. Ron Maly, "Long Sets Girls' Record: 93!" *Des Moines Register*, March 14, 1968, p. 1s; "Olson Duels Long in Title Game," *Des Moines Register*, March 16, 1968, p. 1s; "Union-Whitten Wins It: 113–107!" *Des Moines Register*, March 17, 1968, p. 1s; Jim Moackler,

"Fans against Us, Says Everly Coach," *Des Moines Register*, March 18, 1968, p. 16s.

7. Darrel Bates, "Overtime Needed by U-W to Defeat Everly," *Marshalltown Times-Republican*, March 18, 1968; Chuck Burdick, "Long, Olson Rated Best," *Des Moines Register*, March 18, 1968; "1,000 Cars Join Caravan for Champs," *Des Moines Register*, March 18, 1968; "1,000 Fans Welcome Home Union-Whitten Champions," *Eldora Herald-Ledger*, March 19, 1968.

8. The Langerman twins' success raises questions about social construction and matters of agency and freedom for Iowa women in the 1930s. See Maury White, "Tall Tale: Twins Won Twin Titles for Different Towns," *Des Moines Register*, March 9, 1992, pp. 1s, 5s.

9. White, "Tall Tale".

10. For a thorough analysis of how women manipulated domesticity to gain a foothold in more public arenas, see Shapiro, "History and Feminist Theory," 6. According to Shapiro, " 'permeability' and 'overlap' describe more accurately than does 'separation' the complex and ambiguous relations between the world prescribed for men and the designated realm of women" (6).

11. See Kerber, "Separate Spheres," for discussion on the trope of separate spheres. She suggests that the remnants of separate spheres in today's society are not the cause but only symptoms of a "particular and historically located gender system" whose reconstruction is related to major issues of power.

12. Chuck Offenburger, "Where Girls Become Legends," *Des Moines Register*, March 9, 1995, p. 2A. The twenty-first century ushered in a more ethnically diverse Iowa. According the 2000 census, in the 1990s one of every three new Iowans was Hispanic, boosting the state's Hispanic population to more than eighty-two thousand. Almost fifty thousand Latinos—primarily drawn to Iowa's meat-packing industry—immigrated from a half dozen Central American countries and Mexico (Thomas Beaumont, "Latinos Seek Security, Safety in Iowa," *Des Moines Register*, March 18, 2001, p. 1A). Sports have been used in Iowa to help immigrants deepen community ties. In Storm Lake, where one-third of the high school's 630 students are minorities, girls' basketball coach Stacey Van Der Sloot runs a Sat-

urday basketball program for third- through sixth-grade girls that is geared toward the newcomers and emphasizes participation over competition. "This is the first exposure for some minority groups," Van Der Sloot said. "You have to say, 'This is a ball. It bounces. Here's how to throw it'" (John Naughton, "Newcomers Learn to Play Basketball," *Des Moines Register*, March 4, 2001, p. 4A).

13. Stephen Buttry, "The Way the Ball Bounces: 1971 Champs' Lives Mirror Changing Times," *Omaha World-Herald*, March 6, 1996, pp. 1A, 8A; "Manilla Girls' State Basketball Team Honored on Anniversary," *Denison Bulletin*, July 6, 1999.

14. Rhea Wigg, interview with author, Council Bluffs IA, December 8, 1998.

15. Myrna Hauschildt Feekin, interview with author, Council Bluffs IA, February 16, 1999.

16. Sarah Allen White, interview with author, Omaha NE, May 11, 1996.

17. All quotes from Shawna and Stacey Paskert in this chapter are taken from an interview with the author, Omaha NE, May 11, 1996.

18. Presently the women's basketball coach at the University of Northern Iowa in Cedar Falls, Tony DiCecco has the rare distinction of having coached qualifiers for both the Iowa girls' state tournament and the NCAA women's tourney. DiCecco coached at two Iowa basketball hotbeds—West Central of Maynard (1971–73) and Montezuma (1973–1989)—before moving to the college level at Creighton University.

19. Sandy Van Cleave, interview with author, Montezuma IA, June 5, 1997. Sandy Van Cleave's experiences and opinions mirror those of many other former players. Already five foot ten in the sixth grade, Van Cleave was practicing with the high school team when she was in eighth grade.

20. Beran, *From Six-on-Six*, 202; Women Head Basketball Coaches (November 1, 2000), data provided by the Iowa Girls High School Athletic Union, February 2001.

21. Beran, *From Six-on-Six*, 202; Women Head Basketball Coaches (November 1, 2000), data provided by the Iowa Girls High School Athletic Union, February 2001; Gail Hartigan, interview

with author, November 17, 2000; Lopiano quoted in Cliff Brunt, "Girls Flock to the Court, But Few Women Are Calling the Shots," *Omaha World-Herald*, March 2, 2001, pp. 1–2A.

22. Viv and Charles "Mose" Mosher, interview with author, Allison IA, June 18, 1997; Les Hueser, interview with author, Hubbard IA, June 11, 1997.

23. "Ida Grove to Hold First Girls' Basketball Clinic," *Ida County Pioneer Record*, June 18, 1970, p. 1; Iowa Girls High School Athletic Union, *The IGBA Replay*; "Name Coaches, Girls of Iowa BB Academy," *Ida County Pioneer Record*, July 19, 1973, p. 3; Northern Indiana Historical Society, South Bend IN, All-American Girls Professional Baseball League, 1943–1954, http://www.aagpbl.org (retrieved February 16, 2001). "A healthy mind and a healthy body are the true attributes of the All-American girl," proclaimed the league's charm school guide. Among the rules of conduct were: at no time was a player to appear in the stands in her uniform; "boyish bobs" were forbidden; and all living quarters and eating places were to be approved by the chaperones.

24. Diana Melby, telephone interview with author, February 9, 2001; Deb Kaune, telephone interview with author, February 9, 2001.

6. The Demise of the Six-Player Game

1. Betty J. Sammons, Iowa DGWS basketball chairperson, to Barbara Sipes, basketball clinic director, April 28, 1969, Ruth Johnson personal archives; Division for Girls and Women's Sports, *Report On Basketball 1969–1970*; DGWS, *Philosophy and Standards for Girls and Women's Sports*, 32–34.

2. Gilbert and Williamson, "Women in Sport"; Associated Press, "Doderer Wants to End Dominance by Men over Iowa Girls' Athletics," *Omaha World-Herald*, September 15, 1977; Sue Follon, executive director, the Iowa Commission on the Status of Women, to E. Wayne Cooley, IGHSAU executive director, August 17, 1978, Ruth Johnson personal archives; Iowa Women's Political Caucus, "Women's Sports: From Here to Equality," in 1978 IWPC newsletter; Gordon E. Allen, legal director, Iowa Civil Liberties Union,

to E. Wayne Cooley, December 22, 1976, Ruth Johnson personal archives; George F. Will, "Is Iowa Girls' Basketball a Human Rights Issue?" *Des Moines Register*, October 26, 1978, p. 11A.

3. "Girls Anxious to Compete," *Des Moines Register*, March 5, 1920, p. 8; "Correctionville Girls Win Drake's Invitation Basketball Meet," *Des Moines Register*, March 14, 1920, p. 1s. Nearly one-half of Iowa's high schools had been introduced to *boys'* basketball before the first boys' state basketball tournament was held in Iowa City in 1912. However, there were communities where the girls played basketball before the boys, which was the case in Spirit Lake. There, in the century's first decade, Coach John Webb recalled that girls taught the Spirit Lake boys how to play. Petersen, "Genesis of High School Basketball," 111.

4. Chisholm, *1949 Yearbook*, 26; Beran, *From Six-on-Six*, 122; Women Head Basketball Coaches (November 1, 2000), data provided by the IGHSAU, February 2001; Brunt, "Girls Flock to the Court," 1.

5. Petersen, "Beginnings of Girls' Basketball," 122–24.

6. Petersen, "Beginnings of Girls' Basketball," 127.

7. E. Wayne Cooley, interview with author, Des Moines IA, March 16, 2000.

8. E. Wayne Cooley, interview with the author, March 16, 2000. Opinions varied on what the future held for the Iowa Girls High School Athletic Union when Cooley, who had served as executive secretary for forty-six years, retired in 2000. "The consensus is that the Union will be dissipated when Cooley goes," former board member Connie Shafar said. "No one is being groomed to take his place" (interview with author, Davenport IA, August 16, 1999). Cooley, however, believed just the opposite: "We have strong leadership here. All the employees are very experienced—only another and I are aged—and I have confidence the school administrators will keep the Union in place," he said. Cooley, again, was right: the Union didn't miss a step when he retired on October 1, 2002, turning over control of the IGHSAU to Troy Dannen. "I sense I belong in the past and I want to belong in the future," Cooley told the *Des Moines Register* on his last day in forty-eight years on the job (John

Naughton, "Tearful Cooley Says Goodbye to 'The Iowa Girl,'" *Des Moines Register*, October 1, 2002, p. 1C).

9. Beran, *From Six-on-Six*, 191.

10. IGHSAU, Iowa Girls High School Athletic Union Coaching School program, August 13–16, 1973, Fort Dodge IA.

11. Governor Robert D. Ray to Eugene Evans, March 18, 1974, Eugene Evans personal archives; program for the Retail Merchants Bureau 43rd Anniversary Breakfast for the Girls' State Basketball Championship, March 14, 1974, (Des Moines: Chamber of Commerce).

12. Gilbert and Williamson, "Women in Sport," 50.

13. E. Wayne Cooley, interview with the author, March 16, 2000. After almost a half century of directing the only high school girls' athletic association in America, Cooley couldn't think of anything that led him to this line of work other than his compulsion to have girls on an equal footing with boys. His most memorable accomplishment was already having an equal-opportunity system in place when Title IX was put into effect.

14. Beran, *From Six-on-Six*, 189–90.

15. Beran, *From Six-on-Six*, 189–90; *Iowa Girls High School Athletic Union 1977 Bulletin*, no. 61 (Des Moines: IGHSAU): 15, 20, 24; Eugene Evans, interview with author, Logan IA, November 11, 2000; Report on Iowa Girls High School Athletic Union, audit provided by Nolte, Cornman & Company, Des Moines IA, June 30, 1977; Ivan W. Evans, assistant executive secretary, Oklahoma Secondary School Activities Association, "Organization and Costs of State Events," paper presented at the National Federation of State High School Associations Annual Meeting, Milwaukee WI, July 6, 1977.

16. *Iowa Girls High School Athletic Union 1977 Bulletin*, 15, 16, 20; Tony J. Abramovich, Veterans Memorial Auditorium manager, to E. Wayne Cooley, October 14, 1974, Ruth Johnson personal archives. By 2000 the Union's total income had increased to almost $2,254,000, although basketball ($908,00) provided a considerably smaller percentage than it had in 1977. The biggest change in income activity was that in the year 2000 volleyball's contribution had grown to more than $508,000. The current four-class basket-

ball tournament requires the Union to provide transportation and lodging for thirty-two teams—twice as many as the six-player game's Sweet Sixteen arrangement. Expenses for the 2000 tournament were $344,000, resulting in a gross profit for basketball of more than a half million dollars ($561,000). The financial ruin that six-player supporters believed would result in the changeover to five-player basketball has not occurred (*Iowa Girls High School Athletic Union 2000 Bulletin*, no. 85 [Des Moines: IGHSAU]: 7, 12).

17. Ruth Johnson, "DGWS Secondary Conference," *1971 DGWS Newsletter* (Des Moines: DGWS), 13. In fact the DGWS in 1971 might be described as operating under the jurisdiction of the Union, or perhaps better defined as a liaison organization. Its chairs were listed in the Union bulletin beneath the Union's board of directors. *Iowa Girls High School Athletic Union 1970 Bulletin*, no. 52 (Des Moines: IGHSAU): 4. The DGWS, before becoming a division of AAHPER in 1958, was called the National Section for Girls and Women's Sports, the group that resulted from the 1940 merging of the Women's Division of the National Amateur Athletic Federation and the National Section on Women's Athletics (DGWS, *Philosophy and Standards for Girls and Women's Sports*, 4).

18. Eugene Evans to John McClintock, October 6, 1978, Eugene Evans personal archives.

19. Dr. Judith Bischoff to Merilee Mateer, October 19, 1972, Ruth Johnson personal archives. Robert Smiley, a longtime Union official, recalled that in 1972 HEW's ruling on six-player basketball's compliance with Title IX was still six years away, and whether or not the game violated the law caused confusion among school officials in Iowa and elsewhere. When other states had to adopt girls' athletics in the early 1970s, school officials scrambling for coaches found it easier to adopt five-player basketball rules than six-player because officials and coaches were already familiar with the full-court game (Robert Smiley, e-mail correspondence with author, April 4, 2001).

20. Beran, *From Six-on-Six*, 194–95; Ruth Johnson, interview with author, Davenport IA, August 16, 1999; Ruth Johnson to E. Wayne Cooley, October 7, 1969; Jo Ann Oldorf, IDGWS chairperson,

to women physical educators at junior and senior high schools of Iowa, August 29, 1974; both in Ruth Johnson personal archives.

21. Ruth Johnson, interview with author, August 16, 1999; "'I' Sweater Girls," in *Hawkeye*, 1923, University of Iowa yearbook (Iowa City, Iowa: University of Iowa, 1923), 409.

22. Ruth Johnson to Judith Bischoff, October 28, 1972, Ruth Johnson personal archives; Ruth Johnson, interview with author, August 16, 1999.

23. Ruth Johnson, interview with author, August 16, 1999. Johnson couldn't play basketball because she attended school in Iowa City, which didn't offer the sport at midcentury.

24. Johnson to Bischoff, October 28, 1972.

25. Editorial broadcast on KOEL Radio 950, Oelwein IA, December 15, 1972; Johnson to Bischoff, October 28, 1972.

26. Ruth Johnson to E. Wayne Cooley, November 16, 1972, Ruth Johnson personal archives.

27. The other woman whose name was placed on the final ballot for the "lady chair position" on the board was Connie Shafer, who, in 1974, was a young coach at Hudson High School (IGHSAU *Newsletter* [Fall 1974]). Shafer lost that first election to Johnson, but she later became one of only four women to have held a voting membership in the Union. Shafer was a five-foot, all-state forward whose 48.8 point average was the second highest in Iowa in her senior year at Bedford High School in 1965. She was also the IGHSAU's state tournament program cover girl. With a 322-184 coaching record, Shafer retired in 1996, after her Pleasant Valley team competed in the state tournament. At the time she was the female coach with the most wins in Iowa history, a title Gail Hartigan now holds. In 1979 Shafer coached her Hudson team to state, making her one of the few women coaches to take teams to both the six- and five-player state tournaments (John Naughton, "Shafar to Discover New Passion— Leisure Time," *Des Moines Register*, March 6, 1996, p. 3s).

Ruth Johnson, interview with author, August 16, 1999. She is quick to lay blame for the disappearance of her colleague's "gentlemanly" behavior on "women's lib crap," but hesitant to give the women's movement any credit for forcing the Union to give women a vote on the board. Similarly, Ruth Johnson does not necessarily believe that there should be more than one female board member. "I don't think the [required female] Union vote was to placate the women's libbers," she said. "Sometimes women are not supporting the right things. I don't like the direction of the current women's movement." Johnson said that the Union's constitutional rule that board members must be school administrators, which inevitably results in a male majority rule, is understandable. "We need people who know all aspects of education, and that's why they have the rule," she said. "I won't speculate whether or not it's right. I do know that you ought to pick the person best suited for something, regardless of sex. The best qualified person should be given a job."

28. Thomas A. Fogarty, " 'Little Woman' to Feminism: A Change in Views," *Des Moines Register*, December 22, 1993, pp. 1A, 6A.

29. Henry Rybus, "Title IX, ERA's, 14th Amendment and Sex-Separated Programs," and Matt Otte, "Promoting State Association Tournaments," speeches delivered at the National Federation of State High School Associations annual meeting, Milwaukee WI, July 8 and July 6, 1977.

30. Elizabeth Merrill, "The New Frontier: 25 Years of Title IX," *Omaha World-Herald*, June 21, 1997, pp. 13, 16.

31. Sue Bier, Williamsburg Community High School, to E. Wayne Cooley, November 7, 1969; correspondence between Dorothy Mott, Sutherland Community School, and E. Wayne Cooley, December 8 and December 21, 1970; copies in Ruth Johnson personal archives.

32. "Gain in Girls' Basketball," editorial, *Cedar Rapids Gazette*, October 21, 1972.

33. Russ L. Smith, "Girls Basketball Moving to the City," *Waterloo Courier*, October 22, 1972, p. 2B.

34. "Girls Basketball: What Price 'Equality'?" editorial broadcast on WHO-TV and WHO-radio, Des Moines IA, October 19-20, 1972; Smith, "Girls Basketball Moving to the City."

35. Earl R. Shostrom to Ruth Johnson, April 5, 1974, Ruth Johnson personal archives.

36. Gilbert and Williamson, "Women in Sport," 48; *Iowa Girls*

High School Athletic Union 1975 Bulletin, no. 59 (Des Moines: IGHSAU): 38. For a thorough discussion of high school athletes and social status, see Coleman, *Adolescent Society*; Eitzen, "Sport and Social Status"; Feltz and Weiss, "Impact of Girls' Interscholastic Sport Participation"; Thirer and Wright, "Sport and Social Status."

37. Dr. Peggy Burke, chair, University of Iowa Department of Physical Education and Dance, to Joseph Califano, secretary, Department of Health, Education, and Welfare, August 14, 1978, Ruth Johnson personal archives.

38. Burke to Califano, August 14, 1978.

39. Mrs. L. A. Barchols, "Learn Game before Changing It," letter to the editor, *Des Moines Register*, October 24, 1972; O. E. Lester to John McCaw, October 26, 1972, Ruth Johnson personal archives. Lester took his Oakland teams to eight consecutive state tournaments, from 1949 through 1956, before he left Iowa for California (Beran, *From Six-on-Six*, 202). Cletus S. Miller, superintendent, Prairie City IA, to E. Wayne Cooley, November 10, 1972, Ruth Johnson personal archives.

40. Patricia L. Geadelmann, Iowa Commission on the Status of Women, to E. Wayne Cooley, August 5, 1973, Ruth Johnson personal archives; Iowa Women's Political Caucus, "Women's Sports: From Here to Equality," in 1978 IWPC newsletter.

41. For a description of connections between play and sport, see Huizinga, *Homo Ludens*. Huizinga's "paradox of play" posits the good in *play* against the bad in *play's creations*. The pastoral six-player basketball game can be cast as Huizinga's sacred *play*—the voluntary, unrestrained creator of culture—and the more commodified five-player as profane *play's creations*, which constitute the material end, or the creations of culture.

42. United Press International, "Iowa Girls Dominate National Cage Scene," *Miami Herald*, March 9, 1975, p. C1.

43. Robert Smiley, IGHSAU official, e-mail correspondence with the author, April 4, 2001. Smiley recalled that ABC wanted production control over the basketball tournament telecast, which Cooley refused to relinquish.

44. David Lynch, superintendent, Dallas Community School,

Dallas Center IA, to E. Wayne Cooley and Dr. Robert Benton, state superintendent of schools, Iowa Department of Public Instruction, March 3, 1976; Cooley to Lynch, March 4, 1976; James L. Baker, girls' basketball coach, Altamont School, Altamont TN, to W. Wayne Cooley, December 28, 1976; copies in Ruth Johnson personal archives. Baker and other Tennessee coaches who favored the six-player game appealed the court ruling. "As your state plays the six-on-six style of girls play I know you and the schools in your association will be interested in the outcome of the appeal," he wrote Cooley.

45. Betty Jane Kearns, Ames IA, to E. Wayne Cooley, February 1, 1977, Ruth Johnson personal archives.

46. Schedule of events, Iowa Women's Conference, "6 Player vs. 5 Player Basketball, " Des Moines IA, June 11, 1977, copy in Ruth Johnson personal archives.

47. The Associated Press, "Doderer Wants to End Dominance," September 15, 1977; Linda Hanson, vice-chairwoman, Iowa Women's Political Caucus, to E. Wayne Cooley, September 22, 1977; Sue Follon, executive director, Iowa Commission on the Status of Women, to E. Wayne Cooley, August 17, 1978; copies in Ruth Johnson personal archives.

48. Phyllis Howlett, chair, Iowa Commission on the Status of Women, to E. Wayne Cooley, August 8, 1978, Ruth Johnson personal archives.

49. Burke to Califano, August 14, 1978; North Mahaska (Iowa) High School speech class to Joseph Califano, September 27, 1978; Will, "Is Iowa Girls' Basketball a Human Rights Issue?"

7. ALL DRESSED UP BUT NOWHERE TO GO

1. William (Bill) D. Russell, interview with author, Lamoni IA, March 12, 1998; "3 Schoolgirls Fight Rules," *New York Times*, September 1, 1983, p. 22.

2. Associated Press, "Tennessee's Girl Cagers to Play Boys Rules Next," *Chattanooga Times*, December 24, 1976; Martin Harmon, "Girls Basketball Will Continue Present Rules," *Nashville Banner*,

October 3, 1977; Court citations: *Victoria Ann Cape v. Tennessee Secondary School Athletic Association*, No.CIV-3–76-234, U.S. District Court, Tennessee, November 24, 1976; *Victoria Ann Cape v. Tennessee Secondary School Athletic Association*, No. 77–1153, U.S. Court of Appeals (Sixth Circuit), October 3, 1977; *Cheryl Lynn Jones v. Oklahoma Secondary School Activities Association*, No. CIV-77–0477-T, U.S. District Court, Oklahoma, August 31, 1977.

3. United Press International, "Girl Cagers Fight Suit," *Quad-City Times*, July 24, 1977; Associated Press, "Girls Basket Ruling Reversal Is Sought," *Sioux City Journal*, September 24, 1977; "High School Basketball Guards," *Iowa Girls High School Athletic Union 1978 Bulletin*, no. 62 (Des Moines: IGHSAU).

4. Johnson, "Half-Court Girls' Basketball Rules," 770, 775, 777, 797–98; *Diana Lee Dodson v. Arkansas Activities Association*, No. LRC-77–19, U.S. District Court, Arkansas, April 4, 1979.

5. Cooley recalled meeting with Secretary Califano several times before HEW's favorable 1978 ruling and that Governor Robert Ray and U.S. Senator Dick Clark intervened on the side of six-player basketball. "Both federal and state administrators were protective of the Union," Cooley said (interview with author, March 16, 2000).

6. Department of Education, "Achieving Success under Title IX," archived information, July 10, 1997, http://*www.ed.gov/pubs/TitleIX /part5.html (retrieved May 23, 2003);* Feminist Majority Foundation, "Implementing Title IX," Empowering Women in Sports, Empowering Women Series, no. 4 (1995), http://*www.feminist.org/research /sports12.html* (retrieved May 23, 2003).

7. Bill Russell to E. Wayne Cooley, January 6, 1982; Cooley to Russell, January 13, 1982; copies in William D. Russell personal archives.

8. Bill Russell to 5 on 5 Inc., January 17, 1983, Willaim D. Russell personal archives; Shauna Russell, interview with author, Osceola IA, March 12, 1998; Randy Peterson, "Six-Girl Cage Rules Linked to Knee Injuries," *Des Moines Register*, February 6, 1983, pp. 1B, 5B.

9. Paul Leavitt and Jane Norman, "Suit by Girls Seeks Change in Basketball," *Des Moines Register*, August 31, 1983, pp. 1–2A; Pe-

terson, "Six-Girl Cage Rules," p. 5B; Bill Russell, "Sources for Fund Raising," correspondence to 5 on 5 Inc. members, August 20, 1983, William D. Russell personal archives.

10. Beran, *From Six-on-Six*, 107; Associated Press, "A.D.'s Vote against Move to 5-on-5," *Des Moines Register*, May 6, 1983.

11. Leavitt and Norman, "Suit by Girls."

12. Bill Russell, "Is Iowa Girls' Basketball Unconstitutional?" unpublished essay, December 1983; copy in possession of the author.

13. Leavitt and Norman, "Suit by Girls"; Kari Wolf to Shauna Russell, September 3, 1983; Shauna Russell to Kari Wolf, September 6, 1983; copies of correspondence in William D. Russell personal archives.

14. Shauna Russell, interview with author, March 12, 1998.

15. Paul Leavitt, "Iowa Switch to 5-Girl Game Argued before U.S. Judge," *Des Moines Register*, March 8, 1984, pp. 1A, 8A; Paul Leavitt, "Judge to Hear Suit on Girls' Basketball," *Des Moines Register*, April 27, 1984.

16. Mark Horstmeyer and Randy Peterson, "5-on-5 Game for Girls Passes Test," *Des Moines Register*, May 16, 1984, pp. 1S, 4S; Randy Peterson, "Optional Girls' 5-on-5 Rules OK'd for Schools," *Des Moines Register*, May 19, 1984, p. 1A.

17. Beran, *From Six-on-Six*, 102; Marc Hansen, "Cooley Cools Five-on-Fivers," *Des Moines Register*, May 22, 1984, p. 1S.

18. Horstmeyer and Peterson, "5-on-5"; Mark Horstmeyer, "Switch to 5-Girl Basketball May Be Slow in Sweeping Iowa," *Des Moines Register*, May 20, 1984, p. 7D; Hansen, "Cooley Cools"; Lauren Madden, 5 on 5 Inc., to "Friends of Girls' Basketball," June 1984, William D. Russell personal archives.

19. Paul Leavitt, "Lawsuit Challenging Girls' Rules Is Dropped," *Des Moines Register*, October 24, 1984, p. 1S; Bill Russell, 5 on 5 Inc., to "Friends of Girls' Basketball," June 16, 1984.

20. Bill Russell to Lauren Madden, July 25, 1984, William D. Russell personal archives; "Smith Backs Suit Seeking 5-on-5 Girls' Basketball," *Des Moines Register*, August 18, 1984, p. 4S.

21. "Lamoni Board Favors 5 on 5 Basketball," *Lamoni Chronicle*, August 22, 1984, p. 1.

22. Bill Russell to Mark Bennett, September 7, 1984, William D. Russell personal archives.

23. Leavitt, "Lawsuit Challenging Girls' Rules"; Bill Russell to Jill Kromminga, November 28, 1984; Lauren Madden to Bill Russell, February 4, 1985; copies of correspondence in William D. Russell personal archives.

24. Shauna Russell, interview with author, March 12, 1998; Russell to Bennett, September 7, 1984.

25. Shauna Russell, interview with author, March 12, 1998.

26. Bill Russell, "Iowa Girls Handicapped by Old-Style Basketball," *Des Moines Register*, November 29, 1985, p. 7A.

27. "Basketball Participation Survey Results," IGHSAU, March 2001 (unpublished; information obtained from IGHSAU).

28. Shafar, "A Comparison," 16–35, and Dennis D. Jerome, "Attitudes and Feelings of Iowa College and University Women's Basketball Players toward the Five-Player Game versus the Six-Player Game" (unpublished graduate research paper, University of Northern Iowa, 1978), 13, 14, 17, 21; copy in possession of the author. Shafer was elected in 1979 to serve a four-year term as female member-at-large on the IGHSAU board of directors, succeeding Ruth Johnson.

29. "Iowa Girls Lead Nation in Participation," IGHSAU *Newsletter* (Spring 1982).

30. "Iowa Girls Lead Nation," 3, 4.

31. "Iowa Girls Lead Nation," 1; Jacquie Terpstra, "Who Says Girls Can't Play?" *Title IX Line* 4, no. 4 (Summer 1984): 3.

32. "Comparisons of 1975 Boys' and Girls' State Basketball Tournaments," IGHSAU *Newsletter* (Fall 1975); Iowa Girls High School Athletic Union Statements of Financial Condition, Nolte, Cornman & Company, Certified Public Accountants, Des Moines IA, June 30, 1978, Ruth Johnson personal archives; E. Wayne Cooley, interview with author, March 16, 2000; Beran, *From Six-on-Six*, 189–90; Philip H. Cless, Law Offices of Blanchard, Cless & Hanson, Des Moines IA, to Wayne Cooley, April 18, 1977, Ruth Johnson personal archives.

33. Shafar, "A Comparison," 18; E. Wayne Cooley, interview with author, March 16, 2000.

34. Susan Harman, "Tradition to End: Farewell, 6-Girl Game," *Des Moines Register*, February 4, 1993, p. 1A; E. Wayne Cooley, interview with author, March 16, 2000.

35. Dave Stockdale, "Old Game Dribbles into History Books," *Des Moines Register*, February 4, 1993, pp. 3–4s; Gene Bloom, "Six-Player Basketball to End in Iowa Schools," *Woodbine Twiner*, February 10, 1993, p. 1; Troy Danner, "Six-Player Basketball to End after 1993–94 Season," *Denison Review*, February 6, 1993, p. 1s; Rob White, "Six-Player Faithful Surprised by Game's Conversion," *Omaha World-Herald*, February 5, 1993, p. 19A.

36. "Six-Player Basketball to End after '94 Season," *Iowa Girl Quarterly* 16, no. 1 (May 1993): 1; Harman, "Tradition to End."

37. E. Wayne Cooley, interview with author, March 16, 2000; memorandum to Iowa athletic directors, basketball coaches, and basketball officials, November 18, 1993.

38. Susan Harman, "Iowans Pick Sides on Six-Girl Game," *Des Moines Register*, February 5, 1993, p. 1A; Beran, *From Six-on-Six*, 107; Donald Kaul, "At Long Last, My Mission Accomplished," *Des Moines Register*, February 5, 1993, p. 1A; E. Wayne Cooley, interview with author, March 16, 2000.

39. Michael A. Fletcher, "Changes To Title IX Considered: Proposal Would Allow Scholarship Limits," *Washington Post*, January 24, 2003, p. A1; Richard W. Riley, "Title IX: 25 Years of Progress," archived information, July 10, 1997,*http://www.ed.gov/pubs/TitleIX /part5 (retrieved May 23, 2003)*.Before Title IX, not even Luci Baines Johnson, daughter of President Johnson, could attend nursing school after her marriage—she was refused admission to Georgetown University's school of nursing in 1966 because the school did not enroll married women as students.

40. Fletcher, "Changes To Title IX," A1; Erik Brady, "Time fails to lessen Title IX furor," *USA Today*, June 19, 2002, p. 1A.

41. Brady, "Time Fails to Lessen," p. 1.

42. "Woman Golfer Criticized for Deciding to Play 'Boys'

Game," Feminist Daily News Wire, May 16, 2002, http://*www*
.feminist.org/news.newsbyte/uswirestory (retrieved May 23, 2003).

43. Gerald Reynolds, who has a record of opposing racial and
gender preferences, was appointed to manage the Office for Civil
Rights by President Bush, who campaigned against "strict proportionality" (Brady, "Time Fails to Lessen"). Perhaps most significant,
the commission, cochaired by former women's professional basketball star Cynthia Cooper and Stanford University athletic director
Ted Leland, lacked a commissioner to represent the interests and
perspectives of the almost six million high school students who play
sports (Donna de Varona and Julie Foudy, "Minority Views on the
Report of the Commission on Opportunity in Athletics," February 26, 2003, 19, http://www.feminist.org/news [retrieved May 23,
2003]).

44. De Varona and Foudy, "Minority Views," 5. Between 1994
and 1998 the General Accounting Office reports that more than
two-thirds of the schools the Office for Civil Rights investigated satisfied compliance not through the proportionality prong but
through one of Title IX's two other possible requirements.

45. Valerie Bonnette, quoted in Brady, "Time Fails to Lessen."

46. See John Irving, "Wrestling with Title IX," *New York Times*,
January 28, 2003. Many Title IX supporters blame the "arms race"
in Division I football and men's basketball programs and their ex-
cessive expenditures on the loss of other men's sports (De Varona
and Foudy, "Minority Views," 8).

47. Janet Judge, in Erik Brady and Thomas O'Toole, "Justice
Answers Suit, Not Title IX's Merits," *USA Today*, May 30, 2002, p.
1A.

48. "Bush Commission Releases Report Gutting Title IX," Feminist Daily News Wire, February 27, 2003, http://*www.feminist.org*
/news.newsbyte/uswirestory (retrieved May 23, 2003); De Varona and
Foudy, "Minority Views," 13–14.

49. De Varona and Foudy, "Minority Views," 1, 16; "Bush Commission Releases Report"; Riley, "Title IX: 25 Years of Progress."

50. Jeff Oliphant, doctoral candidate, University of Iowa, "Iowa
High Schools Athletic Gender-Equity Study," summary of results,

June 1995, available at http://bailiwick.lib.uiowa.edu/ge/Iowa Study /iowahs.

EPILOGUE

1. See Geertz, *Interpretation of Cultures*, 412–53, and Strenski, *Malinowski and the Work of Myth*, 121. Six-player basketball, for Iowans, becomes what Geertz called "a story they tell themselves," and a myth by Malinowski's definition was a story told in order to establish or reinforce belief.

2. John Naughton, "Leaping to New Heights," *Des Moines Register*, March 9, 1988, p. 1s; Dan Johnson, "Point Well Taken: At Drake, Northern Iowa, Iowa State and Iowa, the Point Guard Position Is in Good Hands," *Des Moines Register*, November 15, 1999, pp. 1–3s.

3. "Basketball Participation Survey Results," IGHSAU March 2001 (unpublished; information obtained from IGHSAU). For an excellent discussion of the falsity of sport as a social mobility escalator, see Eitzen, *Fair and Foul*.

4. "Don't Curse the Players," from Woodbine Lady Tigers Basketball, official program, Woodbine High School, January 16, 2001.

5. Joy Lynn Conwell, "A Salute to the Iowa Girl: Atlantic All-Stars vs. Atlantic Trojanns," press release from Atlantic High School, November 2, 2000.

Bibliography

Adler, Patricia A., and Peter Adler. *Backboards and Blackboards: College Athletics and Role Engulfment*. New York: Columbia University Press, 1994.

Agar, Michael. *Language Shock: Understanding the Culture of Conversation*. New York: William Morrow and Co., 1994.

———. *The Professional Stranger: An Informal Introduction to Ethnography*. New York: Academic Press, 1980.

———. *Speaking of Ethnography*. Newbury Park CA: Sage, 1986.

Alford, Robert. "School District Reorganization and Community Integration," *Harvard Educational Review* 30, no. 4 (Fall 1960): 350–71.

Babener, Liahna. "Bitter Nostalgia: Recollections of Childhood on the Midwestern Frontier." In *Small Worlds: Children and Adolescents in America, 1850–1950*, ed. Elliott West and Paula Petrik. Lawrence: University Press of Kansas, 1992.

Banner, Lois. *American Beauty*. New York: Knopf, 1983.

Bauer, Douglas. "Girls Win, Boys Lose," *Sports Illustrated* 48 (March 6, 1978): 35.

———. *Prairie City, Iowa: Three Seasons at Home*. New York: G. P. Putnam's Sons, 1979.

Bellah, Robert, et al., eds. *Habits of the Heart*. New York: Harper & Row, 1987.

Beran, Janice A. *From Six-on-Six to Full Court Press: A Century of Iowa Girls' Basketball*. Ames: Iowa State University Press, 1993.

Berenson, Senda. *Line Basketball*. New York: American Sports Publishing, 1901.

Bissinger, H. G. *Friday Night Lights: A Town, a Team, and a Dream*. New York: Addison-Wesley, 1990.

Blais, Madeleine. *In These Girls, Hope Is a Muscle*. New York: Atlantic Monthly Press, 1995.

Bloom, Karen. *A Pictorial History of Harrison County, Iowa*. Logan IA: Bloom Publishing, 1999.

Bodnar, John. "Generational Memory in an American Town," *Journal of Interdisciplinary History* 26, no. 4 (Spring 1996): 619–37.

Brumberg, Joan Jacobs. *The Body Project: An Intimate History of American Girls*. New York: Random House, 1997.

Bryant, M. T., and M. L. Grady. "Community Factors Threatening Rural School District Stability," *Research in Rural Education* 6, no. 3 (1990): 21–26.

Cahn, Susan. *Coming On Strong: Gender and Sexuality in Twentieth-Century Sport*. New York: Free Press, 1994.

Carroll, William E., et al. "The Teaching of History in Iowa Public Schools," *Organization of American Historians Newsletter* 7, no. 2 (January 1980): 13–15.

Cavallo, Dominick. *Muscles and Morals: Organized Playgrounds and Urban Reform, 1880–1920*. Philadelphia: University of Pennsylvania Press, 1981.

Chepko, Steveda. "The Domestication of Basketball." In *A Century of Women's Basketball*, ed. Joan Hult and Mariana Trekell. Reston VA: National Association for Girls and Women in Sport, 1991.

Cheska, Alycie Taylor, ed. *Proceedings of the Annual Meeting of the Association for the Anthropological Study of Play*. West Point NY: Leisure Press, 1981.

Chisholm, R. H. "Girls' Basketball in Iowa," *The Palimpsest*. Iowa City: State Historical Society of Iowa. Vol. 49, no. 4 (April 1968).

———. "Iowa Girls High School Athletic Union," *The Palimpsest*. Iowa City: State Historical Society of Iowa. Vol. 49, no. 4 (April 1968): 125–32.

———. *1949 Iowa Girls' Basketball Yearbook*. Des Moines: Iowa Girls High School Athletic Union, 1949.

Coakley, Jay J. *Sport and Society: Issues and Controversies*. St. Louis: Mosby, 1986.

Coleman, James. *The Adolescent Society: The Social Life of the Teenager and Its Impact on Education*. Glencoe NY: Free Press, 1963.

Coover, Robert. *In Bed One Night and Other Brief Encounters*. Providence RI: Burning Deck, 1983.

Cremin, Lawrence. *American Education: The Metropolitan Experience, 1876–1980*. New York: Harper & Row, 1988.

Davies, Richard O. *America's Obsession: Sports and Society since 1945*. Orlando FL: Harcourt Brace, 1994.

Davis, Peter. *Hometown*. New York: Simon and Schuster, 1982.

Division for Girls and Women's Sports. *Report On Basketball 1969–1970*. Des Moines: DGWS, 1970.

————. *Philosophy and Standards for Girls and Women's Sports*. Washington DC: The National Education Association, 1969.

Edwards, Harry. *Sociology of Sport*. Homewood IL: Dorsey, 1973.

Eitzen, D. Stanley. *Fair and Foul: Beyond the Myths and Paradoxes of Sport*. Lanham MD: Rowman and Littlefield, 1999.

————. "Sport and Social Status in American Public Secondary Education," *Review of Sport and Leisure* 1, no. 1 (1976): 110–18.

Eitzen, D. Stanley, and Maxine Baca Zinn. "The De-athleticization of Women: The Naming and Gender Marking of Collegiate Sport Teams," *Sociology of Sport Journal* 6, no. 4 (1989): 362–70.

Eitzen, D. Stanley, and G. H. Sage, eds. *Sociology of North American Sport*. Indianapolis: W. C. Brown & Benchmark, 1993.

Enright, Jim. *Only in Iowa*. Des Moines: Iowa Girls High School Athletic Union, 1976.

Feltz, Deborah L., and Maureen R. Weiss. "The Impact of Girls' Interscholastic Sport Participation on Academic Orientation," *Research Quarterly for Exercise and Sport* 55, no. 4 (1984): 332–39.

Festle, Mary Jo. *Playing Nice: Politics and Apologies in Women's Sports*. New York: Columbia University Press, 1996.

Ford, Linda. *Lady Hoopsters: A History of Women's Basketball in America*. Northampton NY: Halfmoon Books, 1998.

Fuller, Wayne E. *The Old Country School: The Story of Rural Education in the Midwest*. Chicago: University of Chicago Press, 1982.

Geertz, Clifford. *The Interpretation of Cultures: Selected Essays*. New York: Basic Books, 1973.

Gilbert, Bill, and Nancy Williamson. "Women in Sport," *Sports Illustrated* 39 (June 4, 1973): 48–53.

Goodall, H. L. Jr., *Casing a Promised Land: The Autobiography of an Organizational Detective as Cultural Ethnographer*. Carbondale: Southern Illinois University Press, 1994.

Grundy, Pamela. "From Amazons to Glamazons: The Rise and Fall of North Carolina Women's Basketball, 1920–1960," *Journal of American History* 87, no. 1 (June 2000): 139–40.

———. *Learning to Win: Sports, Education, and Social Change in Twentieth-Century North Carolina*. Chapel Hill: University of North Carolina Press, 2001.

Gruneau, Richard. *Class, Sport, and Social Development*. Amherst: University of Massachusetts Press, 1984.

Gruneau, Richard, and David Whitson. *Hockey Night in Canada: Sport, Identities and Cultural Politics*. Toronto: Garamond Press, 1993.

Guttmann, Allen. *From Ritual to Record: The Nature of Modern Sports*. New York: Columbia University Press, 1978.

———. *A Whole New Ball Game: An Interpretation of American Sports*. Chapel Hill: University of North Carolina Press, 1988.

———. *Women's Sports: A History*. New York: Columbia University Press, 1992.

Higgs, Robert J. *God in the Stadium: Sports and Religion in America*. Lexington: University Press of Kentucky, 1995.

Hokanson, Drake. *Reflecting a Prairie Town: A Year in Peterson*. Iowa City: University of Iowa Press, 1994.

Huizinga, Johan. *Homo Ludens: A Study of the Play Element in Culture*. Boston: Beacon Press, 1955.

Hult, Joan, and Mariana Trekell, eds. *A Century of Women's Basketball*. Reston VA: National Association for Girls and Women in Sport, 1991.

Iowa Girls High School Athletic Union. *The IGBA Replay: A Pictorial Story of the 1971 Iowa Girls Basketball Academy*. Des Moines: Iowa Girls High School Athletic Union, 1971.

Jakle, John A. *The American Small Town: Twentieth-Century Place Images*. Hamden CT: Archon Books, 1982.

Johnson, Janet Junttila. "Half-Court Girls' Basketball Rules: An Application of the Equal Protection Clause and Title IX (Comments)," *Iowa Law Review* 66 (1980): 766–95.

Kammeyer, Kenneth C. W., George Ritzer, and Norman R. Yetman. *Sociology: Experiencing Changing Societies*. Boston: Allyn and Bacon, 1997.

Kemis, Mari, et al. *Perceptions of Educational Quality following a School Closing*. Ames: Iowa State University, Research Institute for Studies in Education, April 1994.

Kerber, Linda K. "Separate Spheres, Female Worlds, Woman's Place: The Rhetoric of Women's History," *Journal of American History* 75, no. 1 (1988): 9–39.

Lasch, Christopher. *The Culture of Narcissism: American Life in an Age of Diminishing Returns*. New York: Norton, 1978.

Lacher, Ira. "The *Register* Regroups: A State Paper Redraws Its Borders," *Columbia Journalism Review* (May/June 1991). Archived: http://www.archives.cjr.org.

Lipsyte, Robert. *SportsWorld: An American Dreamland*. New York: Quadrangle, 1975.

Lynd, Robert S., and Helen Merrell Lynd. *Middletown in Transition: A Study in Modern American Culture*. New York: Harcourt Brace, 1929.

Mandell, Richard. *Sport: A Cultural History*. New York: Columbia University Press, 1984.

Martone, Michael, ed. *A Place of Sense: Essays in Search of the Midwest*. Iowa City: University of Iowa Press, 1988.

McElwain, Max. *Profiles in Communication: The Hall of Fame of the University of Iowa School of Journalism and Mass Communication*. Iowa City: Iowa Center for Communication Study, 1991.

Mergen, Bernard. *Play and Playthings: A Reference Guide*. Westport CT: Greenwood Press, 1982.

Messner, Michael. *Power at Play: Sports and the Problem of Masculinity*. Boston: Beacon Press, 1992.

Messner, Michael, and Donald F. Sabo, eds. *Sport, Men, and the Gen-*

der Order: Critical Feminist Perspectives. Champaign IL: Human Kinetics Books, 1990.

Miracle, Andrew W. Jr., and C. Roger Rees. *Lessons of the Locker Room: The Myth of School Sports.* Amherst NY: Prometheus Books, 1994.

Morgan, William J. *Leftist Theories of Sport: A Critique and Reconstruction.* Urbana: University of Illinois Press, 1994.

Mrozek, Donald J. *Sport and American Mentality, 1880–1910.* Knoxville: University of Tennessee Press, 1984.

Novak, Michael. *The Joy of Sports.* New York: Basic Books, 1976.

Oriard, Michael. *Dreaming of Heroes: American Sports Fiction, 1868–1980.* Chicago: Nelson-Hall, 1982.

———. *Reading Football: How the Popular Press Created an American Spectacle.*Chapel Hill: University of North Carolina Press, 1993.

———. *Sporting with the Gods: The Rhetoric of Play and Game in American Culture.* Cambridge: Cambridge University Press, 1991.

Petersen, William J. "Beginnings of Girls' Basketball," *The Palimpsest.* Iowa City: Historical Society of Iowa. Vol. 49, no. 4 (April 1968): 113–24.

———. "Genesis of High School Basketball," *The Palimpsest.* Iowa City: State Historical Society of Iowa. Vol. 35, no. 3 (March 1954).

Powers, Jane Bernard. *The "Girl Question" in Education: Vocational Education for Young Women in the Progressive Era.* London: Falmer Press, 1992.

Prebish, Charles. *Religion and Sport: The Meeting of Sacred and Profane.* Westport CT: Greenwood Press, 1993.

"Pretty Virginia Harris Leads Hansell to Iowa Basketball Championship," *Life,* April 8, 1940, pp. 41–46.

Reynolds, David R. *There Goes the Neighborhood: Rural School Consolidation at the Grass Roots in Early Twentieth-Century Iowa.* Iowa City: University of Iowa Press, 1999.

Riess, Steven. *City Games: The Evolution of American Urban Society and the Rise of Sports.* Urbana: University of Illinois Press, 1989.

Rooney, John F. Jr., *A Geography of American Sport: From Cabin Creek to Anaheim.* Reading MA: Addison-Wesley, 1974.

Sanjek, Roger. *Fieldnotes: The Makings of Anthropology*. Ithaca NY: Cornell University Press, 1990.

Shafar, Connie J. "A Comparison of the Iowa Six-Player Girl Basketball Competitor to the Iowa Five-Player Girl Basketball Competitor in Relationship to Collegiate Participation Opportunities." Master's thesis, Western Illinois University, 1991.

Shank, Barry. *Dissonant Identities: The Rock'n'Roll Scene in Austin, Texas*. Hanover NH: University Press of New England, 1994.

Shapiro, Ann-Louise. "History and Feminist Theory; or, Talking Back to the Beadle." In *Feminists Revision History*, ed. Ann-Louise Shapiro. New Brunswick: Rutgers University Press, 1994.

Shortridge, Barbara Gimla. *Atlas of American Women*. New York: Macmillan, 1987.

Shortridge, James R. *The Middle West: Its Meaning in American Culture*. Lawrence: University Press of Kansas, 1989.

Shulman, James L., and William G. Bowen. *The Game of Life: College Sports and Educational Values*. Princeton: Princeton University Press, 2001.

Smith, Richard N. *Development of the Iowa Department of Public Instruction, 1900–1965*. Des Moines: State of Iowa Department of Public Instruction, 1969.

Sperber, Murray. *Beer and Circus: How Big-Time College Sports Is Crippling Undergraduate Education*. New York: H. Holt, 2000.

Strenski, Ivan. *Malinowski and the Work of Myth*. Princeton: Princeton University Press, 1992.

Theobald, Paul. *Teaching the Commons: Place, Pride, and the Renewal of Community*. Boulder CO: Westview, 1997.

Thirer, Joel, and Stephen D. Wright. "Sport and Social Status for Adolescent Males and Females," *Sociology of Sport Journal* 2, no. 2 (1985): 164–71.

Tyack, David, and Elizabeth Hansot. *Learning Together: A History of Coeducation in American Schools*. New Haven CT: Yale University Press, 1990.

Van Maanen, John. *Tales of the Field: On Writing Ethnography*. Chicago: University of Chicago Press, 1988.

Vertinsky, Patricia A. *The Eternally Wounded Woman: Women, Exer-*

cise, and Doctors in the Late Nineteenth Century. Urbana: University of Illinois Press, 1994.

Vidich, Arthur, and Joseph Bensman. *Small Town in Mass Society: Class, Power, and Religion in a Rural Community*. Princeton: Princeton University Press, 1968.

Vincent, Ted. *The Rise and Fall of American Sport*. Lincoln: University of Nebraska Press, 1994.

West, Elliott. *Growing Up with the Country: Childhood on the Far Western Frontier*. Albuquerque: University of New Mexico Press, 1989.

West, Elliott, and Paula Petrik. *Small Worlds: Children and Adolescents in America, 1850–1950*. Lawrence: University Press of Kansas, 1992.

"The Whole Town's Talking." woi Television (Ames, Iowa). News broadcast from Winterset, Iowa, January 24, 1952. 54 minutes.

Wiggins, David K. *Sport in America: From Wicked Amusements to National Obsession*. Champaign il: Human Kinetics Books, 1994.

Woody, Thomas. *A History of Women's Education in the United States*. 2 vols. New York: Science Press, 1929.

Zimbalist, Andrew. *Unpaid Professionals: Commercialism and Conflict in Big-Time College Sports*. Princeton: Princeton University Press, 1999.

Index

9 780803 282995